Life's Third Tri

Life's Third Tri:

Wisdom for Mystified Mothers Who Love Adult Children

Charlotte Melcher Smith, Ph.D.

LITT
publishing

Unless otherwise indicated, Scripture quotations are taken from the Holy Bible, New Living Translation, copyright © 1996, 2004, 2015 by Tyndale House Foundation. Used by permission of Tyndale House Publishers, Carol Stream, Illinois 60188. All rights reserved.

Scripture quotations marked (NIV) are taken from the Holy Bible, New International Version®, NIV®. Copyright © 1973, 1978, 1984, 2011 by Biblica, Inc.™ Used by permission of Zondervan. All rights reserved worldwide. www.zondervan.com. The "NIV" and "New International Version" are trademarks registered in the United States Patent and Trademark Office by Biblica, Inc.™

Published by LITT Publishing in the United States of America.

LITT Publishing
Venice, Florida
LITT Publishing.com
CharlotteMelcherSmith.com

Editing by Barbara Kimble, Book design by Andy Towler / Apluss Creative, Cover image of hand prints by Deborah Perpetua, Author photo by Ryan Arford Photography, Cover photo by Vanit Janthra/iStock.com

Paperback: ISBN 979-8-9851298-0-9
eBook: ISBN 979-8-9851298-1-6

Disclaimer: The material in this book is intended for educational purposes only. *Life's Third Tri* provides a collection of ideas, expert opinions, and tools that readers may choose to employ, but not all may be appropriate for your specific situation. Consult a mental health professional for guidance tailored to your unique circumstances. No expressed or implied guarantee of outcomes can be given and no liability taken if you choose to follow the book's recommendations, or if you react negatively to its content. The author and publisher specifically disclaim all responsibility for injury, damage, or loss that the reader may incur as a direct or indirect consequence of reading this book or following any of its suggestions. I am not your personal counselor, and reading this book does not create a client-therapist or client-coach relationship between us. Characters mentioned in this book have either given permission, are fictional, or are disguised composites of many different life stories. I have included no confidential information from any former clients. Other than my family members and my physician, names are fictitious.

This book is dedicated to my beloved
children, Deborah, David, and Daniel.
Thank you for the privilege and joy of being
your mother during all your life stages.

Contents

Introduction 9

Chapter 1 – Embracing Life's Third Trimester 19

Chapter 2 – Longing for a Third-Tri Coach 33

Chapter 3 – Our Great Obsession 48

Chapter 4 – The Humility Factor 66

Chapter 5 – Digesting Humble Pie 91

Chapter 6 – The Peripheral vs. the Central 109

Chapter 7 – Seeking God's Face 130

Chapter 8 – How Tight Is Your Turning Radius? 139

Chapter 9 – Beyond Why 153

Chapter 10 – Communicating the Truth with Love.... 170

Chapter 11 – Thorny Dilemmas. 191

Chapter 12 – Necessary Adjustments................ 217

Chapter 13 – Practicing Flexibility 238

Chapter 14 – What's Next?........................ 256

Chapter 15 – Your Choice: Celebration or Mourning. . 273

Chapter 16 – Grand Finale 290

Notes.. 296

About the Author................................ 304

Introduction

AFTER THIRTY YEARS of sitting in my therapist chair, listening to women unload the deepest secrets in their hearts, I've learned each poignant life story could qualify as a novel. Their narratives include chapters filled with passion, intrigue, betrayals, plot twists and turns, successes and failures, triumphs and tragedies. A common thread weaving through these real-life dramas is the enduring love of mothers for their children.

Although sad exceptions exist, love propels the vast majority of moms to pursue intimate connections with their offspring for their entire lives. Unlike ferocious mama bears who only temporarily defend, nurture, teach, and then launch their cubs, human mothers possess no age limit on mothering instincts. Decade after decade, our "cubs" continue to captivate our hearts. They always remain our beloved "kids," even when they've grown into adults with dozens of candles on their birthday cakes.

Life's Third Tri celebrates a particular group of heroines—courageous moms of grown sons and daughters. These women yearn for love, closeness, and family harmony to prevail during their empty nest years. Parenting adult offspring is uncharted territory, however. Many mothers cannot fathom how relationships with their grown children became so complicated when they've always loved their sons and daughters so dearly. Some heavy-hearted moms feel bewildered because they don't know what next step might foster the healing of wounds and fractures.

In her discussion of intergenerational rifts, Jane Isay, author of *Walking on Eggshells*, asserts, "It takes a lot of work to break up a family. It's almost impossible to stop loving your parents, and even more difficult to stop loving your children. Given this obvious truth, what's the matter with us? Why can't we find a way to be easy with our grown kids, and just be close and relaxed?"[1]

There was never a doubt in any of our minds that motherhood is a life calling. It felt inconceivable that anything or anybody could matter as much as those dependent little human beings who couldn't yet even say, *Mama*. We joyfully accepted our role as our kids' nurturer, comforter, protector, teacher, and life coach. Now, however, they are grown and gone, and they don't cry out for their mama in the same ways they once did.

We face a painful reality. Some adult children not only do not seem to need us now, but they may want little to do with us. To our stunned amazement, they may no longer view us as loving mothers. Instead, some have concluded that we were, and still aspire to be, over-controlling, judgmental moms who are impossible to please. In other cases, they judge us as intellectually inferior, fanatical, prejudiced, racist, self-absorbed, hypocritical, or hopelessly behind-the-times. Many offspring perceive themselves to possess far more wisdom than their parents, often convinced we hold ridiculous priorities and opinions. Sometimes their assessments are correct and sometimes not. So too, after all, were many of us when we flew our own coops.

Because the younger generation's attitudes and choices are so mystifying, we fail to recognize an important truth. Despite our perceived faults, most adult children do deep-down love their moms. However, they desire to relate to their mothers in *redefined* parent-child relationships, and they feel guilty when they neglect us.

Isay interviewed scores of adult children while writing her book, *Walking on Eggshells: Navigating the Delicate Relationship Between Adult Children and Parents.* Her dialogues with the younger generation surprised her. She had expected a litany of frustrations and harsh criticism of parental flaws. Many sons and daughters did resent certain comments or behaviors growing up, and they confessed they remain hypersensitive to their mothers' words now. "Still," Isay said, "these grown children consistently professed admiration, gratitude, and love for their moms."[2]

Isay admitted, "It isn't easy for parents to construe their grown children's behavior as loving when they are not returning our phone calls, when they criticize us, fight with us, and show a certain disdain. But most often the love is there—hiding in plain sight."[3]

As the years since leaving home increase, the younger generation's appreciation grows as they better comprehend the complexities of parenting. Isay spotted a pattern. She recognized how both parents and children were "playing a new version of an old childhood game, blind man's bluff." Isay observed, *"But now both generations are wearing blindfolds, as parents and their grown children stumble around trying to find one another."* [4]

I hold the optimistic view that small changes, even tiny adjustments in how we interact with our offspring, can produce massive returns over time. It is those powerful, permanent alterations that we will emphasize in this book's coaching corners. Then watch for incremental progress in reaching your goal of heartwarming friendships with sons and daughters. The other part of your recovery from empty nest trauma will consist of learning how to build a good life that is not dependent on how the younger generations conduct their lives.

Great news: You can thrive personally and flourish in your family relationships during your empty nest years, but the path may not be what you expect. Mother Teresa, a keen observer of humankind, underscored the realities of intergenerational divergence, but ended with a startling prediction: "You will teach them to fly, but they will not fly your flight. You will teach them to dream, but they will not dream your dream. You will teach them to live, but they will not live your life. Nevertheless, in every flight, in every life, in every dream, *the print of the way you taught them will remain.*"[5]

Your grown children may have left your home, but not your heart. What's more, you are still teaching, and your life continues to impact your offspring.

Consider the following two accounts of mothering challenges. The first mom's empty-nest dilemmas may sound common, especially if grown children distance themselves geographically or contact is otherwise restricted. The second mother's heartbreak contains uniquely difficult elements and troubling value conflicts. In both cases, by the end of this book, you will discern how mom-prints affect all their futures.

Marilyn's Story

"I miss my kids and grandkids so much that my heart sometimes physically aches. Growing up, my son was the loving kid who would proudly wave, 'Hi, Mom,' when he left the field after football games. My older daughter included me in her life almost as if I were one of her close girlfriends. My other daughter was more rebellious, and we sometimes argued during her teen years about her risky behaviors and choice of friends. However, both daughters are domestically inclined, so we relished cooking together, shopping for clothes, tackling craft projects, decorating rooms in our house, and talking intimately. We all reveled in sporting events, camping, game nights, movies, and traveling internationally, with many memorable mountain and seashore vacations. My kids, and now my grandkids, have always been the most fascinating, fun people on earth to me, and I crave time with them.

"It was hard when each daughter fell in love and moved with her husband to opposite sides of the country. I'm proud of their career achievements and admire their devotion to their spouses and my grandkids, but the infrequent contact saddens me. I understand they're busy, but we don't talk as much as I'd like. They send occasional texts, but ration phone calls. They've subtly indicated I am trespassing on their family life if I initiate phone conversations, so silence prevails until they are in the mood. I feel like a pretty low priority on their list. Mostly I learn about their lives from reading their Facebook posts. I try to post responses often, hoping my comments will bridge the gap between us. We're retired now and free to travel, but they're so busy we feel we're imposing if we stay more than a couple of days.

"My son married a little later and moved with his wife and three kids to a farm a few miles from town. My daughter-in-law remains standoffish and doesn't include me in their family life much, preferring to spend weekends and most holidays with other young couples or with her side of the family. Unlike me, my daughter-in-law's mom never had a career, so was available to help extensively as each baby came along. The grandchildren bonded with the other grandma big time. We've offered to keep the grandkids at our house or theirs, hoping to gift my son and his wife some child-free date nights. They rarely take us up on our offer, picking the other grandparents as sitters instead. Our infrequent conversations and times together feel awkward and don't flow naturally. Living just nine miles away makes the emotional distance feel even more glaring. Understandably, my son does whatever pleases his wife.

"I can only describe my mental state as continual low-level sadness. I feel discarded like the stuffed animals they once hugged tightly. What's more, I feel like a beggar when I suggest spending time together. I survive on a diet of relationship 'crumbs.'"

Doris's Story

"No one would have predicted my kids would grow up to make the choices marking their lives. No parents could have treasured their children more, nor tried any harder to bring them up to know God's love and to distinguish right from wrong. Yet we have been hammered by their seeming hatred of us, including caustic verbal attacks on us as persons and as parents. After our son married a woman hostile to Christianity, he transformed into an angry, antagonistic man who wanted nothing to do with us. He refused to speak to us for five long years after one particularly vicious tirade directed at his honorable, hardworking dad.

"When I look back, it is hard to believe we housed three pregnant daughters under our roof at the same time. One was married, but she and her husband didn't make enough money to support themselves, so they needed to live with us temporarily. Two of our pregnant girls were unmarried, and neither father was in the picture nor accepted any responsibility. One of the pregnancies resulted from a bi-racial union, creating additional issues with prejudiced relatives.

"We didn't have enough bedrooms, so people slept on the couch and air mattresses in the family room. Imagine three pregnant women in close quarters undergoing extreme hormone fluctuations. Their emotional outbursts were intensified by resentments toward us as parents, despite the fact we were sacrificing our tranquility to avoid our pregnant daughters living homeless on the streets. Those tension-filled days took on the trappings of a horrific nightmare. Instead of a temporary night terror, however, this period became our new reality—the shattering of our lifelong dreams!"

The heartrending account of Doris's tumultuous journey as a mother of grown children comprised only one of many I'd heard in recent months. It was obvious Doris was suffering from a condition I've dubbed "Third Trimester Mother Syndrome." I added Doris's name to my mental list of heroines—devoted moms who were blindsided and devastated by their adult children's attitudes and actions, yet bravely continue in their struggle to know and do the next right thing, whatever that might be!

As she told her story, Doris identified the villain stalking my list of heroines—stressful intergenerational differences culminating in demolished dreams and splintered families. Doris's dreams had been like those of moms all over the world. All sane, loving mothers wish for their adult children to make wise decisions leading to happiness, spiritual well-being, a promising future, and intergenerational closeness. No mother desires for her child to become a drug addict or criminal or homeless or rejecting and hateful toward Mom and Dad.

I want to mention at the get-go, not all superheroines battling Third Trimester Mother Syndrome have a value system and Christian worldview identical to Doris's. Still, despite holding contrary philosophical and theological positions, most moms share similar aspirations for their children as those possessed by mothers of other persuasions, just based on differing sets of beliefs about what exactly constitutes a moral and good life. It is instructive to remember that cultures all around the globe have been alike in inculcating the rightness of respect for nature, revering some form of deity, caring for one's neighbors/tribe, and esteeming parents and elders.

In his fascinating book, *Messy Grace: How a Pastor with Gay Parents Learned to Love Others Without Sacrificing Conviction*, Caleb Kaltenbach relates his story of "having a mom who was a lesbian and a dad who was gay, of growing up in the LGBT community with my mom and her partner, and of finding Christ and eventually becoming a pastor."[6] In the process of telling his story, Kaltenbach describes the agony experienced by his dearly loved lesbian mom when Kaltenbach revealed he had given his heart to Jesus. His mother was devastated and petrified her adult son's conversion might impact their relationship negatively. Although his mom came from a different worldview, *Messy Grace* suggests that Kaltenbach's mother suffered from the symptoms of Third Trimester Mother Syndrome just as acutely as Doris did.

Some readers might question whether an author who looks to the Bible as a trustworthy source of wisdom has anything to say that they want to hear. My perspective flows from scriptural passages such as, "Fear of the LORD is the beginning of wisdom. Knowledge of the Holy One results in good judgment."[7] I encourage you to open your mind to the possibility that insights from these ancient texts—words guiding humans for millennia—might be a source of truth you need in these unmapped waters. If you are a mother of grown children, then we have "common ground." We all love our kids and want the best for them no matter how old they are, or we are!

Many women pursue spiritual growth more intentionally and diligently as they grow older. For mothers desiring to deepen their relationships with God, I cover the growth process in novel ways, and I suggest pathways. I also want to encourage moms who may have wandered away from, or been disillusioned by Christianity. I identify with you when I look back at my own stumbling progress during my faith journey.

Like moms with many diverse worldviews, Doris had sacrificed to educate and prepare her four kids to launch into adulthood as wise, loving, high-integrity adults who would impact the world for good, live out their God-given purposes, and achieve their potentials. Sometimes mothers' dreams come true, sometimes partially true, and sometimes not at all.

Doris had eagerly anticipated becoming a grandma, having prayed that her son and daughters would marry godly mates and establish loving, flourishing families of their own. Because Doris was determined to correct the parenting deficits she had experienced during her own upbringing, she'd hoped for closeness, affection, mutual support, and appreciation to prevail. When envisioning the future, Doris foresaw harmonious family gatherings filled with love and laughter, with everyone happily at ease. She longed to feel successful at the one job she cared most about—mothering the four beloved individuals God had entrusted to her. But alas, it was not to be. Not without help anyway.

The precise means to help Marilyn and Doris, and to assist other hurting, baffled moms of adult children, has been percolating in me for several years. It all started with a sudden realization: Many of the challenges of the empty nest season share amazing similarities with trials women experienced during the third trimester of their pregnancies. These parallels unlock a whole new way of understanding life stages and how to navigate them. But I am getting ahead of myself. The title of this book and all these allusions to the third trimester must be confusing. Let me take you back to where the first steps toward identifying and managing Third Tri Mother Syndrome began.

CHAPTER 1

Embracing Life's Third Trimester

"HAVE YOU HEARD that Joyce's husband, Randall, died of cancer two weeks ago? He was only fifty-two. I'm gathering a few old girlfriends to try and support Joyce in this terrible time. Charlotte, would you come and teach us like you used to do when we were all young moms?"

The question caught me by surprise. I didn't want to say, "No." Yet I had no idea what I could teach to encourage anyone at such a grief-filled time. Besides, for the last twenty-five years, I hadn't actually interacted much with my friends from that once-upon-a-time young moms' Bible study.

We'd drifted in diverse directions, running on ever-accelerating treadmills, intent on keeping up with our maturing children as they churned their way through childhood, adolescent, and young adulthood challenges. During that same stretch of time, our careers had diverged in time-consuming ways. After my youngest started kindergarten, I went back to school to earn a Ph.D. and dual licenses as a psychologist and a marriage and family therapist. What a whirlwind!

As I sat down with my Bible to pray for the wisdom needed to encourage my old friends at this young moms' reunion, I was swept with nostalgia for the simpler, more hopeful, more predictable season when our lives were defined by the arrival of sons and daughters. Back then, we'd welcomed the assignment to master the art of loving and nurturing children and husbands. Empty nests and mourning dead husbands held no appeal at all!

That's when the Spirit intervened! As I sat with Jesus in my "secret place chair" (otherwise known as my bedroom recliner), a sudden awareness jolted me. An unexpected brand-new crystal-clear thought invaded my mind: *You are in life's third trimester now!*

I knew instantly the idea was from the Holy Spirit. I didn't know exactly what His message meant, but it pierced my heart as truth. Fortunately, I didn't face any deadlines that morning, so I could ponder this revelation for a while. I felt like Mary, meditating on Gabriel's announcement that she would conceive by the Holy Spirit. It was mysterious, but true!

Pregnancies were familiar to me. I'd experienced three blessed nine-month stretches culminating in the births of Deborah, David, and Daniel. I adored being Mom to the world's most incredible kids. A loving family was what I yearned for most, and those three pregnancies provided a passage to my dream. Some of my earliest memories surround the "wishing on the first star of the evening" phenomenon. My deepest desire remained the same every time the first twinkling light became visible: *When I grow up, I wish for a close family with a husband and children who all love each other very much.* I didn't tell a soul, but I harbored my secret longing, and I wished it over and over and over.

More thoughts coalesced, and I arrived at my friend's brunch with a four-page handout and my Bible. It was immensely refreshing to catch up. We unabashedly thrust cellphone photos of our children and grandchildren under each other's noses. While devouring the brunch goodies, we reminisced about the earlier days when I was a young mother ministering on the staff of Cru, and we marveled at how our paths had intertwined and then spun out in unique ways. Even as we celebrated good news and happy times, our hearts felt heavy for Joyce, whose surgeon husband had been a one-of-a-kind wonderful man, and there were others in the group with tough present-day problems, too.

The hostess suggested, "Let's just sit here at the table while you share your thoughts, Charlotte." For the first time, I began to put into words what the Spirit had birthed in my heart. No one got up from the table for four hours, not even to go to the bathroom.

The concept that we were living in our third trimester of life resonated in a way I had rarely experienced when discussing other topics. Instead of anxiously floating through the empty nest and widowhood season without any discernible trajectory, we embraced the familiar imagery of a purposeful third trimester of pregnancy.

Long ago, we had pored over books like the continually updated *What to Expect When You're Expecting.*[8] Now we bonded over the realization that lifespans, just like pregnancies, are designed with predictable developments and milestones, including common feelings and fears. We realized that at this point in our lives we needed a different bonding book, one more appropriately titled *What to Expect When You're Expecting Life Beyond the Empty Nest*!

Acquiring information, guidance, and fellow travelers on the journey could shrink these formidable life transitions, we realized. We had survived, and mostly thrived, during our third trimesters of pregnancy. Now it was time to apply firsthand knowledge of that distinctive season of fertility to our third trimester of life.

I puzzled over how to logically divide our lifespans to match the three-trimester perspective the Spirit had downloaded in my brain. The divisions didn't mesh with calendar measurements based on weeks or months or years or decades, as occurs in a nine-month pregnancy. Instead, it became apparent that two life events serve as dividers between the three life stages.

Trimester #1: From Birth to Motherhood

As during pregnancy, the first trimester of a woman's lifespan, from birth to motherhood, is a time of foundational physical and mental growth and defining of identity. We start this season of life as infants ourselves, and the era ends when we welcome babies of our own.

Environmental toxins and traumas complicate and endanger healthy development during the first critical three-month period in pregnancy. Likewise, events in our early growing-up years permanently affect and shape our life courses, for good and for bad. This important developmental stage lasts until a woman starts her own family, ending life trimester #1.

Since the focus of this book is on mothering adult children, if you have not borne children, you may believe you cannot relate to third-trimester terminology. For childless women, the transitions between the three passages are less clear-cut. Still, women without kids tend to move through the three eras in tandem with their child-bearing peers.

Women without children of their own often become highly involved and hugely influential "special aunts" with nieces and nephews, or function as mentors to other family members and friends. Like biological moms, foster mothers, mothers-by-adoption, and stepmoms, their hearts become emotionally entwined with the younger generation. They similarly rejoice or agonize over the events and life choices affecting the beloved people in their lives.

Trimester #2: From First Baby to Empty Nest

When motherhood occurs, it is a sure game-changer. That first baby might arrive as early as the mother's mid-teens or as late as her forties.

While our babies are growing, developing, and maturing, they need our time, attention, and guidance. The middle trimester of life is a busy, high-energy season of productivity and obvious priorities.

The child-rearing years engage, entertain, and exhaust us. Parenting children through infancy, toddlerhood, grade school, middle school, and high school defines so much about the second trimester of life. Women may be building careers and developing in other ways also, but once we are called to be a mom, those children remain the dominant focus in trimester #2 until . . . the shock of the empty nest.

Trimester #3: From Empty Nest to Entering Eternity

Our beloved birds flying from our nests ushers in trimester #3—often the longest trimester of all. Our third tri frequently starts in our forties or fifties, but the common instigating factor is the departure of children from home. Overnight, noisy bustling households morph into strangely silent museums filled with haunting memories.

Once we cease weeping about our kids' emptied bedrooms, we dread the prospect of living for lonesome decades without compelling purpose and clear direction. Women yearn for a compass, a reliable navigational device, and a new passion equal to our formerly all-consuming call to motherhood. Unfortunately, Google Maps fails to locate any routes through life's third trimester to our final destination. We tend to feel on our own, dislocated, adrift, and bewildered about "what's next?"

What if God built into the third trimester of pregnancy a foreshadowing of this third life phase? There are precedents for such a possibility. Old Testament authors provide partial glimpses, perplexing prophecies, and hazy foreshadowing regarding the arrival of the Messiah on the world scene. Only later did the details become clear. Jesus' life and teachings dissolve the fog surrounding Old Testament characters, prophecies, sacrifices, feasts, laws, and covenants. Jesus revealed and fulfilled much that had remained shrouded and enigmatic for centuries.

The Third Trimester Viewed as a Parable

Jesus routinely taught His closest disciples and skeptical crowds by telling parables. He used metaphors, similes, and allegories. He always chose familiar topics in Israel's culture—stories of planting, harvesting, fishing, weddings, funerals, taxes, and family conflicts. I ask you, what could be more familiar female experiences than gestation and childbirth?

Jesus introduced many profound parables with the phrase, "The kingdom of heaven is like. . . ." For example, Jesus taught, "The Kingdom of Heaven is like a farmer who planted good seed in his field."[9] I am using Jesus' comparison pattern when I say, "Life's empty nest season is like the third trimester of pregnancy." Could twenty-first century women find help navigating their life chapters by applying lessons derived from a pregnancy parable?

Perhaps the presence of a road map for life beyond the empty nest has existed all along, just waiting for our discovery. Have you ever stopped to wonder why American women are blessed in the baby boomer generation with an average life expectancy of 81.3 years, five years longer than men? If you have already celebrated sixty birthdays, you can anticipate a bonus of an additional three years, putting you in the group reaching eighty-four years of age, on average, if mortality rates hold. One hundred years ago, American female life expectancy was only fifty-three years.

For what purpose is God suddenly keeping women around so much longer? I propose that God has a special mission for us third-trimester sisters. He knows many of us are crucial carriers of faith and ancient wisdom. Could it be He depends on us to transport His truth to a world careening off course?

I remain flabbergasted as I consider the similarities between experiences today and those occurring years ago during my pregnancies. You can decide for yourself if the unveiling of these commonalities has been waiting for this exact time in history and for a generation of women uniquely positioned to impact the world during their third trimester of life.

The third-tri concept contends that you have not finished your life work just because your children have launched. Your potential impact on the world has only begun. Since your sons and daughters have moved into the adult world, you might appropriately be asking at this very moment, "What is my next assignment?"

Are You in Your Third Trimester of Life?

To help determine if this book is for you, pretend you are going back in time and are now a young woman coming to your Ob-Gyn's office. You suspect a pregnancy because of certain symptoms, such as a missed period. You might already have used an over-the-counter pregnancy-detecting device, inspecting carefully to be sure a blue line appeared. You will be required to provide a fresh urine sample, and your doctor will perform a physical examination to confirm your status.

Now, just to *confirm* that this book applies to you, I will give some tests to see if you show evidence of being in life's third trimester. Fortunately, I don't need a urine specimen. Instead, I will start by listing some third trimester descriptions and advice available on WebMD,[10] Babyyourbaby.org,[11] FitPregnancy.com,[12] and Parenting.com.[13] Let yourself smile as you remember "back then," and make a check mark by each item if you recognize, "Yep, it's that way again!"

- The mother's abdomen is becoming larger and heavier. You may see stretch marks.

- Your balance and mobility may be changing.

- You may be experiencing indigestion and heartburn.

- You'll likely have to slow down a little, but you also want to keep your energy up. So, do small amounts of exercise. A walk around the block will do the trick.

- Swollen legs and feet tend to occur after standing for long periods of time, but should get better after elevating legs.

- Most women will experience interrupted sleep due to discomfort in back and hips, leg cramps, and necessary trips to the bathroom, leading to more fatigue during the day; taking naps can help.

- It's safe to keep having sex with your partner, though you may be too uncomfortable. Talk with your partner about other ways to remain intimate, including back rubs and foot massages.

- Avoid lifting heavy weights, as they can put too much stress on tendons and ligaments. Whatever your exercise level, scale back if you feel dizzy or lightheaded and try prenatal yoga classes or brisk walking instead.

- Ask for help. If someone offers to lift something for you, say yes!

Indeed, most of us cherished our pregnancies despite unwanted physical trials. It is fun now to look back in a lighthearted way at those challenges. Annoying physical similarities between pregnancy and our encore years certainly will be worth exploring later. Now, however, I want to administer a more comprehensive exam to help you determine if you actually are part of the sisterhood of those in the third tri of life.

To qualify for this sisterhood, a "yes" to question #1 or #2 will suffice. However, questions #3 through #25 identify other commonalities often experienced in life's third season. Third Tri Mother Syndrome describes a cluster of symptoms characteristic of many moms after their nests empty. Not all twenty-five may apply to you personally, but circle each number that does pertain to you.

Third Tri Mother Syndrome Questionnaire

1. Has at least one of your children left home?

2. Do you inhabit a totally empty nest?

3. Do you crave closer relationships with your adult children (or with other beloved young adults central to your life)?

4. Are your grown kids' and grandkids' daily lives a source of fascination, joy, pride, and delight?

5. Are you bewildered by your adult kids' choices and their attitudes toward you or toward God?

6. Do you find yourself in a new era of your life and wondering, "What's next?"

7. Do you feel an urgency to know God's purpose and calling for your life, so you can accomplish it now while there's still time?

8. Do fears, anxiety, and concerns about your children and grandchildren threaten your peace and often rob you of a good night's sleep?

9. Do you feel overwhelmed by problems you feel helpless to solve?

10. Do you long for help managing your complicated life?

11. Are you lonely? Do you feel forgotten or abandoned?

12. Are you still adversely affected by hurts in your family of origin, especially those inflicted by your mother or father?

13. Are you a caretaker for anyone?

14. Are you retired or contemplating retirement?

15. Do you ponder changing careers in hope of finding something more meaningful and fulfilling?

16. Do you wish you had more girlfriends and deeper friendships?

17. Do you battle with unwanted body changes? Wrinkles? Bulging midsections? Drooping boobs? Weight gain? Sexual issues? Acute or chronic health problems?

18. Are you struggling to cope with being unhappily married, single, divorced, or widowed?

19. Does self-pity creep in, stealing your joy and making it hard to face another day?

20. Do health challenges limit you or even consume your days?

21. Because of bitterness, regrets, or addictions, do you find yourself not being the person you want to be?

22. Do you desperately want to "finish well," but struggle with guilt because of past or current failures?

23. Is the ultimate death of your body on your radar?

24. Are you confident about your future after you take your last earthly breath?

25. Do you want to know God better before you meet Him face-to-face?

If you answered *yes* to either of the first two questions, then welcome to the third trimester of life! However, remember that endorsing several of the subsequent questions also puts you in the sisterhood of those experiencing Third Tri Mother Syndrome, even if you've never technically been a mom. Specific needs, defining thought patterns, and certain physical changes generally accompany life's third phase.

Numerous "yes circles" on questions #1 through #25 confirm your membership with millions of other women experiencing an era of life that catches most of us off guard. Our goal is not to just endure these years, but to thrive and blossom instead of shriveling—and to feel we have like-minded company and fellow companions as we figure out this third-tri assignment together.

As I explained previously, once upon a time, in the *first* trimester of life, you were a child in the process of gradually developing into an adult. Those were critical formative years.

You transitioned from the *first* trimester of life to the *second* trimester of life when a sperm and egg combined inside you to begin your own son or daughter's life, and you became a parent. Others attain "motherhood status" by adopting, fostering, becoming a stepparent, or developing close, love-filled relationships with nieces, nephews, or others in the younger generation. Once your babies enter the picture, your life revolves around them. During this busy *second* season of life, you embrace adulthood and explore additional areas of adult development.

The departure of your children from your home ushers in your *third* trimester of life. You are still a mother, but a new stage of life has begun for you, as well as for your sons and daughters.

Maximizing Your Book Benefits

Whether you're reading this book in paper format or as an e-book or listening to it as an audio book, please keep a pen and notebook nearby so you can respond to the various questions and exercises included.

Life coaches ask questions. Then they ask some more questions. Life coaches encourage you to be introspective and find answers deep inside yourself. Coaches make you accountable to take action steps to reach the goals you develop for yourself. Every chapter in this book is followed by coaching questions. Just as swallowing prenatal vitamins and refraining from drinking alcohol gave you a better chance of delivering a healthy baby, taking time to mull over these questions and write down your answers increases your odds of creating a better third trimester for yourself.

I admit it. I'm often in a hurry, and I sometimes skip over the "contemplating and writing down" parts of books. I'm eager to get to the "how-to's" and the author's nuggets so I can rush on with my busy day. In this book, however, the questions in each chapter's Coaching Corner are a crucial tool leading to your own personal life "fixes."

Because it takes time to contemplate answers to serious questions and execute the changes you want to make, you may want to make this book a slow read. Move on to the next chapter only after you've thoroughly processed the coaching questions. This unhurried pace allows you to implement your changes before burying them under new resolves. I would even suggest you enlist a third-tri friend or two to work through the coaching questions together, provide moral support, supply the companionship of fellow travelers, and offer some helpful accountability.

However, if you feel compelled to race through the book without pausing, I understand. If that is the case, then I ask you for a commitment to read the book through a second time after your curiosity is satisfied. Next time around, I encourage you to read no more than a chapter a week and answer all the questions before moving on.

You can rest easy. For over thirty years, I made my living as a therapist and life coach. Naturally, I'll include ideas and suggestions. However, the questions at the end of these chapters possess surprising power to coach you to genuine personal insight and motivate subsequent life change. Bask in fresh revelations illuminating your individual, God-inspired action steps.

Coaching Corner

1. Describe the days when your first and then your last child left home. What were you thinking and feeling back then about the time stretching out before you, minus children in the home?

2. In what ways are you conducting your life differently today than you anticipated when your nest emptied?

3. What did you dread most about the empty nest season? Have those dreaded things happened?

4. What did you look forward to experiencing once the children were grown and gone? Have those desirable things occurred?

5. How would you define a successful third trimester for yourself?

6. What would need to change for your third-trimester vision to become a reality?

7. Write down one step you could take immediately to embrace your vision for your third trimester.

8. What has been keeping you from taking that step?

9. When are you going to take it?

And now, let's move to the next chapter and the first parallel between the third trimester of pregnancy and the third tri of life.

CHAPTER 2

✤

Longing for a Third Tri Coach

YEARS AGO, AS I began my journey through the empty nest maze, I yearned for trustworthy guides. Are you likewise flailing around since your kids exited your home and recognizing you need help figuring out a whole new era of life?

Parallel #1: Pregnant women crave mentors or coaches; in the third trimester of life, we also long for mentors and coaches.

I clearly remember benefiting from labor and delivery coaches once upon a time. My husband and I diligently attended classes and practiced techniques taught by our Lamaze trainer. During my first pregnancy, I sought tutoring in breastfeeding from an experienced La Leche League leader. I brought a list of questions to every doctor's appointment. I devoured books detailing what to anticipate, and I tried to distill and assimilate the experts' best suggestions.

Where is the list of experienced coaches for the empty nest years, those willing to serve as real-life models and provide guidance for this important chapter of life?

Some lucky moms can look at their own mothers' later years for direction. My friend, Annette, talks glowingly about her mom's inspiring example. "Mom didn't become a Christian until she was in her forties, but what a transformation! With every decade, she became kinder, more positive, more fun-loving, more delightful to be around. All of us craved time with her, even when she developed Alzheimer's. When she'd wake up in the hospital, surrounded by nurses and doctors in white coats, she'd invariably ask, 'Am I already in heaven? Are you angels?'

"Mom slid down the high slide at the water park when she was eighty-two, displaying no fear in her later life. After a few months in a nursing home, she still had enough mental awareness, despite her incontinence and dementia, to suggest, 'Wouldn't it be wonderful to spend all our time together. Let's just sell everything I have, and I'll move in with you, and we'll just trust the Lord.' It was a huge privilege to unload a hospital bed into our living room a few days later. Mom was all smiles but lived only two more weeks. I miss her terribly!"

Unfortunately, other friends describe experiences more like those of Trudy. "My mother modeled selfishness and excessive dependence on others her whole life. She suffered from every ailment known to humankind and milked her need for caretaking. For many years, I clocked out two days a week from my CPA practice to transport Mother to dozens of doctors and treatments. She wouldn't even wash her hair or dress herself to be ready to go to the doctor appointments, despite being perfectly capable.

"Mother was jealous and despised all my friends because she wanted me all to herself. However, it was painful to spend time with her because she was so critical, sharp-tongued, and unappreciative. When

I was growing up, as soon as Dad got home from work, he would go out and work in the garden until dark. I, too, longed to flee and hide. After Mother came to live with me for the last eleven years of her life, I found myself fabricating excuses to stay at the office or to sneak out of the house, just like Dad did."

Trudy's sad experiences with her mother's negativity and self-centeredness overwhelmed her as the memories flooded and tears trickled. "Mother was a grudge-keeper, a pouter when she didn't get her way, bitter and vindictive, suspicious, stingy, and materialistic. I knew a lot of Mother's illnesses stemmed from her deep reservoir of toxic bitterness, so I tried to gently suggest to this woman claiming to be a Christian that forgiveness might help diminish the poison inside.

"I hoped Mother might ponder Jesus' plea for mercy on behalf of those crucifying Him and adopt Jesus' inspiring words, 'Father, forgive them for they know not what they do,' so I asked her one day, 'What did Jesus say on the cross?'

"Mother snapped, 'Jesus said, "*Take care of my* mother!"'"

Trudy and I howled with laughter, a coping mechanism Trudy had honed to make life with her self-centered mother more bearable. I queried, "So how did you become such a loving mom and encouraging friend when your mother modeled the opposite?"

Trudy launched into an animated description of two other women in her life. One was her first Bible Study Fellowship teacher, a consistently kind retired math teacher and childless widow the same age as Trudy's own mother. This remarkable mentor took dulcimer lessons at age seventy-five and drove herself to 6 a.m. Bible Study Fellowship training sessions in all kinds of weather. Even when she was in her nineties, she never forgot to send Trudy a birthday card. On her eighty-fourth birthday, the generous octogenarian gathered a houseful of friends and proceeded to give away her prized collection of baby dolls to those at the party. Eventually, Trudy's beloved friend broke a hip and went to a rehabilitation facility, only to return home and live alone while using a walker. Soon she was well enough to accompany Trudy to movies again, bringing coupons to buy the popcorn.

Trudy's next third-trimester model was her dad's mom, a woman Trudy described as "incredibly fun." Her grandmother offered warm hospitality and patiently taught Trudy to crochet. Together they picked yummy strawberries and other garden goodies. Grandma stayed up late when her granddaughter visited and watched old movies with her, a treat Trudy cherished. Her grandmother also delighted in playing cards and board games together.

"Grandma made angel food cakes with me, and she let me frost them with any color of icing I wanted. Then Grandma would carefully ease a little flowerpot into the cake's hole and plunk a real flower in the pot. I loved her warmth and enthusiasm. I decided at a young age that I wanted to be the most fun woman around when I grew up and not a sourpuss like my mom."

Barb was sitting next to Annette and Trudy on the patio the summer evening when a group of us had gathered to discuss our mothers' roles in shaping life's third-trimester expectations. Barb described her mom as a mixture of positive and negative influences. She admired how her mother fought tenaciously against debilitating chronic conditions. Although previously a guilt tripper, Barb's mom changed midstream and became more appreciative of Barb's help and started saying "I love you" readily. Barb gave her mother credit for growing and changing over the years. Still, Barb missed having a spiritual role model and observed that she was drawn like a magnet to women ten or fifteen years older than herself, specifically those who have vibrant relationships with God.

She said wistfully, "I've deliberately surrounded myself with wise women who challenge me spiritually with their words and lifestyles because I've never experienced that before."

The last thing you may desire is to duplicate your mother's choices, attitudes, and behaviors during her later decades. Even if that is sadly the case, you are halfway there, because you have a good idea of how you do *not* want to spend the coming days and years. I hope this book, along with wisdom from other sources and some new role models, will help you fill in the blanks for how you want to conduct your life instead.

Cries for Help

Since I am proposing that *Life's Third Tri* can serve as a coach-in-print, let's consider the role a life coach plays. Most of us think of coaches as knowledgeable, experienced, sports-savvy gals and guys who train, drill, teach, prepare, critique, motivate, and perhaps yell and curse at players on their teams.

Tom Landry, the former coach of the Dallas Cowboys, whose record includes two Super Bowl titles and the fourth most wins ever for an NFL coach, described a coach as "someone who tells you what you don't want to hear, who has you see what you don't want to see, so you can be who you have always known you could be."[14] By the way, Landry won his victories without yelling and cursing, and I promise you I intend to follow his calm, composed model in that regard. Like Landry, I am also committed to helping you become who you always wanted to be.

As you read, there may be times when, similar to Landry's football players, you don't feel like doing what is suggested. It may seem too exhausting, time-consuming, unnecessary, or useless. However, most of the time I think you will understand the benefits and enthusiastically join me in running toward the goalposts, keeping your eyes on the prize.

Landry was famous for saying, "Today you have 100 percent of your life left."[15] Landry was working with young men in their twenties and thirties, and I'm writing to women age 45 to 105, but it is true that you also have 100 percent of your future life ahead of you. At any age, a life coach can come alongside to assist the growth process by helping you learn strategies and act on what you've learned.

Life coaching borrows elements from sports coaching, but life coaching is also an entity all its own. It likewise duplicates some components of therapy, especially listening on a deep and intuitive level. However, unlike therapists, coaches don't treat mental disorders.

Like therapy, effective life coaching boosts self-esteem and confidence in the one being coached and aids in building a toolbox of strategies to apply to life's most formidable challenges. A life coach facilitates these desirable outcomes by posing thoughtful questions and holding the one answering the questions accountable for her action steps.

A coaching textbook lists certain circumstances when life coaches can make a huge difference through empowering the stuck person to move forward. I've paraphrased a few situations from the textbook's list. Please circle the bullet point if you need empowerment in any of the following areas:

- You've encountered obstacles and feel discouraged.

- Your goals appear blocked and unattainable, and you are blind to potential stepping-stones to achieve them.

- You've lost the vision you once had and need a fresh look at the possibilities.

- Your inner voice sounds discouraging and negative. An empowering coach replaces the negative tapes in your head, so you hear your coach's optimistic, compassionate voice instead.[16]

Any bullet points circled? We've discussed how women yearn for mentors and coaches when they contemplate bringing a child into the world. Similarly, if you are a third-tri mom who wants to maximize your influence, make this world a better place, prepare for the next world, relate better with the younger generations, and leave a lasting legacy for beloved kids and grandkids, could a coach help?

People of all ages long for help—to solve our problems, to carry the load, to save us from disaster. Babies need help to survive and children need help to learn and grow. Teenagers need help to figure out who they are and their place in the world. Young adults need help to launch careers and establish new families. Middle adults need help raising their brood, caring for their homes, and building financial security. Is it surprising that once the nest empties, we need help adjusting once again? As we age, it feels as if we require more help than ever—and we have fewer helpers to provide it. Many of us are in a season when we need assistance, but simultaneously carry heavy responsibilities to help others.

I know what it feels like to be desperate for help. As I struggled to care for my suffering husband during the last nine years when he was in physical decline and homebound, my first word as I woke up in the morning often took the form of a single syllable prayer, "Help!" Sometimes the word inhabited my dreams, and I'd startle my husband awake in the middle of the night as I unknowingly screamed, "Help!" at the top of my lungs.

Our knowledge and ability gaps dismay us. Many find it humbling, even embarrassing, to need assistance navigating unfamiliar high-tech terrain. We are at a loss how to confront alien worldviews and lifestyles. We come undone trying to decipher the incomprehensible language, attitudes, and behaviors of the younger generations.

As our years increase, we may need transportation to and from doctor appointments or the grocery store. We will probably require help to lift heavy objects and eventually to perform ordinary household tasks or even to walk. Most of us are far more familiar and comfortable with giving rather than receiving, and we hate asking for help. *Who lives close enough and is free enough to ask for help anyway?* we wonder!

Many of us forget how our kindergarten teachers once set a sensible rule for everyone in the class to get a turn standing first in line for lunch and recess. Mothers typically go last while raising their families. We gladly ate the backs and necks from the fried chicken platter and the heels from the loaves of bread during our second trimester season. We all, kids included, grew accustomed to that system. Your grown children may not comprehend that the "kids first" rule has been modified to include a "mom's turn now" clause. When you're on the receiving end of help, expressing copious thanks, with no complaints about how the help was delivered, is the spoonful of sugar that makes the role reversal go down easier.

Angrily demanding "my turn" is unattractive whether we are four years old or one hundred and four. Even subtle entitlement hints can backfire. Your children will want to sprint in the opposite direction from a self-centered mom who suggests her children "owe" her. You can be a squeaky wheel determined to get the grease, but I warn you of the resulting high relationship cost. Keep your lips zipped. Remember Trudy's story and how she found ways to avoid going home because of her mom's self-centeredness and sense of entitlement.

The Wisdom Prize

The first empowerment strategy I want to add to your toolbox is a priceless one. When I urged you in the preceding paragraphs to discard any tendencies toward laying guilt trips on your adult kids, I was pointing you in a precise direction—the direction of wisdom. My aim in writing this book is to help you acquire more of this enormously valuable asset.

Wisdom will help you know how to act and speak in various life situations. Wisdom is vital to healthy relationships. Wisdom not only enables you to avoid problems; wisdom will also help you manage difficulties when they arise. We are not talking about simple intelligence but God-inspired understanding and an ability to see a bigger picture. The kind of wisdom we need in life's third trimester is available for the asking. "If you need wisdom, ask our generous God, and He will give it to you. He will not rebuke you for asking."[17]

Part of being wise in our older years lies in cherishing this stage of life instead of lamenting our limitations and lost youth. How about revising how you think about encroaching age? It is unnecessary to swallow our culture's disdain for old bodies, old kitchens, old vehicles, and old technology. Young and new don't always mean "better." Research on the relationship between age and happiness supports the opposite view.

A *Wall Street Journal* article declared in its headline, "Despite Covid-19, Older People Are Still Happier." In her article, Alison Gopnik summarized research conclusions comparing people from age eighteen to seventy-four. The results showed that the happier outlook of older people was independent of income, class, or culture. Even though older participants accurately ranked themselves to be at greater risk from Covid-19 than younger people, they were still "more calm, quiet and appreciative, and less concerned and anxious." Gopnik concludes, "Age grants us an equanimity that even Covid-19 can't entirely conquer."[18]

Journalist and Brookings Institution Senior Fellow Jonathan Rauch writes about the upturn in contentment levels as people enter their fifties. "Studies show quite strongly that people's satisfaction with their life increases, on average, from their early 50s on through their 60s and 70s and even beyond—for many until disability and final illness exact their toll toward the very end."[19]

Rauch mentions Princeton University economist Hannes Schwandt, who used data from an intriguing German study to uncover a unique age advantage. Schwandt asked people from two different cultures to estimate their current life satisfaction and their satisfaction expectations for five years in the future. The researchers checked back with the study participants after five years and discovered, "Younger people consistently and markedly overestimated how satisfied they would be five years later, while older people *underestimated* future satisfaction. So youth is a period of perpetual disappointment, and older adulthood is a period of pleasant surprise."[20]

Rauch also describes the findings of distinguished research psychiatrist Dr. Dilip Jeste, who focused his medical career on helping the elderly age successfully. Jeste noticed in his interactions with senior patients, including those suffering from schizophrenia, that aging people felt better, not worse, as they progressed through life's decades. He admitted great astonishment when even the onset of chronic health problems didn't stop the march toward more life satisfaction as years passed.

Jeste began questioning whether increased wisdom might explain his findings, so he conducted brain-imaging experiments to learn how seniors process tasks related to compassion, one element of wisdom. He found the wisdom concept has stayed amazingly similar over many centuries and across diverse geographic areas. He reported, "The traits of the wise tend to include compassion and empathy, good social reasoning and decision making, equanimity, tolerance of divergent values, comfort with uncertainty and ambiguity. And the whole package is more than the sum of the parts, because these traits work together to improve life not only for the wise, but also for their communities."[21]

No wonder many world cultures value their elderly citizens so highly as storehouses of wisdom and experience. Unfortunately, in the United States, not so much!

Good news: Research indicates wisdom can grow year after year. However, we must choose the wisdom path. After Rauch had considered the research findings described in the preceding paragraphs, he concluded none of these statistics "proves that people automatically get wiser with age (or more satisfied, or more calm, or more grateful). Many young people are wise, and many old people are not. It does hint, however, that aging changes us in ways that make it *easier* to be wise (and satisfied, and calm, and grateful)."[22] It sounds like aging primes us for wisdom, so let's look at some thought processes leading us in that direction.

Some time ago, a colleague of mine, Dr. Steven Smith, sent me a book he'd written after years as a therapist. A core theme, "Nothing Has to Happen My Way," expressed the wisdom Smith gained over decades as a counselor:

Nothing Has to Happen My Way

"Nothing has to happen

. . . the way I wish it would

. . . the way I think it should

. . . the way I expect it to

. . . the way I want it to

. . . when I want

. . . with whom I want

. . . any differently than it is right now

For me to be at peace."[23]

You might want to stop and read those lines again. Ponder their relevance to your own life circumstances. Do you need to attach Smith's words with a magnet to your refrigerator?

Peace had been unusually elusive for me in the days before Smith's book showed up in my mailbox. It suddenly occurred to me that I had possibly swallowed a lie about my life situation. Was it true I must feel persistent sadness because my main life desire was seemingly unmet? It felt true, but was it?

Almost immediately, a familiar Bible verse jumped into my brain, "Always be joyful. Never stop praying. *Be thankful in all circumstances,* for this is God's will for you who belong to Christ Jesus."[24] How could I be so deluded when I knew this Scripture so well? I recognized how the embedded lie had been the enemy's sneak attack to steal, kill, and destroy my peace and joy and make me ineffective in my relationships.

Secular coaching books refer to a concept developed by Richard Carson called the "gremlin."[25] Gremlin voices are defeating inner thoughts that keep us from moving forward. The gremlin loses its power over us when we can identify it for what it is, resist the gremlin's accusations and discouragement, notice our options in the situation, and then consciously choose what it is we really want. Naming this lying, accusatory entity a "gremlin" may help some readers relate better when I refer to opposing, discouraging thoughts as "enemy" voices and lies.

As I started sharing Smith's "Nothing Has to Happen My Way" wisdom and my revelation about resisting the enemy's lying voice, one woman after another in my counseling room admitted to believing she possessed "the single most unwanted circumstance or unmet desire" in her life. Consequently, these women had felt doomed to sadness. Together we renounced this falsehood; no one is doomed to despair by the particular thing happening, not even disappointing occurrences involving our adult children.

Moms-to-be invariably profit from the insight, encouragement, guidance, and inspiration they receive during their pregnancies from wise, experienced coaches, teachers, doctors, and mentors. The same can be true for you now in your third-tri season. I suggest you use this book as a coach-in-print to encourage the continual acquisition of wisdom throughout your lifetime. I want to motivate, educate, and cheer you on to a heightened awareness of the life-enhancing choices available to you. I hope to raise your sense of personal potency and help you identify your signature strengths so authentic happiness, deep peace, and true fulfillment become a reality during this final stage of your life development.

Coaching Corner

1. Looking back at your mother's example in her later years, what traits do you want to emulate in your own third-tri season?

2. In what ways do you want to be different from your mother's model as she aged?

3. Name two wise older women you admire and whose traits you want to adopt. Which of their qualities do you want to make your own?

4. What advantages of being in the third trimester do you want to acknowledge and celebrate?

5. When you cry out in your spirit for help, for what kind of help are you longing?

6. If you had a one-year goal and the continuing encouragement of a coach to help you make it happen, and if money were not an issue, what would that goal be?

7. What difference could a wise coach make in helping you achieve your goal?

8. What persistent enemy/gremlin messages will you need to resist in order to move forward toward your goal?

9. What strategy do you intend to employ this week to send the gremlin packing?

10. Do you buy into the concept that nothing has to happen your way for you to be at peace? Why or why not?

11. Has anyone laid guilt trips on you? Name them. How did you feel about those individuals?

12. Do you feel convicted about guilt-tripping any of your grown children or grandchildren?

13. When are you tempted to lay guilt trips on people in your life? What could you do instead?

14. The psalmist wrote, "Fear of the Lord is the foundation of true wisdom. All who obey his commandments will grow in wisdom."[26] Do you agree or disagree with the psalmist? Why or why not?

15. In your pursuit of wisdom this week, to what source will you go?

16. When will you go to that source?

CHAPTER 3

Our Great Obsession

WHEN YOU WERE pregnant, it was hard to carry on conversations with friends or family without the topic circling back to the child soon to be born. You discussed due dates, recent developments, ultrasound images, worrisome symptoms, room decorating ideas, and naming possibilities. And what do you suppose all my friends have in common during their current third trimester of life? You probably guessed right—every sister confesses feeling consumed over something going on in her adult kids' lives. The person of interest might be her son or daughter, grandson or granddaughter, or perhaps a niece or nephew taking center stage, but I guarantee some younger adult is on her mind and heart.

Parallel #2 between the third trimester of pregnancy and the third tri of life: Relating to the next generation and obsessing about developments in their lives dominate mothers' thoughts.

Our emotions take the form of delight over our beloved's good fortune, hard-earned achievements, and positive relationships, or grief over the opposite. Sometimes grandmas sigh with relief over the safe delivery of a grandchild, celebrate good news from a medical report, or applaud the next generation's grand accomplishments.

Other times, fear, hurt, bewilderment, guilt, or sorrow hold sway. Many mothers readily admit, "My life can only be as happy as my least happy child." Another way of stating this reality is to say that third-trimester moms find themselves emotional hostages to their offspring. Our children hold our heartstrings in their hands.

When women gather after entering an era of life without any kids in the house, one might suppose happy conversations would prevail. After all, moms now possess the freedom to focus on themselves for a change. You would envision hearing about exciting plans for travel with a spouse or friends, exhilarating dreams of new career ventures, and reveling in the reclamation of time for long-neglected hobbies, self-development, and leisure pursuits. Such bravado might actually be *all* you'd overhear if you were stuck in a superficial cocktail party setting, but *not* when honest women take off their masks and talk frankly.

A discerning counselor friend of mine reflected on years of personal observation in his Facebook post about motherhood today. He wrote, "Wired deeply into the soul of a mom is a highly complex, but ever-present connection that never goes away. It's like an emotional high-speed fiber-optic cable—1,000 megabits per second! A father can compartmentalize his emotions and feelings quite easily, but a mom? *No way*! Whether she's twenty-eight or seventy-eight, she's always thinking about her kids, and nothing in heaven or earth will change that. Did I mention worry? Is there a mother alive who doesn't worry about her 'babies?' I've not met one, ever."[27]

"Can you believe this text on my phone, Charlotte?" My widowed friend's face was damp with tears as she handed me her phone. I scanned the short message: "Now you know why I never come to see you!"

Laura explained, "My youngest son drove ten hours with his wife and toddler to spend four days visiting our family. To my dismay, once they'd arrived in town, my son texted me saying they didn't want to include me in any family activities. No explanation! Instead, they stayed all four nights and ate every meal with his sister's family in a nearby subdivision. He made it clear I was not invited to join them. He promised they'd 'stop by my house' and finally did bring my little grandson for forty-five minutes on their way back out of town. I offered to feed them, but they didn't want anything. I was nervous about the visit because my daughter-in-law seems to hate me for some unknown reason. However, I was pleasant and kind and interacted with all of them. I hugged them enthusiastically and played with my grandson as much as he'd let me. I gushed about how smart and adorable he is. I thought everything went well, so I was shocked the next day when my son sent his text, 'Now you know why I never come to see you.' What on earth is he talking about?"

During recent conversations, Lucy, Teresa, Kim, Anne, Donna, Carla, Betsy, Delores, Beth, Shirley, and Peggy all spilled their anguish involving adult kids. These eleven women represent multitudes of others with similar heart-wrenching stories. Some of the vignettes may seem negative and extreme in comparison to your family's situation, but look for elements relating to your experiences. As you hear the confusion and sorrow of these moms, *keep in mind that these scenarios do not have their last chapter written yet.* God promises us hope and wise guidance for a better tomorrow.

Lucy: "My forty-two-year-old son is going through a divorce, was just released from a treatment center for alcoholism, lost his trucking job, and refuses to accept any family phone calls. At the treatment center, he told the counselors that a neighbor had sexually molested him. I want to give him emotional support, and I'm willing to drive the fourteen hundred miles to show up on his doorstep, but I'm afraid he'll slam the door in my face. I have diarrhea and haven't slept in three nights over his revelation of sexual abuse. I feel responsible for not protecting him."

Teresa: "My thirty-three-year-old daughter looks to everyone like she's on top of the world. She's landed a great career, but I just found out she has slept with more than thirty men, some married and as old as her father. She's gorgeous, smart, and talented, but she craves attention from males even though she had a good, involved dad. I've devoted my life to her, but I don't know how to save her from this reckless course. She wasn't raised to live like this."

Kim: "My thirty-nine-year-old son has a painful digestive condition and doctors haven't been able to figure out exactly what's going on. He's had every test, but no clear diagnosis or remedy. His sweet wife is right by his side, so that is a blessing, but it kills me when he doubles over in pain. I am so worried. I've had cancer, you know . . ."

Anne: "My thirty-five-year-old daughter just moved in with a new boyfriend who plays video games all the time. I strongly suspect he's a drug addict. I'm pretty sure he uses porn, and I know he's hit her. She lived with another deadbeat guy for three years and had two kids with that creep. She was always such a sweet and smart child and good student, but she went crazy her last year of high school and started hanging out with drug users. She flunked out of college her freshman year and lies around doing nothing. We cashed out my 401k to pay for two stints of rehab already, to no avail. I'm raising her two little girls because she was neglecting them. They are sweet, like she was once upon a time."

Donna: "My youngest told me today that he and his wife are expecting again—their fifth baby in six years. He's such a good dad to his brood, but I worry about another pregnancy so soon. I love the thought of this precious grandchild about to join our clan. Still, I worry I won't have the energy to keep up with all the little ones who need Grandma's lap and babysitting time. It's exhilarating, but exhausting, to be Grandma to thirteen grandkids. When everyone gathers at our house for meals, it's fabulous to be together, but I collapse for two or three days afterwards.

"Family traditions mean so much to me, and I'm immensely grateful we live close to each other. However, it is getting harder than it used to be to entertain the kids and clean our big old house and cook the complicated family recipes they expect when we gather. I can't bear the thought of disappointing them by not cooking their favorite childhood dishes. They help, of course, and we often do potluck, but I don't know how much longer I can keep up my end, and I'd feel guilty for letting them down."

Carla: "My forty-six-year-old unmarried daughter was a missionary for more than two decades, but I asked her to leave her assignment in Brazil to help me care for her cancer-afflicted, bedridden father. I was wearing down after eight years of nonstop caretaking for an invalid husband. She criticizes everything I do, and I think she is slipping into a depression. I try hard to be a fun person to be around, and I know to give her space. Despite her courage in traveling all over the world, even braving the rigors of the Amazon River, she's now too anxious to apply for a job. I should never have asked her to come home."

Betsy: "I homeschooled my three highly intelligent sons and paid for their college educations at prestigious universities. They all have successful careers and are financially well off, but none of them goes to church, and they obviously despise me. Two refuse to set foot in my house. I've had health problems develop since their father died last year, but they don't care about any of my challenges as a new widow. They've all made it clear they would consider it an imposition to help me in any way when I undergo a hip replacement and rehab next month. I tried so hard to be the ideal mother. I simply don't understand!"

Delores: "My thirty-seven-year-old daughter just goes off on me. She frequently asks me to fly up and help with her new baby and two preschoolers, so I've closed my law practice earlier than I anticipated to be available whenever she needs me. She's terribly uptight and stressed by motherhood, although she graduated third in her class from Auburn's School of Veterinary Medicine. She's a competent person and handled other pressures just fine, but motherhood has her bamboozled. I always looked forward to being a grandma, and I dearly love the grandkids, but whatever I do is never quite right. She doesn't seem able to cope and takes it out on me, to the point of being abusive. I apparently am letting her down somehow. She took it hard when her dad walked out of the house and into the arms of another woman. I fear she has entrenched anger and bitterness leaking out because of our divorce."

Beth: "I'm proud my son makes a good living as a cardiac surgeon, but he's married to a controlling wife, and she has totally stiff-armed me since their wedding day. My husband and I have tried to make friendly overtures, but she takes offense over nothing. I have no idea what I've done wrong. I just know she's written me off and makes a point to keep my son and grandkids away from us too. Holidays are tense and miserable if we're together, but usually they go to her side of the family and ignore us completely. I dread every birthday, Mother's Day, Thanksgiving, and Christmas because I feel so unwanted, lonely, and unloved."

Shirley: "My daughter's wedding is next month. We don't like the guy she's marrying, and his parents are a piece of work. In opposition to our wishes, they've already lived together for three years. How on earth am I going to pull off the happy mother-of-the-bride look when I'm so worried she's making a huge mistake? Two bridal showers require my smiling attendance next week. She expects us to pay the bills for dresses and flowers and musicians and photographers and sit-down meals at $35 a plate for 160 guests. I've looked forward all my life to Heather's wedding day, but I didn't expect it to be so conflict-ridden. She doesn't express gratitude for anything, although we've depleted much of our retirement savings to give her the wedding she wants. She says we 'owe' her, but for what?"

Peggy: "My kids are all doing great. Well, that's not exactly true. All four married smart and talented spouses, dearly love their kids, and are super-involved in their activities. They work hard and are successful in their jobs. They're generally kind and generous people, but they show little interest in continuing the relationships with Christ that they established as kids. They are raising my grandchildren with no exposure to the Bible whatsoever. They've subtly communicated I shouldn't sing songs like 'Jesus Loves Me' or read their children any Christian-themed stories. What did I do wrong that's made them run from the God they loved as youths and keep their kids away from the world's best-selling book?"

Welcome to a reality you didn't anticipate when your nest emptied. Your kids (and grandkids) are *still always on your mind*. Your heart aches with love for them. You yearn for their well-being and for close, healthy relationships. Your greatest desire is for their eternal well-being. And there are still sleepless nights spent tossing and turning due to discomfort and worry.

A sixty-four-year-old friend lamented, "Diapers, sibling rivalry, cleaning up messes, and school hassles were a breeze—tiring, of course, but I felt like a competent, nurturing mother back then. Today my adult kids make me feel like an abject failure, and my life is full of tension and conflict. Parenting grown children constitutes the brutal chapter, not when they're little."

When our kids leave, our hearts go with them! Sure, we tried to appropriately cut the apron strings and allow them to fly. We know releasing them to live their own lives is part of being a good mother. We intentionally occupy ourselves with other pursuits. Replacement activities seem hollow, however, if something is out of kilter with our sons or daughters or grandchildren. And most of us flat out "miss" our kids, but attempt to hide it because it's not their fault they grew up and left us behind!

Listen to third-trimester women chatting candidly, and you won't need to wait long before the subject of a son or daughter comes up. The range of heart-wrenching emotions accompanying these discussions is vast: unbridled joy, pride, relief, gratitude, and optimism—but often worry, anger, hurt, regret, confusion, or hopelessness as well.

Comparisons Steal Your Contentment!

Do you remember how awful you felt on particularly rough days of your pregnancy, but then you felt even worse when a friend appeared to be breezing through her nine months, constantly basking in her motherly glow? The feeling that your friends were handling pre-birth challenges better than you, though probably not accurate in retrospect, hit a sensitive nerve. Years later you recognize other mothers in your group most likely suffered through some painful, uncomfortable, and miserable days too, but your assessment was skewed because you were not privy to the whole story.

The same is true with life's third-trimester comparisons. Because mothers tend to cover up tender, vulnerable places to protect their parental nakedness from judgmental eyes, we assume everything is hunky-dory between the generations at the houses of most others in our neighborhoods or churches. Facebook certainly gives that impression. Every day we see impressive tributes to *other* moms. It appears so obvious the younger crowd relishes time with *other* parents and grandparents. We view photos of hugging family members and frequent intergenerational birthday and holiday bashes. New grandbabies gaze with adoring eyes at doting grandmas who were invited into the inner circle for birthings and other intimate family events. We try not to think about being deliberately excluded from the happy occasions people are gushing about online.

The next posts display smiling faces on exotic family trips that include beloved grandmas and grandpas. You know the true story behind some of the lovey-dovey pretense on social media sites and recognize a lot of hypocrisy and careful curating of posts. Even so, if you don't feel valued as one of those esteemed and successful parents or grandparents yourself, you may surrender to weeping after viewing social media!

The message to remember is that *comparisons rob you of your joy*! You need to know the truth: you are not alone if you experience distance (either emotionally or geographically) from the generations following you. You are not alone if you tiptoe on eggshells for fear of offending one or more of your children or their spouses and driving those you love even further away. You are not alone if your child is rejecting you and the God you serve. You are not alone if you desperately desire to improve relationships but don't know how.

You are not even alone if your adult kids are non-achievers, self-focused, unappreciative, resentful of you, and avoid spending time with you. They may say mostly critical things to your face or behind your back. Perhaps they only show interest in you as a convenient babysitter or source of money. You are not alone if you don't feel honored, respected, or loved, and if you feel like a parental failure because of destructive choices you see your grown children making.

On the other hand, you are also not alone if you cherish every minute spent with your adult kids and grandkids and crave their company above any other, and they feel the same about you. Family time together is the highlight of all your lives, and you get together frequently. No one else has such ability to make you laugh yourself silly or prompt you to cry and pray when they're hurting. You are so proud of them for what they've achieved. You're flooded with grateful thoughts about your joy-filled friendships. Being helpful to the younger generations and planning ways to be part of your sons, daughters, and grandkids' lives dominate your thoughts. Welcome to a diverse, emotion-filled third-tri club!

New Strategies

First-time mothers frequently describe their third trimesters of pregnancy as an anxiety-filled time with looming complications at every turn. It turns out third-tri parenting, particularly in America at this time in history, is often even more anxiety-producing and surprisingly complicated. I've pondered feedback from focus groups and contemplated information gathered through surveys and interviews. Combined with comments in my counseling room from children and adolescents, young singles and young marrieds, as well as third-tri parents, I am convinced that clearing the intergenerational minefield is critical to safe passage for all ages.

I am not undertaking this hazardous cleanup job because I have all the answers. To the contrary, I've ignorantly detonated numerous relationship landmines myself! Therefore, we will be leaning on wisdom from multiple experts and sources. I will attempt to filter human opinions, including scientifically derived ones, through the ancient truths God has generously made available for centuries to people of all ages.

Remember, we are in life's third trimester *together* and need to lock arms with one another, supporting, encouraging, and caring for injured and suffering sisters. We may be the walking wounded, but we are also seasoned, astute, dedicated mothers and grandmothers, intent on developing and implementing strategies to gain victory over the crafty enemy of our family's souls. The cruel prince of this world, not a wayward child, is the evil one endeavoring to steal our dreams, kill our joy, and destroy our legacies.

One clue to winning this war is evident in the Lord's instructions to Solomon, advising the king that if calamities strike the land, he should react in a specific way. The Lord urged, "If my people who are called by my name will humble themselves and pray and seek my face and turn from their wicked ways, I will hear from heaven and will forgive their sins and restore their land."[28]

Are you called by the Lord's name? Do you aspire to wear the label of *Christian*? If so, then restoring your land (and specifically your family territory) starts with humbling yourself. Not one of us was perfect, despite all our great intentions when our children were growing up, and not one of us is perfect now.

The Lord promises to heal our land if we meet the fourfold criteria to (1) humble ourselves, (2) pray, (3) seek the Lord's face, and (4) turn from our sinful ways. He then goes on to pledge, "But if you or your descendants abandon me and disobey the decrees and commands I have given you, and if you serve and worship other gods, then I will uproot the people from this land that I have given them. . . ." They will ask, 'Why did the Lord do such terrible things to this land?' And the answer will be, 'Because his people abandoned the LORD . . . and *they worshiped other gods instead and bowed down to them*. That is why he has brought all these disasters on them'"[29] (emphasis mine).

According to the Lord's explanation quoted above, turning from sinful ways includes remorse and actions consistent with forsaking allegiance to non-God gods. Let's consider what alternative gods might be competing for your worship and loyalty. As mothers, we sometimes err by making our children our gods, allowing their wishes to dictate our courses of action. Compromising our beliefs in an attempt to get grown children to like us can easily take precedence over pleasing God.

I trained for seven years to become a psychologist but am well aware my profession is not a worthy god. Replacement gods of this culture (academic degrees, wealth, beauty, power, science, pleasure, enter-tainment, sexual gratification, politics, celebrities, and esoteric spiritu-ality) fail us. Many of us are dumbfounded by the cesspool our country has become as non-gods proliferate. We mothers face a huge cleanup job, starting with ourselves. The first thing we need to sweep out are our own false gods.

Therefore, a prime strategy involves focusing on *changing yourself instead of changing others*. Obstetricians repeatedly remind mothers how important it is for the health and well-being of the developing baby to first focus on the nutrition, exercise, and emotional support of the preg-nant mom. In the same way, achieving third-tri health begins with hum-bling ourselves through personal repentance and turning from false gods.

Why is this so important? The answer: When you focus entirely on changing your adult child, you turn into an irritating manipulator, incite further rebellion, and cause more harm than good. One of the anger-charged, negative descriptions of mothers I frequently hear from young adults in my counseling room is some variation of, "My mom is so controlling."

Shortsighted, unwise mothers set goals that can be obstructed. You may repeatedly try to force your adult daughter to get off drugs. You may lecture her because you are intent on your daughter getting a better job or treating you with more respect. You might be pushing her to marry a quality guy instead of just living together or allowing men to take advantage of her. You may be vociferously opposing a sexual life-style that defies your beliefs. Since such objectives targeted entirely on changing your children can be thwarted by their wills and the actions of others, you run the danger of appearing to be an annoying, judgmen-tal control freak in their eyes.

The Lord's advice to Solomon suggests an alternative goal: Become the godly woman the Lord desires *you* to be, and concentrate on getting rid of false gods in your *own* life. Follow the Lord's prescription, and look to Him to heal your family territory. Jesus asks us, "Why worry about a speck in your friend's eye when you have a log in your own? . . . Hypocrite! First get rid of the log in your own eye; then you will see well enough to deal with the speck in your friend's eye."[30]

Please don't misinterpret my message. Not every adult child's foolish decision, bad behavior, unfortunate life circumstance, or lack of affection for you is related to your mothering behaviors. In coming chapters, we will look more closely at what God has to say about our misguided tendency to take responsibility for our adult child's choices, both bad and good.

The truth? We cannot legitimately claim credit for our sons' and daughters' successes, nor their failures. Some mothers pridefully look down their noses, believing they did everything right as a parent, as confirmed by their adult kids doing so well now. These arrogant mothers are insufferable to moms drowning in despair and guilt. I want to drain away some of the guilt you are swimming in, not add to it, so you can peacefully breathe again.

I wish to convey that there is an *order* to recovery that starts with *looking at ourselves first*. Taking steps to make your own corrections instead of obsessing over, and trying to control, what your child needs to do, can provide better opportunities to meet your adult children where they are and foster healthier communication down the line.

Among the Ten Commandments, the only one with a promise attached is "Honor your father and mother. *Then* you will live a long, full life in the land the LORD your God is giving you."[31] More than anything, we want our descendants to be blessed with long, happy, full lives serving God here on earth and eventually receive rewards in heaven.

However, we dislike the thought of *grudging* obedience to the commandment to honor father and mother. One mom confided, "Just as sex performed out of duty isn't pleasurable to either party, when I sense my kids are mechanically doing the dutiful act of calling or visiting me because they feel guilty and obliged, little satisfaction occurs. I detect they hope our interaction won't last long because they have more important and enjoyable things on their schedules. I want to be honored because they truly value me and treasure my company."

If you view your adult child as dishonoring you, it may not seem fair that *you* must work to become more honor-worthy. Unfortunately, no matter how hard you tried to be an ideal parent through the years, your adult child may remember you as hurtful or unloving or angry or selfish or controlling or judgmental or impossible to please. The biblical pattern is consistent: *we* must humble ourselves and repent and pray, so that forgiving and honoring us become a little easier. Then, God can do His work of healing and restoration in our families and in our land.

Almost none of us with empty nests expected our kids, when they reached adulthood, to feel so much disapproval of us, or turn against Jesus as God's Son, or torpedo their lives with addictions or sexual immorality. We thought there might be a few tough teen years and anticipated maybe they'd think we were pretty dumb during the college years. But we'd loved them, nurtured them, taught them, and prayed for them. Therefore, we assumed any rejection or rebellion would be temporary, surely not lasting decades. Many hurting moms are still waiting as they travel through their third tri of life, beginning to wonder if they will live long enough to see their blind sons' and daughters' eyes open.

Your nest may have emptied two, ten, or fifty years ago, but your kids stay constantly on your mind, and you would willingly drop everything if they needed you. It is no exaggeration to say our children and grandchildren are in peril. An anti-Christian worldview increasingly invades our culture at a hyper-warp speed none of us would have predicted a few years ago. We stand as holders of ancient wisdom desperately needed by the younger generations, but we find ourselves sadly marginalized and fear our influence is waning.

The good news: All is not lost, and you are not left without a prescription for progress toward healing strained relationships. Exactly like a pregnancy with serious complications needing medical intervention, there is still hope for healing in your family, leading to a shared and loving future together.

We are all sheep who have gone astray and require a good shepherd to rescue us. Once we became moms, we accepted the challenge to shepherd those entrusted to us. Because I grew up on a sheep farm, I have experienced my share of shepherding adorable but foolish animals. My most beloved pet ever was our sheepdog, Sparky. Sparky rounded up those stubborn balls of cotton far better than I could. He wasn't afraid of the menacing rams, but as a little girl, I was.

Over lunch this week, a pastor friend described his visit to a sheep ranch. He wanted to educate himself about the makeup of good shepherds. After observing the sheep at the farm, he concluded that a well-trained canine is the singular component most responsible for shepherding outcomes. He had watched with fascination as the small energetic dog circled the flock and nudged the lagging or straying members to follow the shepherd leading his snow-white recruits.

But what about those intimidating rams, easily twice the size of the dog, the ones that ferociously threatened to charge the shaggy shepherd? When a hulking ram tried to intimidate, the sheepdog refused to step back. Instead, our canine hero stood still and *leaned in* toward the defiant ram. He didn't bark, growl, or bare his teeth; he just stood firm and *leaned in*. And the bullying rams backed off and fell in line. It reminds me of Paul's advice to persecuted first-century Christians, "Be on guard. Stand firm in the faith. Be courageous. Be strong. And do everything with love."[32]

Coaching Corner

Today the coaching questions are tough and challenging, but they originate from my heart of love for hurting moms. Please sense me in your corner, asking you to make some needed adjustments and encouraging you to stagger back into the boxing ring with your head held high. Hear my voice as soft and affirming, never stern nor judgmental. My heart aches for all of you pummeled by a ferocious opponent. I want the victory for you as much as you want it for yourself.

1. In what ways are your relationships with your adult children different from what you anticipated when they were younger?

2. With which of the mothers' stories in this chapter did you most identify? Why?

3. How do you feel about being asked to work on improving your-self *first*, as a prelude to dealing with unwanted family dynamics?

4. If I had secretly filmed your life this past month, what non-God gods might I suspect were competing with Jesus for first place in your life?

5. What do you want to do about those false gods?

6. What would it look like to forsake your false gods?

7. Which of the four criteria for healing our land and restoring lost territory (humble yourself, pray, seek the Lord's face, turn from your sinful ways) sounds hardest to you?

8. What is one step you could take to overcome the obstacles preventing implementation of the four criteria?

9. Would any of your adult children accuse you of being too controlling?

10. What two things could you change to come across as less controlling?

11. When are you going to make those changes?

12. Identify any struggles you experience when you compare yourself with other third-trimester moms? What do you want to do about tormenting comparisons?

13. What does your inner gremlin mutter to you about your child's unwise choices?

14. What is one thing you could tell yourself when the enemy accuses you of failing as a mom?

CHAPTER 4

The Humility Factor

DO YOU SOMETIMES wonder if you have what it takes to be a good mother to your adult children? When describing the heroines and heroes who inhabit every novel and movie ever created, author and screenwriter, Donald Miller, asserts, "Feelings of self-doubt are universal, as is the desire to become somebody competent and courageous."[33]

Previously, in our *second* trimester of pregnancy, we wondered if we had what it takes to go through childbirth and take care of a baby. However, because there were trustworthy authorities to guide us and we wanted so much to be successful, we tackled the assignment of getting ready for the challenges. In this empty-nest stage of life, we often stay paralyzed by even greater feelings of self-doubt and inadequacy when our offspring make bewildering choices or display incomprehensible attitudes.

It turns out having a warm attachment in the growing-up years is no guarantee you'll never be estranged. A friend related, "My daughter and I were so close. I was the fun mom who hosted slumber parties, helped out in the classroom, and entertained her pals at our vacation house on the shore of Lake Michigan. I took her and her friends skiing in the winter and swimming most summer days. She seemed particularly proud that I was the involved den mother of her Girl Scout troop. Her years at nursing school were also a breeze, and our strong relationship continued when she started working at the hospital.

"Then she got married. I expected her husband to be her first priority, so I backed way off, avoiding any advice-giving or asking for her time. I had no idea she had resentments festering toward me. I was shocked when she confronted me, accusing me of being "abusive" during her growing-up years, and self-centered and uncaring about her life now. She indicated I'd ruined her life and proceeded to distance herself physically and emotionally. I feel like she can't stand me, and it's the most painful thing I've ever experienced."

Another girlfriend asked, "What happened to the confidence I used to have when raising my kids? As a young mom, I read lots of books about raising kids and conscientiously applied what I learned. I found biblical guidelines making sense to me about the importance of abundant love and appropriate discipline. I tried to mother my two perfectly, believing they would then harbor no reasons to revolt once they reached adulthood. By the estimation of anyone knowing and admiring my family, we were affectionate and close and our kids would be the least likely to ever rebel.

"I urged their dad to soften his harsher approach by reminding him of specific directives such as, 'Fathers, do not provoke your children to anger by the way you treat them. Rather bring them up with the discipline and instruction that comes from the Lord'[34] and 'Fathers, do not aggravate your children, or they will become discouraged.'[35] I objected to my husband's sterner approach, but I knew he loved them dearly. However, considering their current lifestyles, opposing worldviews, and lack of interest in enjoying time with their dad and me, I now feel the cloud of failure hanging over me to such a degree that I'm walking around in a fog most of the time. I have no idea how to salvage anything but the most superficial of relationships."

Unfortunately, by the time offspring in our American culture enter adolescence, many are already provoked and aggravated by one or both parents. If not as teenagers, then later as young adults, countless sons and daughters baffle their mothers with their hostility, immoral lifestyles, self-sabotaging choices, and disdain for parental values. The same children who could not bear to be separated overnight now act like they wouldn't care if they ever saw their parent again, and some even say exactly that. Mothers keep hoping their children will grow out of this stage, and many do, but not as many as you'd wish. It's not surprising that moms of wayward children choke over the ultimate self-doubt questions: Is this my fault? What did I do wrong? And how on earth am I supposed to handle these impasses now?

The pervasive sense of failure among my third-trimester sisters weighs heavily on my mind, and I've felt it myself. I experienced seasons when self-doubt stole my joy and immobilized me. Therefore, I want to clothe all our heads with new superhero hats—fresh thoughts based on different beliefs from replays of our constant "if only" variations such as:

- If only I'd homeschooled
- If only I had not homeschooled
- If only I hadn't let sports activities dominate our schedule and steal church time and family life
- If only I had taken out a second mortgage and sent her to a Christian university instead of to the affordable state university

- If only I hadn't become so frustrated and angry and said hurtful things

- If only I'd been a stay-at-home mom instead of a working mother (or vice versa)

- If only I hadn't pushed rules and youth group attendance so strongly (or vice versa)

- If only their dad and I had modeled the Christian life better, prayed more, and defended Bible truths more intelligently.

- If only I hadn't worked so hard, but instead had been more playful and fun and taken more vacations

- If only . . .

Gary Thomas, author of many insightful books about family relationships, points out, "As parents, we ultimately wear our kids' failures as though they were our own. No, I'm not saying we *should*, just that we usually *do*. We tend to take too much credit for kids who turn out well and too much blame for kids who rebel. It can be a difficult truth, that none of us can be such good parents that God becomes obligated to save our children's souls. Yet on the encouraging side, none of us can mess up so badly that our children are somehow beyond the reach of God's mercy."[36]

I agree with Thomas when he clarifies, "I am not saying that children can't be led astray and even damaged by deficiencies in our parenting. But the failure of kids does not necessarily mean we have failed as parents, even though it does probably mean we'll *feel* as though we've failed."[37]

In light of the Bible's acknowledgment that many children will not adopt parental beliefs and values, Thomas urges moms and dads to "recognize that a child's rebellion *doesn't mean they've failed as parents.* In other words, Jesus said this not to condemn us, but to prepare us."[38] Yes, we need to be *prepared* to examine our own hearts, grow in our own love relationship with Christ, and cope with disappointments if sons or daughters sabotage their lives.

However, my fellow third-tri heroines, what do we *do* with all those failure and guilt feelings? Our guilt hammers us with the likelihood that we bear some degree of responsibility for our children's mystifying behaviors and attitudes. How do we get to the place of moving on with competence and courage?

Hard challenges confronted you in your pregnancy's third trimester, just as they do now. Sometimes the pregnancy was unexpected, unwanted, or perhaps physically or financially risky. Since 1973 in America, the choice to abort or not abort has existed. The decision whether to marry the baby's father is a life-altering choice, as is whether to give a child up for adoption. Recognizing the immensity of the consequences of choices made by pregnant women leads us to the third parallel between pregnancy and our current third trimester of life:

Parallel #3: Whether in pregnancy's third trimester or in life's third trimester, when mothers face difficult quandaries, a successful outcome depends on making *wise* responses.

In the previous chapter, I introduced an initial fourfold "to do" list based on 2 Chronicles 7:14. By way of review, the Lord's promise to heal our family territory, (our "land"), rests on God's people engaging in the following four actions:

1. Humble ourselves.

2. Pray.

3. Seek the Lord's face.

4. Turn from our sinful ways, especially worshipping other gods.

The four mandates address a set of problems the Lord predicted Israel might experience, "At times I might shut up the heavens so that no rain falls, or command grasshoppers to devour your crops, or send plagues among you."[39] All those dire circumstances don't seem worse disasters than the broken heart you may be experiencing today over an adult child's path.

Originally the healing referenced in 2 Chronicles 7:14 specified the nation of Israel, but healing in families often precedes healing of the country. We can turn each of God's four conditions for healing into guidelines for mothers of adult children. Let's start with some prerequisites and ramifications of humbling ourselves.

Guideline #1: Humbling ourselves necessitates examining relationships with our parents. Be sure you have been diligent to process and forgive wounds from your own upbringing.

In a third-trimester workshop I taught, I asked participants to fill out a worksheet answering three questions:

1. Thinking about your own mother, what was the most *helpful* thing she did or said *when you were an adult* to build or improve your relationship?

2. What was the *worst* thing your mom did or said in your adulthood that has hampered your relationship with her?

3. What do you wish your mother had said or done?

You will notice I was trying to focus the group members' attention on how their mothers had hurt or helped interpersonal dynamics *after* their kids left home. In reading my participants' feedback, I detected an enormous degree of simmering resentments. Only 39 percent responded with appreciation for their moms' efforts to make relationships better. However, one group member's mother healed a bunch of wounds when she complimented her daughter's parenting style by saying, "I wish you could have been *my* parent." What a powerful affirmation!

This mother's praise of her daughter's parenting demonstrates the power of a single positive affirmation to turn things around. Alas, few of the participants seemed to have heard the sentences they craved. Instead, these women remained trapped with bad feelings about their mothers, and they supplied a list of grievances they'd carried for many years, sometimes long past their mothers' deaths. Several resentments were based on a single offensive sentence their mom once uttered—one permanently stuck in the craw of their adult child. The persistence of bitterness in our hearts toward our mothers surfaces another similarity between an expectant mom and those of us with empty nests.

Parallel #4: It is necessary for both moms-to-be and third-tri moms to "grow up" because the younger generations depend on us to be examples of maturity and responsibility.

Why do women judge their moms so harshly when we want mercy from our own kids? Few of my third-tri peers connected their internal lack of forgiveness and honor for their own mothers with lack of honor from their offspring.

The reality of my mother-daughter journey reminded me that my mother was eighty years old before I grew up enough to fully humble myself and write a long-overdue tribute. For decades, I was stuck on how she favored my brother and never once said she was proud of me and other perceived offenses. I was ensnared in grudge-keeping until God convicted me and helped me to repent.

Until the last couple of generations, when it became common for offspring to disrespect parents, many of us went through the motions of "honoring." Still, in our hearts, many of us nursed grudges, even if we covered them up with less overt in-your-face hostility than many mothers receive now from the generations following us.

Finally, as a gift for her eightieth birthday, I humbled myself and wrote a tribute to my mother. I printed my words out on parchment paper, framed my tribute, wrapped it in pretty paper, and delivered it to her. My mother immediately hung it in the place of honor over her television set where she could see it every day. Along with a couple of family photos, Mom insisted on bringing my framed tribute to adorn her nursing room wall until the day she died at age ninety-two. I wish I had changed my heart, appreciated her more, and written her tribute decades sooner, but I will share with you what I wrote.

A Tribute from Your Daughter

Time has passed far too quickly since you gave me the gift of life, lovingly welcoming me into the world of rural life. Over the years I've come to cherish my farm heritage with all its opportunities to interact with the animal kingdom and the cycles of nature. With consummate skill, you taught me to clean and cook and sew, often against my protests, which I'm glad you ignored. You made our home beautiful with your eye for color, expressed in wallpapering and painting and curtain making. You were the original recycler—using bits and scraps and whatever you had to create something new and functional and lovely. You inspire me to this day with your ingenuity and resourcefulness. From you I learned to value order and beauty and the smell of homemade bread and fresh, clean sheets.

You passed on your esteem for lifelong learning and education, honing your own keen intellect. You continue to amaze me with your wealth of knowledge. All your descendants have been challenged to develop their minds and love books, and thank you for passing on your high-IQ genes to all of us. Even as the years advanced, you've persisted in your creativity, turning quilting projects into works of art, authoring rich treasuries of fascinating family history, and doggedly mastering new technology, including the frustrating medium of the computer in your seventies.

You modeled commitment to your wedding vows in countless ways, the most profound being your rock-solid decision to stick by Dad's side through thick and thin, for better and for worse. You also modeled commitment to your church, honesty, hard work, a job well done, and moral choices. You deeply honored your own parents and extended family, and you taught me to sacrifice for my children and the generations to follow, through your example.

You faithfully made gargantuan efforts to involve me in church activities, where obedience to God's laws and love for Jesus got planted in my earliest days. Of all the gifts you've given me, a heart tender toward God matters the most—for both you and me. As we age, it is increasingly clear that earthly life is fleeting, so loving God passionately, and drawing strength from Him to *love our families and neighbors as ourselves, is the most important legacy anyone can bequeath.*

Throughout the years, you've loved me to the very best of your ability, and you've given me so much I value and cherish. God has used it all to mold me, even your well-meaning mistakes.

It occurs to me that probably the true "best" at this stage of life is to extend boundless mercy and grace to each other and walk humbly with our God. I ask you to forgive me for not being a perfect daughter, and I forgive you for not being the perfect mother. Despite all our noble intentions and all our enormous efforts, we're both still fallible human beings. How liberating to know God forgives generously and completely, and loves us fervently, despite our imperfections. I want to celebrate our mother-daughter relationship in the same spirit, loving and forgiving with abandon.

Happy 80th Birthday, Mom! I love you!

The level of humility needed to quick start the healing process begins with admitting we have not honored our own parents as God commands. We did not have flawless parents, but we weren't faultless children either! You see more lashing out and avoiding family get-togethers and harsh accusations today, but the dishonoring issue is the same. We didn't like things about the way we were raised, nor how we were treated once we reached adulthood. Ditto for our kids. Yet, all generations want to be loved and appreciated for what they did get right.

Even if your mother had few redeeming qualities, she will have demonstrated how you do not want to behave as a parent. Through her bad example, she taught you important information you can put to good use. And no, you do not have to be an alcoholic, abusive, self-centered, or full of self-pity because she modeled those things. You can choose the opposite.

I introduced Guideline #1 first because it applies to making peace with the generation ahead of you. However, the same humbling process will also be necessary to make peace with the generation behind you. We will visit the important themes of confession, repentance, and forgiveness repeatedly.

We each have our own way of humbling ourselves and expressing sorrow for being so tardy in recognizing all the good things we learned in our homes of origin. My Cajun husband, the godly man I married after I had been a widow for two years, didn't wear shoes to school until the fourth grade, nor have an indoor potty until he went away from home on a college scholarship. Yet he is far more eloquent in expressing his repentant feelings than I. He also arrived at his place of humbling sooner. One Mother's Day years ago, he read his raw, honest account of his unfortunate feelings about his mother in front of the entire congregation where he pastored. Now that is humbling oneself!

Tooger's Repentant Letter to His Mom

Dear Mom,

I am in my forties now. You are bedridden and no longer able to recognize me. Only a few people on this planet have ever seen you. Your picture has never been in a newspaper or magazine. Now your world is limited to only Dad's constant care and a few others who help him. One day your body will die, like your mind has already done. But Mom, you will live forever.

As I pondered what to talk about this Mother's Day Sunday, I felt compelled to write to you. I know you can't under-

stand, and yet I sense you understood for many years what I now have the spirit to confess to you and to God and before the congregation. I am impressed with my blindness and stupidity and your wisdom and love.

When I was growing up on our sharecropper's farm, I saw you as fat, uneducated, poor, and old. You were ignorant of most of this world and its concepts. You spoke broken English. You could read a little and write essentially nothing—hardly equipped to raise six children. It did not matter those conditions were essentially beyond your control. You had been born into that environment and equipped the way God provided. And you had risen steps above your 13 brothers and sisters.

I quickly grew to dislike fat, uneducated, poor, and old. As a teenage student in school, I did not want to be seen with you. All I saw was the dilapidated car, the homemade feedsack dress, the butchered language, the eating habits, the lack of money—the list seemed endless. You were an embarrassment to me. What would my friends say? May peer pressure be eternally accursed!

Mom, I'm so sorry. I've prayed often since I've grown up that God mercifully blinded you to my stupidity and sin during those years. Please forgive me. I'm sorry for the times I hurt you. Thank you for doing your best for me in spite of me. I know now that's what love is—doing the best for your child in spite of your child. I could not tell you before, while you were still able to communicate; I hoped maybe God had protected you from knowing my wicked thoughts during those years. If He had hidden my foolish judgments from you, I did not want to hurt you with my adult apology.

Mom, according to this world's standards, you still are fat, uneducated, poor, and old. Like the rest of the world, I was blind to real beauty, but now I see. Once I was blind to real wisdom, but now I understand. Once I thought gold and silver were real wealth, but now I know differently. Mom, I am so proud of you.

I understand now the pain you felt when you could not help with my homework. I understand the pain you felt when you could not provide material things that were so important to a teenager. I understand the pain of feeling out of place in a society that bases status on youthful appearance and social and economic standing. I understand the pain of parenting a rebellious, ungrateful teenager.

During college years I grew some, and then I was able to hug you and give you a kiss, and tell you I loved you. I started getting you a watermelon every Mother's Day, because you enjoyed juicy watermelon more than flowers. I suspect there will be something like watermelon in heaven for you.

You did not leave when it got tough. You hung in there when Dad was so sick for so long. You were strong enough not to answer my rudeness with rudeness. You were indeed a class act. Now I realize you are a champion among mothers.

I thought I was tough because I played football, but toughness is being true to the challenge of continuously performing as a Christian mother in today's world. Toughness is saying "no" when "no" needs to be said. Mom, you spent countless hours in prayer to be so strong, so much like Jesus. I know you prayed, because I spied you on your knees at the end of every exhausting day of serving your family, often falling asleep with your head resting on the edge of the bed.

Now, Mom, I see how beautiful you really were during all those years. You really did do it all. You took care of me and five others. It was not Dad's fault he could not read or write and was nearly completely blind. Nevertheless, you still had to care for everything, from money matters to discipline and most everything else in between. I remember, Mom, there was always food to eat. You spent countless back-breaking hours growing most of it in your huge garden.

Why did I change my foolish judgments? And why are your six children and twenty grandchildren all Christians? And why do my five siblings also love you today like I do? Because of the one outstanding concept you instilled in all of us: JESUS! You see, Mom, no matter what I said, nor how I behaved, I had to see that you loved Jesus and He was real to you. You lived it every day. This is how I remember you, Mom.

I remember no profanity ever came from your lips. You never cursed at Dad, nor me, nor any human, animal, or occurrence. You never called a person a fool. You saw humans as special, and you were rather alone in caring for the black people in Louisiana. You never got out of control. I know because I heard you every day for eighteen years. Your English was broken, but never profane. You couldn't read much, but read us the Bible. Now I know anyone who knows the Bible and Jesus is not an uneducated person!

I remember, Mom, you never turned your back on anyone in need, no matter their race. You took care of my ailing grandparents in our home for years, although you were old, infirm, and poor yourself. For years you cared for my uncle even though he had mental problems and epilepsy. For years you fed the many hungry relatives. You really were wealthy because you possessed the wealth of giving to others. What wealth will be yours in heaven!

I remember, Mom, I never had to worry about whether you would be at home when I got back from school. You were always there. You missed only one day in eighteen years! What security you were. I was the youngest, fourteen years younger than your firstborn, but you persisted in your parenting responsibilities year after year.

I remember, Mom, never feeling you had spanked me without just cause, but I do remember having to go cut the switch you used on me. I still remember the bush it came from, but you never screamed at me.

I remember, Mom, you never verbally degraded me. You always were an example of winning by being a tough, loving, trusting Christian. And you are my Mom! How ashamed I am to confess that for years I thought of you as an embarrassment. God, forgive me.

One day, probably soon, your body will die and Dad and the six of us kids will get together to bury your body. And I will cry some more like I have done while reading this letter. I will cry because you were so good to me and I was so stupid for so long. I will not be crying because of where you are, however. I know you will be with Jesus!

Mother's Day Despair

Since Tooger's profound apology occurred on Mother's Day, it seems appropriate to address here the feelings generated in many third-tri moms on that holiday. The following list of Mother's Day meltdowns includes a sampling of comments heard in May of this year:

- Life's third-tri mom to her friend: "I wish the country would abolish Mother's Day. I have felt nothing but pain for years on this miserable day of unmet expectations when it seems every mother on the planet except me is elaborately celebrated by her adult children."

- Husband to his wife: "Please don't hurt yourself by reading all those 'eulogies' to other mothers on Facebook today. Some of those Mother's Day posts lavishing praise on their mothers bear little resemblance to how those moms are treated by their kids the other 364 days of the year."

- Third-tri mom to her sister: "During the thirty-one years I was raising my kids, they thought I was a loving, kind, caring, supportive, and lovable parent. Now they're grown and seem unable to acknowledge any of that, almost like they are rewriting history to turn me into a bad, unwanted, worthless parent. I had to dig into my old collection of scrawled, handmade Mother's Day cards to reassure myself that long ago they thought I was a good mom."

- Third-tri mom sharing her feelings at her small group meeting on Zoom: "I'm so tired of generic 'Happy Mother's Day' and 'Happy Birthday' text messages identical to the ones my kids send to lots of other people on their phone list. I want my sons and daughters to be thankful *I'm* their mother and tell me why! On their birthdays and special occasions, I go out of my way to list things I admire and respect about them, but it is never reciprocated.

– Third-trimester mom to her husband at bedtime: "I wish Mother's Day wasn't even on the calendar. I feel like such an unimportant afterthought, with only a brief phone call after Amanda and Don celebrated Mother's Day extravagantly with their own kids. I'm disappointed because Amanda is such a talented artist and poet, and I'd secretly hoped she'd make time to draw me one of her masterpieces and write a special poem just for me."

– Spiritually mature third-tri mom processing the weekend with another mom: "I know it shouldn't bother me, and every year I tell myself not to hope for much recognition on Mother's Day or other special occasions. Unfortunately, my emotions tanked today anyway. Despite my best resolve, I listened to the enemy's lies accusing me of not being the mother my sons wanted, and I succumbed to feeling unappreciated and sad, *again*. I'm discouraged I didn't internally handle their neglect better.

– Woman in life's second trimester to her therapist: "I spent hours at the Hallmark store trying to pick out a suitably truthful card to send my mom for Mother's Day. I don't want to lie and say I cherish her as a wonderful mother, when I actually view her as hurtful to me for years now. I hate the whole idea of Mother's Day because I feel pressure to say complimentary things that aren't true and that I don't mean."

Guideline #2: Don't engage in self-pity. It's normal for the next generation's "first love" to become their own spouse and children.

Consider it a victory if your children and grandkids make it a big deal on Mother's Day to celebrate "Mommy" in the homes they established. Make peace with the fact that empty-nest mothers generally feel greater desire for time and communication with their adult offspring than grown offspring feel for their parent.

The sad feelings that assert themselves on special days like birthdays or Mother's Day reflect our deep desires to feel loved and treasured by the kids we raised. We want them to crave our company like we crave theirs. When you feel neglected and not valued on other days of the year, you deliberately choose not to dwell on your hurt and get busy doing something productive. But on Mother's Day you feel so vulnerable!

Many of you are inwardly wondering if your son or daughter felt paralyzed at the Hallmark store like the last example in my meltdown list above. Or you may feel convicted because of your own hesitancy to send a gushy card applauding your mother's love for you.

Guideline #3: If your own mother is still living, treat her like you would wish to be treated. Your kids are watching and building a view of how to treat the older generation through your modeling.

If your adult children witness you attempting to reverse intergenerational schisms by humbling yourself and honoring your parents more than you have in the past, it will plant a seed in their hearts. Let your kids see you taking responsibility for your attitudes and behaviors even if justice and equality were denied in your home of origin.

Justice and equality are prime values driving the younger generations. They may believe the way you disciplined them was not fair, or that other siblings received preferential treatment. Some may feel justified to remain angry and harshly confrontive, and even to cut you out of their lives. We live in a time of raging fury, and mothers are a common target, with their therapist sometimes "piling on." Some counselors may even recommend children terminate contact with their mom because they're convinced the kids need such a boundary to protect their feelings from continuing to be hurt by their parent.

When the children you raised see you changing because you now find reasons to applaud your own parents, the very same moms or dads you previously bad-mouthed or avoided, fruitful discussions about your growth process may ensue. You might get an opening to admit you regret your judgmental stance and withholding of forgiveness. Also, humility toward the generation above you is good exercise because you are building "humility muscles" to deal with the generation you birthed.

If your mom is still living, decide to work on identifying a few ways you benefitted from her mothering. If you feel stuck, look at an old photo album or ask a sibling to brainstorm with you. Put those memories into written words and make your mom's next Mother's Day the best ever. You don't even need to wait for Mother's Day. Would you want to wait for the words you crave hearing?

If you remain convinced your sons or daughters can't find appropriate Mother's Day cards because they don't respect you or value their upbringing, I'm going to offer a few guidelines with the potential to improve the picture. Because of three decades in a counseling room listening to people's feelings about their parents, I have noticed patterns worth considering. Rather than being just a repudiation of the nurturing we provided when they still lived at home, a lot of the negative intensity from the younger generation surrounds behaviors we're exhibiting now in our third-tri years.

Guideline #4: Humbling yourself includes giving up believing you are always right.

Believing you are always right forces others with differing opinions into the position of being "wrong." The natural reaction to "You are wrong!" is defensiveness. Spending time with dogmatic know-it-all offspring can be torturous. You may want to consider whether it is equally unpleasant for your child to be around a know-it-all mother who thoughtlessly spouts her opinions.

In order to decrease our defensiveness when confronted by the younger generation's positions on issues, it is going to require an internal confession that we have been wrong about quite a few things. Can you admit you've said hurtful, contradictory, shortsighted, hypocritical, or just plain dumb things, and you regret certain life choices? I remind you I am not recommending you debase yourself and conclude you are always wrong and a bad person. A proper perspective requires recognizing we are fallible, like all human beings, with plenty of examples to prove it.

What an irony: The more life experiences we acquire, and thus the more we "know," the less of a know-it-all we can become. There is a beautiful humility available at this stage if we choose to walk in that direction. It's liberating to invest less in being right and proving others wrong. We've lived long enough to recall feeling certain about vast numbers of things, only later to discover we were flat-out mistaken. How unbecoming to dispense our opinions in this third trimester as though we are smarter and better informed than anyone else possibly could be.

We have the opportunity to acquire greater humility by recognizing our track record of mistakes and proneness to wrong thinking about so many areas of life that fall into the category of opinions. At the same time, we can simultaneously grow in certainty about a few foundational convictions standing the test of time.

Perhaps the most influential theologian of the twentieth century was Karl Barth. He refused to take the oath of unconditional allegiance to Adolf Hitler and pitted the revelation of Jesus Christ against the lies of the Fuhrer and National Socialism. Barth wrote numerous volumes on diverse subjects to express his unique combination of evangelical passion and the social concerns characterizing his life. Yet when asked in 1962 how he would summarize his theology and the essence of the millions of words he had published, he replied simply, "Jesus loves me; this I know, for the Bible tells me so."[40]

I've been surprised in life's third trimester to find myself less sure I'm right about many debatable topics, but I'm increasingly sure about a few bedrock things. Opinions about politicians and the way they should solve our world's problems or how people should dress and adorn themselves are generally personal sentiments and culturally-derived viewpoints and not worthy of quarreling about or obnoxiously pontificating about.

However, humble discussions, listening, and learning from one another's ideas do have merit. Openly exchanging viewpoints with others in younger generations can help keep our minds sharp, our logic skills keen, our information-seeking current, and our influence felt. Humility constitutes the unique ingredient allowing our conclusions to go down smoothly without leaving the lingering bad taste of a know-it-all personality.

Guideline #5: In America these days, adult kids often see politics and religion as enmeshed. You won't win any points or open any hearts by arguing politics.

You are a fortunate parent indeed if you see eye-to-eye with your off-spring about political matters. Likewise, if biblical topics are fodder for enjoyable conversations among the generations, you are in the minority of Americans today.

When family members hold strongly opposing worldviews, voicing your sentiments leads to rolled eyes, at the very least. More likely, you diminish yourself in your kids' estimation and calcify their belief that you are an opinionated relic of the past. Even if your son or daughter throws in snide and sarcastic political comments, you don't have to take the bait. You can ask if they are interested in a reasoned debate about the merits of each other's views, or you can ignore their provocation. Just don't be the person inciting anger-filled arguments that drive you further apart, no matter how rational you consider your political position to be.

Levels of animosity toward supporters of the "other" political party skyrocketed before and after the contentious 2020 presidential election cycle. Even earlier, after the election in 2016, both the left-leaning *New York Times* and the right-leaning *National Review* published articles describing schisms occurring in homes because of political differences. The *NY Times* reported in its headline, "Political Divide Splits Relationships—and Thanksgiving, Too."[41] The article described typical American families suddenly blown apart and estranged because of strongly-held feelings about presidential candidates. Angry partisans refused to be in the presence of relatives endorsing the other candidate or opposite party policies.

A contemptuous attitude toward those who support a different political party has become a common one. If offspring hold contrary political views, incredulity and disdain toward their parents' positions often manifest.

Advice given us by Paul serves as an appropriate guide, "Get rid of all bitterness, rage, anger, harsh words, and slander, as well as all types of evil behavior. Instead, be kind to each other, tenderhearted, forgiving one another, just as God through Christ has forgiven you."[42] Whether or not your sons and daughters live in obedience to those instructions, you can decide to do so! Choosing humility when your political buttons are pushed is not easy but requires maturity and dependence on the Holy Spirit for self-control.

Humbling ourselves is such an important act of obedience. Understanding additional aspects of humility is worthy of another chapter, but take time first to answer some probing questions.

Coaching Corner

1. Which descriptions best describe your feelings as a mother of adult children?

    a. Proud of your "successful" mothering

    b. Grateful for how well your children turned out despite your parenting mistakes

    c. Shamed by your mothering "failures"

    d. Embarrassed by your grown child's choices

    e. Sad for the consequences your rebellious adult children experience

    f. Angry and defensive when your opinions are criticized by your kids

    g. Confused by mixed feelings

    h. Angry, hurt, and bitter

    i.   Grateful for progress over time

    j.   Peaceful

    k.   Hopeful

    l.   Prayerful

2. Which descriptions would you like to be true of your internal world?

3. Do you need to renounce parental pride in how your parenting "resulted" in an exemplary adult child?

4. From your vantage point as the mother of devoted and godly sons or daughters, have you secretly suspected other families made mistakes "causing" their child to veer off course and judged them for their "failures?" Are you now questioning that stance? Why or why not?

5. What does it mean to you to "humble yourself"?

6. What "if only" questions torment you? Is it time to let them go?

7. Do you still hold ill will toward your own mother for how you were raised or for how she treated you in adulthood?

8. How would humbling yourself play out with your parents?

9. What would be required for you to forgive your mother for the ways she wounded you?

10. When are you going to pen a tribute to your mother?

11. Could you write the first paragraph of your tribute this week? Why or why not?

12. What is your plan to deal with political differences between you and your kids in the future?

13. Have gremlin voices made you miserable on Mother's Day or other holidays? How do you want to respond next time?

14. What is your reaction to the following message one mother posted on Facebook? She specified that all she wanted for Christmas was just *time* with her young adults—maybe a long walk and a nice home-cooked dinner.

Message to my Adult Kids

"My children ask me each year, 'What do you want for Christmas?' After thinking about it, I decided to give them my real answer:

- I want you to keep coming around.

- I want you to ask me questions. Ask my advice.

- Tell me your problems.

- Ask for my opinion. Ask for my help.

- I want you to come over and rant about your problems, rant about life, whatever.

- Tell me about your job. Your worries. Your classes.

- I want you to continue sharing your life with me.

- Come over and laugh with me, or laugh at me. I don't care; hearing you laugh is music to me.

- I want you to spend your money making a better life for you. I have the things I need. I want to see you happy and healthy.

- When you ask me what I want for Christmas, I say, 'nothing' because you've already been giving me my gift all year. I want you!"[43]

CHAPTER 5

Digesting Humble Pie

MOTHERS FEEL "EXPOSED" when our adult kids make what we consider to be a mess of their lives. Our underwear flaps in the breeze. We cannot hide evidence of our "imperfect parenting"—not when we must admit our kid is in rehab again, in jail, just had her third abortion, or our son announced "she's" our daughter. The reality of our family skeletons falling off high shelves and smashing our heads reminds me of Parallel #5 between pregnancy and life's third tri.

Parallel #5: Your inner developments grow increasingly visible to others.

Jane Adams, a psychologist and respected authority on thriving despite intergenerational conflicts, writes, "We have watched our dreams fall apart, betrayed by the children we raised to know better. We feel helpless in the face of needless waste, frightened when we think about what the future has in store for them, ashamed in front of our friends and neighbors."[44]

Adams provides all too familiar examples: "Catherine, a regular churchgoer, sneaks into early Mass and leaves before it's over so no one will see her, and Pat tells people his son, who's doing time for armed robbery, works for a secret government agency, which is why he couldn't come to his sister's wedding. Good, caring, committed parents all, unable to reconcile the ideal child we hold in our hearts with the one in the orange jumpsuit who sits across from us at a table, separated by shatterproof glass and a life we never imagined could turn out this way."[45]

Even though many third-trimester moms are strangling on personal guilt about adult children's paths in life, massive shame will not help the situation. Humility and shame are not the same animal. Humility is a positive trait implying awareness of one's own fallibility, and the accompanying desire to be forgiven when we miss the mark. Associated elements include gentleness, gratitude, graciousness, and modesty. A humble Christian knows when observing others' mistakes, "There, but for the grace of God, go I."

Pride is the opposite of humility. Synonyms of pride include arrogance, smugness, conceit, and self-importance. Pride is an obstacle to establishing equal relationships because prideful people project an air of superiority. Pride makes owning one's faults and apologizing nearly impossible. Pride is ugly!

Shame can also be the opposite of pride, but shame suggests worthlessness, disgrace, humiliation, embarrassment, and self-degradation. Neither pride nor shame constitutes an acceptable alternative to humility. We do ourselves no favors when we despicably strut with pride nor woefully wallow in shame.

If we have succeeded in acknowledging our human fallibility, as discussed in previous guidelines, we are equipped to move forward as humble, mistake-prone persons. And whom is the hardest person to forgive for their mistakes? If you said *yourself,* you are correct. Many Christian sisters attest to believing God has forgiven them for contributing to their offspring's rebellious path, but they insist, "I just can't forgive myself."

It is possible you are stuck here because you have not yet asked for and received God's forgiveness. If that is the case, please jump to Chapter 15 for help in understanding God's love for you and knowing all is right between you and your Heavenly Father, and then return to this page.

Guideline #6: Develop self-compassion and forgive yourself.

Self-compassion comes hard for mothers. Because moms desire to be ideal mothers, and because some of us were so hard on our own mothers for their hurtful errors, we are unrealistic in our expectations. Can you choke out these words? "As part of the human race, all mothers make mistakes, and I will let both my mother and myself off the hook for being human. Then, I will intentionally take steps to correct my wrongs."

A *Huffington Post* article on "The Right Way to Learn from Your Mistakes" highlights research on what psychologists call the *negativity bias,* a tendency to let errors take center stage in one's thinking. Many of our minds get stuck on personal failures, elevating our screwups to life and death importance. Neuroscience experiments suggest it is critical to *admit* slipups to rouse ourselves and eliminate failure patterns, but people tend to fall into two camps in regard to what they *do* about the mistakes they acknowledge making.[46]

The *fixed mindset* group believes they are defective individuals who will never do any better, so they deny, ignore, or suppress their failures *without learning from them.* Other individuals display a *growth mindset* and regard their mistakes as *wake-up calls*. They decide to invest energy in learning from their errors, enhancing their neural activity, and making their mistakes work for them.[47]

Fortunately, even if we have not navigated mistakes expertly in the past, it is possible to alter our responses. Perceived mistakes don't need to become shame and anxiety-ridden rabbit holes. A whole body of research suggests a requisite ingredient to improve our reactions is *self-compassion*. Experiments showed self-esteem boosting and outside validation didn't matter as much as *self-compassion* enhancement—deliberately choosing to be patient and merciful toward one's own struggles.[48]

Guideline #7: Admit you've overestimated your importance and power.

Mothers get lots of messages about what a critical role we play in turning our kids into well-adjusted, God-honoring, successful adults. While I would never downplay the significance of moms, I realize buying into the belief that all outcomes depend on mothers overstates the case. When kids are little, moms and dads truly are their primary nurturers, their main teachers about life, and the major influencers in their lives. Siblings affect them early on, too. However, over the years, more and more sources of influence enter the equation.

If you were like me, you tried to protect your sons and daughters from negative influences and attempted to mitigate the damage when sinister forces impacted them. None of us totally succeeded in that endeavor, and we may even have inflicted injuries while trying to protect them from harm. Just a partial list of openings for attacks on their bodies, minds, and souls is mind-boggling:

Influences on Your Offspring

- Genetics
- College roommates
- Dating relationships and breakups
- Spouse or partner
- Teachers
- Professors
- TV programming
- School recesses
- Social clubs like Boy/Girl Scouts and 4-H
- Radio broadcasts
- Facebook, Twitter, Instagram, YouTube, and other social media
- Song lyrics
- Internet content
- Overheard adult conversations
- Rock bands
- School classmates
- Grandparents
- Gymnastics or karate classes
- Arts and crafts, ballet, theatre, violin, piano, drums, guitar, voice, and other involvements in the arts
- Movies
- Neighborhood or school bullies
- Health problems
- Library books
- Family reading material
- Video games
- Babysitters
- Disabilities (their own or siblings' or parents')
- Hypocritical church members
- Mental health issues like depression, anxiety, and bipolar disorder
- Neighbors
- Parental divorce
- Best friends
- Friends' parents (with different values about alcohol, food, religion, R-rated movies, etc.)
- Priests, pastors. rabbis, and church youth leaders
- Commercials
- Alcohol use by parents or other adults in their circle
- Cross-cultural experiences

- Step-parents
- Brothers, sisters, or step-siblings
- Pop stars and other celebrities
- Mission trips
- Conservative or liberal politics
- Sports teammates and sports heroes

- Coaches
- Public or private school curriculums
- Therapists
- Sexual predators
- Cousins, aunts, and uncles
- Drug pushers
- Fraternities and sororities
- Bosses and co-workers

Assignment: Go back and underline any influences you believe may have negatively impacted your children up to this point in their lives. Go through the list again and check positive influences. Would you have underlined and checked the same items when your children were much younger? Can you see how unclear it was at the time which exposures were going to bring negative results? Maybe some peers, adults, and activities you trusted ended up adversely affecting your off-spring in ways you could never have foreseen.

Considering the host of influences on your children's development, do you still believe mothers should be able to counteract it all? No human is that powerful. We must be satisfied with knowing we gave them the best we could at the time knowing what we knew then, and humbly move forward.

Now that we've determined we are important, but not *all* important in our adult kids' development, we can turn to a source of real power in the next chapter. First, however, I want to discuss two more guidelines involved with humbling ourselves.

Guideline #8: Relinquish shame, pride, and defensiveness.

Thank God for revealing our tendencies toward shame, pride, and defensiveness so we can surrender them and grow during our third trimester into a more Christlike person. When Guideline #8 recommends we relinquish shame, pride, and defensiveness, we are talking about surrendering three detrimental attitudes and pursuing humility as our normal posture. However, the shame, pride, and defensiveness we want to abandon stubbornly resist eradication. We need a plan for demonstrating progress to our children.

I will describe how an incident played out in my own life, starting with a word picture from a book and some communication skills I'd learned as a therapist.

Defusing Armadillo Defensiveness

A friend gave me a copy of Lysa Terkeurst's book, *Craving God,*[49] for Christmas. She praised the slim volume as the most influential book in her life that year, so I was intrigued. In glancing at the chapter titles, my mind jerked to a halt when I saw "The Underbelly." I flinched, aware of my own persistent abdominal roundness. *Does the author have the answer to this formidable problem,* I wondered? Generally operating in life as a rule keeper, I started in proper sequence by perusing the first inspiring chapter. I admit I then cheated and flipped to Chapter 37 to read about the ominous "underbelly."

Unfortunately, I discovered no suggestions for my anatomical problem. However, the author did present interesting ideas about a daunting relationship challenge. That problem is, "How do I deal with hurtful criticism and perceived attacks, especially from family members?"

Terkeurst described her Google search for the word "underbelly." She ultimately stumbled upon an article describing the soft underside of armadillos. With tough prickly scales, these desert lizards intimidate any attackers by wrapping their armored bodies protectively around their one susceptible spot—their soft vulnerable tummies. The remainder of leathery armadillo shells are strong and impenetrable. People have been injured by bullets ricocheting off these animals' scale-encrusted armor.

As third-trimester mothers, we can play the role of intimidating armadillos in crouched defense mode. We're tempted to hunker down and protect our vulnerabilities, especially our need for love and approval from our adult children. We can simultaneously be terrified by the sharp barbs aimed our way and also appear terrifying in our defensiveness and counter attacks! Is there any way to avoid both generations behaving like a bunch of razor-edged, hunkered-down armadillos?

Terkeurst's book urges us to consider that our critics may be spewing out judgmental, rejecting comments because they are trying to protect their tender interiors. Terkeurst admits, "I sometimes get all wrapped up in myself and tragically forget the underbelly of my critic—the place they are vulnerable and the things they might be hiding and protecting beneath the harsh words and prickly exterior. This is a place they may never let me see. It's the storage place for their hurts and disappointments. It holds the root cause of their skepticism and the anger that probably has very little to do with me."[50]

If I am mindful of the other person's hidden wounds, I have a greater chance to detach from personal criticism that seems over the top or even totally undeserved. Turkeurst referenced Jesus' words, "This will result in your being *witnesses* to them. But make up your mind not to worry beforehand how you will *defend* yourselves. For I will give you words and wisdom that none of your adversaries will be able to resist or contradict."[51]

How wonderful to be able to turn our responses to unwanted attacks into a witness, even when our grown child may be aiming arrows at our hearts. The focus needs to be on recognizing the pain and vulnerability our adult child is carrying, not on defending ourselves. Defensiveness is not God's way; *He* is our Defender! Instead, take responsibility for any part of the accusation that may be true.

Admitting responsibility *disarms* our critics in a way that makes them unable to resist or contradict. The premier researcher on creating harmony in marriages, John Gottman, labels defensiveness, along with criticism, contempt, and stonewalling, as the destructive "Four Horsemen" who instigate destruction and devastation as they gallop through our family relationships.[52]

In graduate school, I learned to employ the "Disarming Technique" whenever I felt attacked by critical comments. I often taught this communication method to husbands and wives locked in criticism and defensive standoffs.

Let me illustrate how the disarming technique works by using an analogy. Imagine a police officer walking into the room where you are sitting, intending to "disarm" an assassin in your midst. If the villain has a weapon in his backpack, the officer will confiscate it. A knife in his pocket? The policeman removes it. A bomb strapped around his midsection? The officer calls a special unit to disconnect the explosives. When the policeman and bomb squad complete "disarming" the assassin and putting him in handcuffs, the attacker is no longer capable of hurting anyone. You are safe. Similar to a scenario where a cop removes a handgun from your critic's purse, you render your critic weaponless when you voice responsibility for your contribution to an offense.

Wait a minute, Doctor Charlotte, you may be thinking. After all, the criticism your son or daughter directs toward you seems ridiculously unfair and undeserved.

The disarming technique proposes that you find some truth in what the other person is saying, even if it feels totally off-base. Cognitive therapist pioneer, David Burns, recommends, "Agree *in principle* with the criticism, or you can find some *grain* of truth in the statement and agree with that, or you can acknowledge that the person's upset is understandable because it is based on how he or she views the situation. Agreement with whatever truth exists in their complaint is how you short-circuit criticism attacks and how you take away any reason for more hurtful jabs."[53] Look for even a tiny bit of truth in the accusation, admit that small piece, and thereby remove the need for your opponent to keep stabbing you over and over in attempts to convince you of wrongdoing.

Starting your reply with the magic words, *You're right,* or *I agree,* often helps defuse the situation even more. It is a law of life—the more aggressively you verbally defend yourself when someone believes you are in the wrong, the more criticism you invite, and the more you lose the chance to have a positive witness. Angrily and stubbornly insisting you are right and they are wrong is counterproductive.

Please hang with me. I am not trying to turn you into a doormat for abusive words. I want to equip you to defuse a situation, reduce resistance, de-escalate emotions, and create positive communication patterns with the sons and daughters you love so much. In the heat of the moment, choosing the disarming technique can calm you and your offspring enough for you to remember you are dealing with an armadillo.

On a recent occasion, I felt verbally ambushed and almost forgot everything I knew about armadillos and disarming techniques. There was tension in the air between my adult daughter and me that day. You know the kind of day when you are getting clipped, tight-lipped responses to any questions or comments, followed by a plea not to say anything at all because you are so irritating and distracting to her concentration. My daughter and I were strapped in the driver and passenger seats for a three-hour trip in uncomfortable silence through barren Florida marshland, headed for a college visit with her daughter, my granddaughter.

The accusation came out of nowhere. "Mom, you have a negatively skewed view of life because you spend so much time with depressed clients."

Ouch! Everything in me wanted to take the low road and blast back with a sharp denial of habitual negativity, a scathing correction about the nature of my clients, and then take the offense with an unnecessary reminder, "At least I have an income as a therapist, so I can help pay for Sequoia's college."

Fortunately, I paused before I responded. The only part of my daughter's criticism seeming true was that I spend a lot of time with clients. I started there. "I agree, Honey. I do hear a lot of life stories." Then I offered a bit more information, hoping she'd drop her gun. "Mostly the people I counsel are a lot like the people I know outside of the counseling room, just ordinary likable people trying to figure out life." I tried to keep my tone pleasant and noncombative.

What evidence did Deborah possess that I had a negatively skewed view of life? I internally wondered. I didn't have to wait long for my answer. "Mom, you said a while ago when I was talking about missing

Sequoia while she's away at college that 'Life is hard.' You always say that. I don't think life is hard. It's just because you deal with people in crisis all the time."

Here we go again, salvo number two. My professional training helped me to start with another of the magic agreement phrases. "You're right, sweetheart," I said. "I guess I do think life tends to be hard in various ways. Life is not *always* hard, but it is often for me and everybody I know—clients, friends, and family alike."

All the while, I was trying to keep in mind that Deborah was covering with prickly bravado the multiple hurts and considerable life difficulties that constituted her soft underbelly. Indeed, I viewed her life as a single mom to be very difficult indeed. In fact, I was proud of Deborah for her dedication to her daughter and wanting the best for Sequoia despite financial constraints and cross-country separation. We were two armadillos in the trenches!

I wish I could say we eliminated all mother-daughter friction as a result of our exchange, but it wouldn't be true. Both of our underbellies were still too soft and vulnerable. Nevertheless, I made progress in my "witness," instead of adding another reason for Deborah to judge me as someone she didn't want to be around.

In retrospect, when I think about our mother-daughter conversation, I believe Deborah was accurate in stating I had been more affected by hearing so many client stories of troubled family relationships than I realized at the time. Even in writing this book, I recognize I describe mom-child schisms more often than recounting all the heartwarming relationships existing in families today.

Therefore, I now say, "I'm sorry" to Deborah and to you, my readers. I am probably a bit like a dentist who notices teeth problems when they meet people because they've spent so much of their life peering in people's mouths. Likewise, cops who are frequently dispatched to investigate parking lot crime scenes tend to view parking lots differently from those who've never experienced that kind of trauma.

To facilitate the humbling process required in our third tri, we need to be sure we accomplish Guideline #9 next.

Guideline #9: Forgive sons or daughters for ways they've hurt you.

Do you love your daughter, your son? You do realize those we love have the most power to hurt us! For one thing, we want them to treasure us as much as we cherish them. Sometimes, however, they act like they wish someone else had been their mom. As comedian Jeff Allen so eloquently describes it, "Teenagers are God's revenge on us. Now you know how it feels to create somebody in your own image who rejects you and acts like you don't exist."[54] Still, God's love for His children never stops, and neither does ours, even if an adversarial teenager grows into a rejecting and disapproving adult.

Sometimes parents are overwhelmed with soft loving feelings, as when we see our four-year-old cuddled with a plush teddy bear in her bed sound asleep. Somehow those warm feelings cool when our forty-four-year-old is sleeping with yet another person to whom she's not married. It feels like an offense against you when she flaunts behavior opposite of the values you taught her growing up. It is so tempting to make the mistake of taking our adult children's choices personally.

Because we often romanticize love to consist only of fuzzy feelings, I am turning to the New Testament's definition of love, an action-packed kind of love: "Love is patient and kind. Love is not jealous or boastful or proud or rude. It does not demand its own way.

It is not irritable, and it *keeps no record of being wronged.* It does not rejoice about injustice, but rejoices whenever the truth wins out. Love never gives up, never loses faith, is always hopeful, and endures through every circumstance.[55]

Perhaps the toughest part of the Scripture's description of love is the phrase, "*it keeps no record of being wronged.*" Since our children are so much on our minds in the third trimester, nursing the grievances stoking our pain can be a frequent, even daily, occurrence. Each new infraction or reminder of an old one can prompt us to stew and rehearse old offenses. Sometimes a mother and dad feed off each other as they recount the latest undesirable words or behavior at mealtime or bedtime. How do we get off that sour note?

If we buy into Guidelines #4 and #7 to the extent that we have humbled ourselves by (1) giving up our beliefs that we are always right and (2) stopping overestimating our own importance and power to determine the choices our kids made and still make, we are off to a good start. The life decisions your child makes are so much more complex than simple reflex negations of everything you stand for.

What your children think, believe, and do as adults does not constitute a reflection on you as much as you suppose. Instead, they are an indication of their deliberately chosen paths. True, genetics play a part and nurture plays a part. Nevertheless, humans still have options. Going clear back to Cain and Abel, offspring choose differently depending on their own selected beliefs and worldviews. The cumulative effect of multitudinous influences piled on top of your nurturing resulted in those beliefs and worldviews. Yes, we feel *sad* and grieve mightily for them when we see them make choices we deem foolish; we dread the consequences we fear will follow. We hurt *for* them. However, we easily become angry if we are hurt *by* them.

Certain expectations prevail in human societies. Hurt enters in when we feel wronged. People like to be thanked for generous gifts, so ingratitude hurts. Neglecting and ignoring us hurts. Harsh, angry accusations hurt. Rejection hurts. Being used hurts. Puncturing our dreams hurts.

Forgiving our children for hurting us is paramount if we are to live a tranquil life, free of bitterness. Forgiving them is essential for a good relationship with them, but forgiving is also necessary for our internal peace and for us to forge a right relationship with God. One of the scariest verses in the Bible is a section of the frequently recited Lord's Prayer, "Forgive us our sins, *as we have forgiven those who sin against us.*"[56] Jesus goes on to emphasize, "If you forgive those who sin against you, your heavenly Father will forgive you. But if you refuse to forgive others, your Father will not forgive your sins."[57]

There are two keys to easing the difficulty of forgiving an adult child's minor or major offenses. Remember, the goal is unconditional love and forgiveness to such a complete extent that we hardly even notice when our child does us wrong, and we scarcely remember previous provocations.

Key #1: An awareness of the armadillo condition we have previously discussed. Your child may be dishonoring you in certain ways and possibly lashing out because s/he feels in jeopardy. An accumulation of perceived parental offenses, combined with combat wounds separate from anything you've inflicted, may churn in your child's underbelly. It isn't surprising they're hunkered down and ready to intimidate.

Key #2: When hanging in excruciating pain on the cross, Jesus uttered the unfathomable words, "Father, forgive them, *for they don't know what they are doing.*"[58] The Roman soldiers knew good and well they were hammering spikes into the wrists and feet of Jesus. What they didn't know at the time was *whom* they were crucifying—the Son of God! They were simply carrying out orders, displaying loyalty to the Roman government, amusing themselves by gambling for Jesus' garments, showing off their muscles, laughing, and entertaining themselves with the spectacle. Jesus was a nonentity in their minds, somebody whose suffering didn't matter. The soldiers were not actually thinking about Jesus at all, but about their own agendas.

Most of the time, when your children bewilder you with attitudes and behaviors seeming bizarre or self-sabotaging, their minds are not on how their choices will affect you. Instead, their actions spring from their own agendas. Their chief aim in life is not to snub their noses at your values and bring you sorrow. Rather, the pursuit of personal pleasure and perceived happiness beckons. If you consider all the media and cultural input, plus the influences of peers, professors, and popular God-denying role models, you will realize their choices make sense to them.

The generations coming behind us are driven by the universal human desire to love and be loved. Many also fixate on politically correct definitions of equality, equity, and social justice, and they want to be liked and admired by their peers. Think about all the agendas competing for their loyalties. For some, food, alcohol, or drug highs dominate their lives. Financial advantages, novel experiences, harmony with nature, artistic expression, independence, international travel, scientific knowledge, technological prowess, musical rapture, planet-saving activism, entertainment, sexual gratification, and career success all compete for priority. These are all normal human pursuits. To one degree or another, moms are attracted to many of the same quests.

Jesus knew his executioners were clueless about His real identity and worth, and our adult children can be similarly clueless. They aren't convinced their mom possesses valuable wisdom refined through experience. They don't realize how advantageous peace with God is. They don't comprehend that trusting Jesus, loving Him, and following His teaching lead to serenity and contentment. So many other influences have said otherwise, promising that man's intellect and the pursuit of personal pleasure comprise the route to what they crave, not a relationship with God. And mom's biblical values seem irrelevant, old-fashioned, not very smart, and expendable.

Forgive them! They don't know what they are doing. Keep loving them. Let your anger go. Let their choices be between themselves and God. And pray!

Coaching Corner

1. What progress have you made in forgiving yourself for your mothering mistakes?

2. How does humility relate to self-compassion?

3. When do you intend to take the next steps toward self-compassion and self-forgiveness?

4. What insights did you gain from the assignment to evaluate your ability to control influences impacting your children?

5. What armadillo characteristics have you observed in yourself or in your offspring?

6. How would viewing your child as an armadillo affect your responses to criticism from them?

7. What relevance do Jesus' words on the cross, "Father, forgive them for they know not what they do," possess for you?

8. Why is forgiving your children for the ways they've hurt you so hard?

9. What would it look like for you to forgive your son or daughter for dishonoring you and/or God?

10. On a scale of 1 to 10, how far along are you in deciding to let your child's choices remain between him/her and God? What reservations keep you stuck?

CHAPTER 6

❦

The Peripheral
vs. the Central

IN MY HASTE not to forget, I fumbled to find the closest pen and notepad. I was frantic to capture Alistair Begg's provocative sentence, "Father, forgive us for making the peripheral things central and the central things peripheral."[59] I instantly intuited that those words extracted from Pastor Begg's national radio broadcast were life-changing!

I hadn't grasped yet that neglecting the second condition in the Lord's promise to heal our land, specifically to *pray*, epitomizes the deadly reversal of peripheral things and central things. What was worse, I erred in making that mistake in other forms when raising my kids.

My mind races to example after example of my blindness in my second trimester, when I blundered by committing exactly that swap of the peripheral and the central. I remember the winter my teenage daughter opted to wear a shabby, moth-eaten man's overcoat she'd scrounged from the Salvation Army's thrift piles. I particularly cringed as she insisted on flaunting her disregard for "what people will think" at church. In those days, women dressed in their "Sunday best," and men usually sported suits and ties. Ostensibly, churchgoers honored God with their respectful attire. However, 99 percent of the time folks chose their apparel to impress others. Deborah, always an activist at heart, was making a statement about that twisted thinking.

I was embarrassed by how Deborah's ugly overcoat with its torn lining reflected on her and on me as her mother. Since the ridiculously big coat had once obviously belonged to a man, Deborah rolled up the too-long sleeves, exposed their faded purplish lining, and persisted in wearing the garment in lieu of her regular coat. We argued about the overcoat, and I lost. I not only lost the arguments; to some degree, I also lost my daughter.

Deborah was stung by her parents' disapproval and poorly concealed embarrassment, and she smelled our hypocrisy. After all, going to church is not about showing off one's fashion sense and seeking admiration from people in the pews. Rather, we go to celebrate God's love and grace, to worship Him, and to learn how to be like Him. Stylish attire as a measurement of how one honors God is so peripheral it counts for nothing! In fact, Jesus was disgusted when the hypocritical Pharisees paraded sanctimoniously in their elaborate robes with tassled hems!

I also wince as I remember the day our whole family responded to our minister's prodding and joined a courthouse rally to demonstrate against a proposition on the ballot to allow alcohol sales on Sundays in our city. At the time, it seemed like the right thing to do, in obedience to the commandment to keep the Sabbath holy. What was I thinking?

As the crowd gathered to protest the legislation, the *Lexington-Herald Leader* photographer snapped a photo of our fourteen-year-old son, head bowed in prayer. The editor prominently posted our son's picture in the newspaper, along with headlines about the demonstration against Sunday liquor sales. I proudly snipped out the article and mounted it on David's bulletin board. Eventually, the clipping just disappeared from his wall. I didn't know why.

Many years later, David told me about the ridicule he experienced when high school peers reacted to his face in the newspaper. He was mocked at school, where alcohol was considered "cool," of course. He described his outrage at realizing he was expected to carry, at age fourteen, the impossible burden of saving the world from Sabbath abuse via alcohol, when he knew good and well Jesus had turned water into wine at a wedding banquet.

I think David could have handled the pressure of being different from his peers if he had been caught in the act of taking a stand for the central message of Christianity. Instead, a candid camera had exposed him and his family in the act of marketing the peripheral. Yes, alcohol abuse devastates countless families, but alcohol use on Sunday (or any other day of the week) is not the central theme of the New Testament. The Pharisees were the judgmental, compassionless group constantly monitoring what people did on the Sabbath. Unfortunately, on all seven days of the week, these self-righteous frauds were themselves guilty of pride, greed, and mistreatment of the poor. Jesus called them white-washed tombs.

My kids were smart. They read the Bible for themselves and correctly discerned that their mom and dad sometimes succumbed to a focus on the peripheral, a kind of legalism more like the hypocritical Pharisees than like Jesus.

I can't turn back the clock and erase hypocritical blunders affecting my kids so negatively during their impressionable years. I can't eliminate history's record of the many days I relied on my own wisdom instead of on God's power accessed through prayer. I can learn, however, from my mistakes and chart a different course now in my third trimester. That's where prayer, the most central of activities for third-tri mothers, comes in.

Guideline #10: Commit to prioritizing prayer as a central focus.

Stop for a minute and consider how a change in focus during these third-tri years resembles what happens during pregnancy's third term.

Parallel #6: Priorities change. Many things that meant so much to you during pre-pregnancy days lose their allure. Your mind is fixed on your growing offspring and finishing your trimester well. Likewise, priorities need to change in life's third tri.

Numerous helpful books about prayer have been written by saints more qualified to teach on that subject than I am. Some prayer warriors I admire have worn threadbare areas in their carpets from so many hours on their knees, pouring their hearts out to God. Some pray while prostrate, calling out from a humble, worshipful stance. Although I've tried those postures, at my current rate, my rugs will last for years.

My mind tends to wander, or I fall asleep when I silently pray. Group prayer often seems like a competition to win the excellent prayer contest. Mealtime prayers can easily become mere routine rather than a genuine connection with God. Corporate public prayers rarely engage my spirit with His. I am getting better at talking out loud to God in the privacy of my office or car, or while walking, but speaking aloud to God the Father, Son, and Holy Spirit doesn't come naturally to me. Sitting at my computer right now, I just whispered out loud to my Father that I desperately need His Holy Spirit's help to write through me. I once read that Mother Teresa described herself as "a pencil in His hands," so I asked Him to flow through my fingers.

While admitting my prayer deficiencies, I can't get away from Old and New Testament teaching about the necessity of going to God through prayer and believing He hears and responds. In my first and second trimesters of life, I put more stock in my own efforts, and prayer was a peripheral activity. I once heard Francis Chan warn against overestimating what I could accomplish and underestimating what Christ could accomplish. Of course, I wouldn't say it out loud, but I was more interested in reading the

Bible and knowing what was in it and listening to human experts so I could navigate life skillfully, than in praying. Foolish me!

The total inadequacy of my personal efforts and strategies humbled me, and I was primed to believe Jesus when He said, "I am the vine; you are the branches. Those who remain in me, and I in them, will produce much fruit. For apart from me you can do nothing."[60] To escape the "nothing" results in my life, I needed to discover a way to achieve persistent connection and communication with Jesus.

Any prayer style that builds intimacy with the Father, Son, and Holy Spirit and results in fruit-bearing is commendable. I want to tell you what works for me, not because it is superior to any other forms of prayer, but because some of you may also have made prayer a fringe part of your life, and you desire a way for prayer to become more central. You may realize you have prayed too little, too shallowly, with too few results, and without much faith.

The path to where I am now was incremental. I completed the *Experiencing God* study[61] a number of years ago. It was formational in helping me understand God wants to communicate to His people, and we can listen to His voice and join Him in His work.

Shortly thereafter, I learned how lies embedded in our long-ago memories of events and interactions affect our lives negatively. I discovered how pivotal it is to sense God's presence in my past and present circumstances and then ask, "What does Jesus want me to know about that?" Listening to the new thoughts subsequently impressed upon my heart resulted in the revelation of profound truths to replace destructive lies.

I had been in the habit of journaling much of my adult life, and I was aware that writing down my prayers made them more real and substantive. I had a record of what I'd prayed, so I could distinguish between praying and just thinking about something. However, due to the recognition that prayer is not just a one-way activity but a two-way conversation with God Himself, I added the new habit of *focused listening*.

I begin by systematically reading a chapter in Scripture, looking for what God wants me to internalize that day. I pay special attention to what those verses reveal about God's character. I then begin a response in my journal to what He's said to me through His Word. First and foremost, I seek to note what He's shown me about Himself. I begin with the phrase, "Thank You, Father . . ." After thanking Him for aspects of His character that the passage illuminated, I continue writing in my journal and tell Him other things on my mind. The journaling flows effortlessly because starting the page is always the hardest. By scribbling "Thank You, Father . . ." automatically at the top of my day's entry, I only have to finish the sentence and pour out my heart.

At some point in the process, I feel an urge to listen to Him again. I've already listened to Him through reading the Bible passage, and I've responded back to Him in my written journal entry addressed to Him. Sometimes I ask Him questions. Now I enter a capital "L" for "listen," and I sit quietly and expectantly for Him to speak again, this time for His Holy Spirit to communicate needed information to my spirit. I record the thoughts as they come to me. Naturally, I discard anything contradictory to Scripture. However, most of the time the thoughts impressed on my heart are spot on. Amazingly so! Often what He tells me immediately adjusts whatever skewed thinking has been present. I sit there and ponder what His words mean. Many times, the Holy Spirit's messages require an adjustment of my life in order to obey.

In 2015, God revealed an additional level of intimacy in prayer. The experiences I am about to describe are intensely personal. I disclose this information because many of you may want to move to a deeper, more intimate relationship with God but don't know if it is possible. If you are not already practicing two-way prayer journaling, I want to encourage you to begin that habit as I have just described. You will become familiar with God's voice, like a sheep knows the unique vocal sounds of his shepherd. It was because of my listening prayer habit that God could interact with me at one of the lowest points in my life in an astonishing encounter.

God Speaks Through the Thunder

In my seventieth year, God gave me a *sign*—a sign shockingly similar to Moses' burning bush spectacle when he was eighty. I record this experience for the same reason John recorded specific miraculous signs from Jesus' ministry. "These [signs] are written so that you may continue to *believe* that Jesus is the Messiah, the Son of God, and that by believing in him you will have life by the power of his name."[62]

Doubting Thomas saw the evidence of Jesus' nail holes and placed his hand into the wound in Jesus' side per Jesus' instructions, so Thomas would be faithless no longer but "believe."[63] Signs do that. They help us to believe with a whole new certainty.

Moses was tending his flock at the base of Mt. Sinai when God's voice called to him from a burning bush. "'Moses, Moses, do not come any closer,' the LORD warned. 'Take off your sandals, for *you are standing on holy ground... You must lead my people Israel out of Egypt... And this is your *sign* that I am the one who has sent you: When you have brought the people out of Egypt, you will worship God at this very mountain.'"[64] My own subsequent holy ground sign took me completely by surprise.

My first husband, Chuck, had been homebound for nine years, leaving the house only for doctor appointments and, toward the end, via ambulance. He lived in constant pain. I was his sole caretaker until the last year and a half of his life. I then hired caretakers to provide company and assistance between 10 a.m. and 8 p.m., while I continued my counseling practice and got a break from constant caretaking.

As his blood cancer progressed despite chemotherapy treatments, Chuck became weaker and woke me more often during the nights. He'd fallen and broken a knee the last time he attempted to get out of bed, so now his world had shrunk to his adjustable hospital bed. His helpers and I could no longer get him out of the house for blood transfusions or other medical treatments.

Hired caretakers (and eventually Hospice angels for the last eight months) were a blessing because I could not do all the required lifting and turning and bathing, or be on duty twenty-four hours a day, day in and day out. However, their presence also usurped the unique helpmate role I'd previously played in our marriage. I felt tormented, frustrated, and helpless as his suffering mounted. Still, I stubbornly resisted having helpers stay overnight. I wanted to preserve our husband-wife love relationship, but I was at the end of my strength and totally exhausted physically and emotionally.

It was Thursday of Easter week of 2015 when Chuck stopped eating and drinking and lost his ability to speak. For the past few days, following every swallow of water, he'd choked, gurgled, and coughed endlessly. The week before, Chuck had reported seeing a "blue angel" at the foot of his bed and described interactions with his long-departed mother and my dead parents, who were surrounding him. He was agitated and disturbed by the ceilings and walls closing in on him and by blindness overtaking him. Every breath was an enormous effort.

Two girlfriends brought me dinner that Thursday evening, and one offered to spend the night. Because Shawn was an Ob-Gyn, she claimed to be accustomed to not getting much sleep at night, so I relented and said she could sleep in the room directly across the hall from Chuck.

Before she could come, my doctor friend needed to deliver a baby, so she didn't arrive at our house until after 10 p.m. I had no reserve left. As she bopped into the house, Shawn smiled and said cheerily, "I feel like I am entering *holy ground* here tonight." I replied wearily and dejectedly, "Oh no, this is *abysmal ground.*"

Shawn stared at me briefly because my comment seemed so out of character, but then she kindly said, "Go to bed!" Immediately, without another word, I disappeared into the master bedroom and crawled between the sheets.

Then the storm started. It is difficult to convey the intensity of the storm that ensued. For seven hours, waves of record-breaking thunderstorms battered the house. Six inches of rain fell in torrents. Repeated rounds of deafening thunder rocked the house. Despite my exhaustion, I couldn't sleep for more than short periods before crashing thunder would awaken me. I repeatedly got up and checked on Chuck even though I knew Shawn was a capable doctor and on duty.

At 4 a.m., an explosive boom of thunder again shook me awake with an instantaneous thought, *Charlotte, this thunder is not going to stop until you get up and go* pray *with Shawn.* I recognized the message as being from God, and I jumped out of bed and headed immediately toward Chuck's wing of the house. When I looked in Chuck's room, I was so astonished that I stopped dead in my tracks.

Totally opposite of his usual craving for warmth, Chuck had found the strength to throw off every stitch of clothing, his sheet, and blanket, and he lay there with only a white strip of a disposable brief draped across his emaciated skin-and-bones body. He was spread-eagled on the hospital bed, arms stretched out to either side, his chest heaving, eyes closed, gasping for breath. Maybe I've seen too many passion plays with actors portraying Jesus hanging on the cross, but that is what I beheld. I suddenly realized it was now early Good Friday morning, and Chuck had entered into the agony of Gethsemane while I'd been fitfully sleeping. Shawn joined me at Chuck's bedside, and she saw the same image: Chuck entering into, and portraying, the suffering of his Savior on the cross.

Chuck seemed totally unaware of Shawn's and my presence as we slipped on his pajama top and covered him with his bedclothes. With quivering voices, Shawn and I warbled, "We Are Standing on Holy Ground," while wobbling weak-kneed next to Chuck's bed. And, yes, we began to pray! And it was mostly *listening* prayer, as I experienced the Holy Spirit downloading truth into my mind and spirit. We slipped across the hallway, lay down on the bed next to each other, and I began to tell Shawn the revelations God gave me in those moments, while she and I had stood on holy ground with angels all around. Not generally given to many tears, I totally soaked the pillowcase that night as we lay in bed praying while the storm raged.

Tears streamed as I grasped the enormous cost of sin. In my inner being, I now knew it had been no small consequence when God required the death penalty because of Adam and Eve's defiance. A hatred of sin overtook me as I comprehended the horror disobedience brings. What's more, I realized God also *hated* the excruciating deaths of His loved ones, including Chuck's deathbed agony.

God had longed for obedience from the beloved humans He'd created and planted in Eden. He didn't want to pronounce the death penalty on humankind. But because of Adam and Eve's refusal to obey, it had required His Son's gruesome death to provide a chance for eternal life beyond the grave. I realized how hideous Jesus' death was—how much He did not want to go through the torturous hours and agonized breathing and far more pain during His scourging and hanging on the cross than even my suffering husband was enduring.

I knew Chuck on that Good Friday was struggling like Jesus in the garden (complete with sleeping disciples nearby) to choose, "Thy will be done!"

The Holy Spirit also implanted a surprising truth concerning my inability to "be there" for Chuck in his darkest hours. My craving for sleep sometimes won out. I felt guilt-ridden about longing for more than an hour of undisturbed sleep. I dreaded the chime's jarring interruptions when Chuck pushed the button over and over during the exhausting nights. In the past, I had read the Gospel account of the failure of Jesus' sleep-deprived disciples to keep watch and pray while Jesus anguished in Gethsemane. I'd always interpreted Jesus' rebuke as harshly scolding, "Couldn't you watch with me even one hour? Keep watch and pray, so that you will not give in to temptation. For the spirit is willing, but the body is weak!"[65] However, the Lord's love enveloped me, and His tender voice now affirmed and comforted me with the very same words, but spoken in a loving, gentle tone.

The Lord let me understand that He saw my willing spirit and even commended it. Jesus dismissed my failure as mere "body weakness." He understood I was doing my best to love and serve Chuck during the long, difficult nights. What counted to God was my willing spirit, my abiding desire to steadfastly love my husband these fifty years, and He lauded my commitment to fulfill my wedding vows, "in sickness and in health, until death do us part."

Jesus let me know He was advising His beloved disciples and all of us who would follow Christ in years to come to overcome temptation by spending time with Him, watching, and praying. Christ was not shaming either His disciples or me for succumbing to exhaustion, just compassionately teaching us what we would need to know after He was gone: Prayer is necessary so we can resist temptations.

Another clear perception as I sensed Jesus' whispering in my heart was the truth that my husband's spirit had also been willing, but his flesh had likewise been weak.

Those of you who have cared for extended periods for critically ill loved ones may have struggled with attitudes displayed by sick family members. It is common for caretaker spouses to feel like the afflicted person regards them mainly as someone to meet their many urgent needs. Our loved one may act self-centered and ungrateful as they claw for their relief and comfort at the expense of their caretaker's well-being.

Numerous times I wondered if I would end up dying before Chuck because of the toll caretaking took on me. It was important for me to know that Chuck's spirit of love and concern for me remained in his heart's core even when it was no longer visible. After Chuck's body died, I was buoyed by knowing Chuck loved me intensely to the end. Jesus told me so.

I use the terminology, "Chuck's body died," because Chuck's essence, his spirit, went to be with Jesus and lived on. This is how I view the deaths of all Christians—as deaths of their "earth-suits" only.

After an hour of tears and revelation, the storm outside abruptly stopped, and peace filled my heart. Like Moses, I felt assured the Lord loved me and would be with me. The Holy Spirit had downloaded into me what I needed to know for the journey ahead. My doctor friend recognized the emergence of complete peace and sensed her role as a witness to this momentous night was over. She left before sunrise to go work out at the gym, but I was so glad Shawn had been with me, or I might have wondered if it was all my imagination.

As God predicted in Moses' burning bush encounter, Moses returned to Mt. Sinai months later, accompanied by all the Jews he'd miraculously led out of Egypt. God again spoke to Moses, this time in awe-inspiring thunder, providing a confirming sign that it truly had been God speaking to Moses the first time in the burning bush. Little did I know God would give me a confirming sign in regard to my thunder encounter with God.

On the third day, on Easter Sunday morning, my spiritual leader and beloved husband slipped into eternity to celebrate Easter with his risen Savior. Knowing the end was near, our youngest son had arrived to be with his dad, and our daughter was catching a plane from Seattle. The Hospice nurse had predicted it might still be several days before Chuck's body died.

I fell asleep after midnight while listening to Chuck's oxygen-assisted breathing. I awoke at 1:45 a.m. on Easter Sunday morning, but not to any sound. I was instead startled awake by the sudden absence of sound. Chuck had taken his last breath and he was gone.

God had already spoken to me in the thunder on Good Friday and told me what I needed to know as I now shifted from being the bride of Chuck Melcher to a widow whose provider and protector is Christ. God's communication to me in the thunder had been a burning bush sign enabling me to believe more deeply, know Him more fully, and be prepared to obey Him in the days ahead. Like Moses at the burning bush, I had stood on holy ground and received His initial message and directions. More was to follow!

A Confirming Sign

The first Christmas after Chuck's body died, I wrote a letter to my three children to send with their "Merry Christmas" checks. I also enclosed copies of the book, *Secrets of the Secret Place*.[66]

I'd chosen not to join any of my family for the holidays, although they'd all issued invitations. David had urged me to come with his family to Italy, and Daniel begged me to take a Caribbean cruise with them. They couldn't understand why I would want to be alone the first Christmas after their father died. No one in my family knew yet that my decision to stay home resulted from a confirming sign occurring within days of Chuck's funeral, and the book they were receiving would explain that sign.

I had related the God-infused thunderstorm encounter to a few Christian friends who came to support me in my loss, and the kids overheard those conversations during the week of their dad's funeral, but they didn't seem interested in discussing it further. For all I knew, they were assuming "Mom has finally lost her mind completely!"

Talking about God and spiritual things had become awkward, really taboo, after each of the kids went away to college. They no longer felt comfortable discussing Christian topics after serious doubts about God and the legitimacy of the Bible prevailed. They didn't want to hurt their mom and dad with their belief and lifestyle changes, so they preferred not to talk about "controversial" topics, nor hear our contradictory views. Does this sound like some of your homes?

While my kids were moving further from Christ, I began moving into a more intimate relationship with Him. After some unfruitful discussions, I recognized that the God they'd ostensibly rejected was not the true Christ, but a caricature their dad and I had portrayed in our spiritual immaturity. I asked them to forgive me for sometimes wrongly acting like a Pharisee, but they didn't want to talk much about any of it. I didn't know to confess that I'd fixated on the peripheral rather than the central aspects of Christianity because I didn't understand that concept yet. However, God was poised to invite me to "dive into the central" immediately after the funeral flurry ended.

Within thirty minutes of putting Deborah on a plane back to Seattle after the two memorial services, an unexpected *sign* occurred, a confirmation that it was God speaking to me through the thunder on Good Friday. By way of explanation, I will include a copy of the Christmas letter I wrote to my children, beginning with an opening paragraph describing their dad's and my courtship, and followed by a description of my confirming sign. It felt like a risky move after so many years with a gag in my mouth.

• • •

Dear Deborah, David and Daniel,

Your dad maintained he fell in love with me the first night we met, in the lounge of the dormitory where I was staying at the University of Kansas Science and Math Camp. I was jaded already at 16, and dubious of the sincerity of your dad's avowed feelings for me that summer. I even requested he not say "I love you" again, because I was so cynical about men's "lines" on that 4th of July night, 1961, when he first uttered those words with fireworks blazing in the sky. My trust in your dad's love gradually grew as he steadfastly pursued me, persistent and undaunted, while I struggled with crushes on other guys over the next three years. Then we both gave our hearts away, first to Jesus, and then absolutely to each other, declaring our commitment until death do us part with wedding vows before our senior year of college.

Too soon, after 49½ years of marital belonging, faithfulness, and spiritual togetherness, the Lord took my soulmate to heaven on Easter Sunday morning, and his body was buried in a grave a mile away. You three kids came (David all the way from inland China), grieved with me, and supported me through those first surreal days. Inevitably, I dropped off the last helpful offspring (Deborah) at the airport and returned alone, for the first time, to the newly empty house.

As I unlocked the door and walked solemnly into the living space, I forgot my churning emotions because my eyes riveted on two strangely out-of-place objects lying on the seat of my recliner where I always sat to read or watch TV. For years I held hands with your dad in his matching "Daddy Bear" chair next to mine, while we praised God together with Gospel music videos.

I immediately stepped to investigate and discovered the unfamiliar objects lying on my recliner seat were two identical books. I felt sure the volumes had not been in my recliner when I left for the airport, and Deborah later confirmed she had not seen them there either. However, I had locked the door when I left for the airport, so no one could have brought them into the house. They simply had not been there, and suddenly there they were.

In trying to solve the mystery of the books' origin, I later discovered a couple from church remembered bringing copies for your dad and me about three years earlier, but we had set them aside and never opened them. We routinely housed all books we weren't currently reading on bookshelves downstairs. How they ended up upstairs in my chair is still a mystery—or a miracle.

I sank down in the recliner and started reading *Secrets of the Secret Place* for the first time. I was hooked from page one, but soon the hairs on the back of my neck began to stand up. On page 10, Sorge began to talk about God's thundering voice at Mt. Sinai. He referenced the Psalmist's description of that scene in Psalm 81:7, "*I answered you out of the thundercloud.*"[67]

Sorge wrote, "God has always designed that the secret place be a place where He answers us and speaks to us. Sometimes He even apprehends us by thundering to us with His awesome voice. There is nothing more glorious in all of life than hearing His voice. . . . 'The secret place of thunder'—what an awesome description of the place where we come aside to be with our Lord!"[68]

Reverential awe overcame me because I was obviously in the middle of a personal "God event," a confirmation of my experience with the Lord less than a week before on Good Friday. What resonated for me at that moment was my recollection that your dad's death on Easter Sunday morning had been preceded by a completely supernatural experience of Jesus communicating to me "in the thunder" on Good Friday, during a record-setting, deafening seven-hours-long massive thunderstorm. My friend, Dr. Shawn Campbell, had witnessed the messages I'd received in the wee hours of Good Friday morning as we stood on thundering, holy ground with angels all around.

Although I have read hundreds of Christian books, I had never before read anything emphasizing the possibility of present-day believers hearing God's voice "in the thunder." *Secrets of the Secret Place* became God's unique vehicle to deliver me a confirming sign bringing peace during the coming months of grieving. Through it, the Holy Spirit delivered comfort, help, and direction. I can say with Sorge, "My paradigm of kingdom living was radically realigned because I was awakened to the fact that everything changes when I *hear* from God and act upon that word."[69]

The supernatural communication, both in the messages I received during the Good Friday night thunderstorm and the bizarre, mysterious appearance a few days later of a book talking about God speaking through thunder, gave me goose bumps. At a crucial time, these signs led me to believe and relate to Him on an increasingly deep, experiential level.

It has now been over eight months since April 5, 2015, and the words in *Secrets of the Secret Place* continue to move me as I am now rereading it for the fourth time. Its 52 chapters are highlighted in purple, green, pink, and blue, as I see something new to ponder with every reading. I have learned to never process more than one chapter a day because of their richness and depth.

I was already conscious God promised to care for widows,[70] but now I embraced the experience of God being like a husband to me, caring for me, protecting me, cherishing me. Spending extended time with Him in our "secret place" is balm for my heart and soul. Even before your dad's body died, I had chosen my 2015 life verse to be the Lord's promise in Psalm 32:8, *I will guide you along the best pathway for your life. I will advise you and watch over you.*[71] I have found astounding intimacy with Jesus in my secret place. There, in my Mama Bear chair, I read and process God's love and guidance in the Bible, and I supplement with the *Secrets* book, prayer journaling, and listening prayer.

I am aware that because the Lord miraculously put me on this path to intimacy in our secret place where we hang out together, I have navigated this first year of widowhood with far less agony than many widows I know. It is why I can face Christmas in Lexington without any family members at my side and not be miserable or depressed. Although there is a natural longing to be with you, my children and grandchildren, I am content to view this season as my "honeymoon Christmas." I willingly devote this season to joyfully spending time with the One who cares for me now, and who loves me unconditionally and forever, even when all my family members are far away. Future Christmases will likely offer different possibilities.

Just as it was a process for me to gain trust in your dad to love me and care for me, it has been a process for me to surrender to God's love and believe in Christ as the "Lover of my soul." The book of John, which is my favorite Gospel account, talks about the signs and wonders performed by Jesus for the sole purpose of people being able to *believe* in Him.[72]

I am sending copies of the *Secrets* book to each of you three kids in hopes it might resonate in some way, just because it has meant so much to me. I have pondered the question, *"Why **two** copies in the chair?"* I have concluded it is because I was to read one and share the other with appropriate people. You kids are among those "appropriate people." God called Moses to lead His people, the Jews, to the Promised

Land. Moses was astounded and felt inadequate to be chosen for such an assignment. Likewise, God called me, a most unlikely person, to lead third-tri moms and you, my beloved children.

For some reason, it has been awkward to have spiritual conversations with my own three kids for many years now. I regret the pressure you felt as teenagers and young adults to gain your parents' approval through certain spiritual practices, some of which smelled of hypocrisy and Pharisaism. Your spiritual path is between you and God, not between you and me.

I do feel assurance that each of you has belonged to Him since childhood and that He is your Good Shepherd and holds you safely in His hand. I believe He is answering your dad's and my prayers and is helping you find your way to authentically know and love Him better and better, just as He is doing with me. However, I feel Dad and I hid the deepest parts of ourselves once you were adults because of trying to respect an unwritten code of silence surrounding our faith for fear of further offending or turning you off. I greatly desire to be genuine, open, caring, and loving, and to express myself naturally without being fearful, and I want you to feel free to do the same.

You remember Dad always saw to it that we read the nativity story on Christmas Eve before we dove into piles of presents and cinnamon rolls and games and Chex mix. The Son of God being born on earth is what Christmas was ultimately about to us, even though those events probably happened in the fall while shepherds were out in their fields, not in late December. Those signs and wonders still excite me and lead me to believe! Glory to God in the highest, and on earth, peace and good will toward men!

With oodles of love and hugs,

Mom

•••

My mentor-in-print, Bob Sorge, related that during his period of intense study of Jesus' teachings, it became clear to him, "The word 'hear' is the most important word in the Bible! The most important treasures in the kingdom are predicated upon the necessity of hearing God."[73] Jesus Himself cried out after teaching the parable of the farmer planting seed in four different soils, "Anyone with ears to *hear* should listen and understand."[74]

Sorge maintains, "Nothing can replace the confidence and authority that comes from hearing God. . . . For this reason, I strongly advocate for a prayer life that is comprised mostly of silence. . . . *Things don't change when I talk to God; things change when God talks to me.* When I talk, nothing happens; when God talks, the universe comes into existence. So the power of prayer is found, not in convincing God of my agenda, but in waiting upon Him to hear His agenda."[75]

I am thinking of all the third-tri moms who will be reading this account. I admit I feel inadequate to usher you into God's throne room when I still have so much to learn myself. I have simply borne witness to my own prayer transformation over time. Prayers for the Holy Spirit to draw your children to God, and prayers for them to "hear" the voice of their Good Shepherd, are anything but peripheral add-on activities in your day. Rather, prayer emerges as the most central and powerful force available to you as the mother of grown children.

To help you develop and deepen your prayer life while you are undergoing a transformation into the thriving third-trimester mother you want to be, I recommend *Secrets of the Secret Place* and a blank prayer journal to supplement your daily study of Scripture. Both will be invaluable in accelerating your progress.

According to God's promise about restoring our family territory, humbling ourselves and praying are the first two criteria. The next chapter moves us to condition #3: Seek the Lord's face!

Coaching Corner

1. What peripheral motivations have reigned as inappropriately central during your second and third trimesters of life so far? What results have resulted from emphasizing the peripheral?

2. What central focus do you want to accentuate now in your third trimester?

3. What one change would accelerate your focus on prayer?

4. What do you believe about my experience of sensing God's voice in the thunder?

5. What is your reaction to Bob Sorge's assertion that *hear* is the most important word in the Bible?

6. Bob Sorge also states, "Things don't change when I talk to God; things change when God talks to me." What has been your main deterrent keeping you from hearing God's voice in your heart?

7. What is your plan to overcome that deterrent?

8. How could you implement that plan this week?

CHAPTER 7

Seeking God's Face

"CONGRATULATIONS, YOU ARE going to have a baby," your physician once said based on your urine analysis. From that moment, you eagerly looked forward to beholding the precious little face of your son or daughter.

Whose face would you like to materialize in front of your eyes right now—perhaps your sweetheart, your cherished child or darling grandchild, your dear mother or father, your beloved grandma or grandpa, a brother or sister? Anxious mothers with a soldier son or daughter serving in some dangerous distant place would be ecstatic to see their child in battle fatigues walk through the door this very minute. Those with terminal illness sometimes put off dying because they long to see the faces of their much-loved children one more time. People we treasure, whether we saw them an hour ago or they have already departed this life, possess faces we adore, so we constantly crave another glimpse.

How much do you long to behold the face of God? Perhaps the Lord has been living inside you for many years now. Do you seek the face of the beloved One you've carried in your heart, as a pregnant mom fixates on her soon-to-be-born child's characteristics?

Looking at an online collection of pregnancy photos recently, I was struck by the picture of a tiny clenched fist visible through the skin of a protruding abdomen. We gaze at ultrasound images of unborn grandsons and granddaughters, relishing their developing facial features. We celebrate and throw parties the day the sex of a grandchild-in-utero is clearly revealed by high-tech equipment.

Despite all the ways we garner information about our new family member before delivery, the first total view of our newborn takes our breath away. Mamas-to-be may develop theories about eventual temperaments by analyzing the kicking and churning inside their ever-expanding bellies. However, they are utterly captivated by the son or daughter they finally hold in their arms, as waves of previously unimagined motherly love sweep over them.

Once again, stop and think about the striking parallels between the third trimester of pregnancy and your third trimester of life, the era that commenced once your children grew up and left home.

Parallel #7: During pregnancy, and again now in your empty nest years, you look forward to meeting the beloved One you carry inside. You long to see, hear, hold, know, love, and be loved by Him.

As third-tri mothers, we know the infusion of joy when our grandchildren pop through the door. We just can't get enough of their beloved faces. Let me remind you of the Lord's directives to Solomon, "Then if my people who are called by my name will humble themselves and pray and *seek my face* and turn from their wicked ways, I will hear from heaven and will forgive their sins and restore their land."[76]

Guideline #11: Don't let seeking connection with your adult children replace seeking God's face.

I don't mean to downplay the totally appropriate thrill of connection with family members. Our children are inadequate and inappropriate *gods*, however. The reality of knowing Christ energized Paul through years of hard labor, personal sacrifice, relationship heartaches, missionary journeys, beatings, and imprisonments. Paul declared, "Everything else is worthless when compared with the infinite value of knowing Christ Jesus my Lord."[77]

In all of life's trimesters, there is a tendency to get distracted by the cares of this world. Therefore, we fail to invest much time in the deliberate process of getting to know the One we've invited to live in our hearts. We are "too busy" with other things, with peripheral things. We thought we would have lots of time on our hands once the children moved out, and the pace of the hectic child-filled years slowed down. However, the mundane activities of everyday life and frequent urgent deadlines seem to consume our minutes and hours, and even more so during holiday seasons.

There is a second problem. The Pharisees of Jesus' time made a lethal error in how they approached knowing God. They studied and memorized Scripture intently, but they only succeeded in knowing the contents of the Book, not the Author Himself. Likewise, mothers of grown children can pray, attend church, and read the Scripture regularly without actually *loving* the Lord and becoming enthralled by His person and His "face." An intimate relationship with Him doesn't seem as compelling as the bond with our human loved ones.

Sorge revealed the surprising truth: *"Your reading in the word can be a dynamic and living encounter with the person of the Lord Jesus Christ!* Don't come to the word out of a sense of rote duty to knock off your daily quota of chapters; don't come merely to master spiritual principles or to glean clever insights; come to *gaze* upon the majesty and mystery of the altogether Lovely One, the One who has captured your heart! . . . Come with a cry in your heart to *see* Him and *know* Him."[78]

Moses is the unique biblical figure who possessed a face-to-face relationship with God. The blinding reflection from those encounters required Moses to wear a veil when he left the tabernacle after meeting with God. Moses is the one to whom God spoke from the burning bush and from the thunder on Mt. Sinai. The Bible also describes Moses as "very humble—more humble than any other person on earth."[79] We are checking off the boxes for Moses:

- Humility

- Prayer

- Seeking God's face

How do we get beyond checking off boxes and experience the real deal implied in "seeking God's face"? Remember my question about whose face you would most like to see today?

The birth date on our driver's licenses would indicate we are mature women, but many of us have failed the maturity test in our relationships with God, and we are still looking to earthly relationships for our main satisfaction. That is not an indictment, but an invitation to consciously spend more focused time with Him so we can grow to love His voice and His face. Many of us are too distracted, and we don't yet comprehend the benefits that "He rewards [to] those who sincerely seek Him"[80]

"I've gone to five different women's Bible studies in the past three years," Rita lamented. "In the end, they all turned out to be about diabetes," the forlorn young mother insisted.

Rita's statement floored me since we'd both just finished participating in an eight-part series titled "Seizing Hope" an hour prior. I also knew this mom had attended a Beth Moore study on Esther with me the previous summer. The word *diabetes* had not come up once in either series.

Then Rita divulged that she had a daughter afflicted with childhood-onset diabetes. Now I understood. This mom's heart and mind were entangled with the day-in and day-out problems of caring for a cherished child dealing with a dangerous health condition. Therefore, Rita viewed every Scripture and teaching point through the lens of a mother consumed with concerns for her daughter.

Can you relate to this phenomenon as I do? When my heart is heavy over a child's path in life, many verses in the Bible, as well as my pastor's sermons, seem to apply to those situations and dilemmas. I've concluded God intended it to be so.

Whatever struggle dominates our brain space, the Living Word, full of wisdom, love, and compassion, offers His guidance. If three third-tri moms were swaying gently back and forth on my porch swing this afternoon, my mind might be focused on a health problem, yours fixated on a prodigal child, and our friend's mind troubled with financial worries. Jesus could be speaking equally to each of us, "Come to me, all of you who are weary and carry heavy burdens, and I will give you rest."[81] In all three cases, His invitation and His promise would be personal and true.

Yes, the Lord wants us to seek His face when we are burdened and need comfort or direction. Jesus also wants us to seek His face because we desperately want to be in His presence and enjoy our intimate relationship. He wants to be in the center of your life, and you want Him in the center of everything. He's your #1 confidante, your companion, your friend, your mentor, your guide, your helper, your source of hope, your Almighty God. You light up when you see Him in Scripture and at work all around you, just as you light up when you see your beloved sweetheart enter the room. For me, this happens most often in the "secret place," the meeting place I've carved out to spend time together with God without distraction.

Guideline #12: Ruthlessly seize focused time with Jesus in your secret place.

It isn't easy to untangle the activities that happen in the secret place. Paying attention to the specific things the Lord wants you to hear and apply from Scripture each day, praying to your Father, writing in your journal, listening to the whispered counsel of the Holy Spirit, experiencing love and wisdom flooding you—all feed on each other and enrich each other.

The essential prerequisite, to ruthlessly seize focused time, requires exactly what it says—ruthlessness! The early morning, before the distractions of the day hit, seems far more potent than any other time in amplifying our experience with God. If you examine the lives of spiritual giants throughout history, you will find, almost without exception, their devotional time occurred early in the morning. It is a battle every sunrise. We're sleepy, and it's hard to get up. Even if we win the contest with the bed, we haven't yet successfully seized the time because we have so many pressing tasks and needy people depending upon us.

When I was still a full-time therapist and also caretaker for my husband, I found I could not leave my bedroom or someone would grab me. The phone was ringing; Chuck needed my attention; I noticed an unfinished task or a mess to clean up and told myself, "It will only take a minute." I was tempted to check my phone for newly arrived texts or emails from clients. I steeled myself with the thought, "It can wait," and dared not open the bedroom door, or my hour of opportunity evaporated. Consequently, I carved out a corner in the bedroom to establish my regular secret place.

After I retired at age seventy-two, I acquired more discretionary hours and flexibility, but I still find mornings in the secret place more productive than later in the day. I need what the Holy Spirit imparts in the morning in order to navigate the rest of the twenty-four hours.

In a favorite chapter titled "The Secret of Radiation Therapy," Sorge declares, "*When you're in His presence for extended periods, the molecular composition of your soul gets restructured. You start to think differently, and you don't even know why.* You start to have different passions and interests, and you don't even know why. God is changing you on the inside in ways you can't cognitively analyze. All you know is, sinful affections that once pulled at your soul no longer have their former power over you. The secret is simply this: large chunks of time in God's presence—loving Him and imbibing His word."[82]

As third-tri moms, our hearts are still intricately attached to our grown offspring. We never expected our feelings to be so intense at this stage, but they are. What I am proposing is also to make room in your heart for intensity in your relationship with the Father, Son, and Holy

Spirit. Maybe an intimate connection with God is something you also didn't anticipate earlier in your life, but here we are now, drawn to seek His face! As we seek His countenance, we can petition with the psalmist, "May *His face smile* with favor on us."[83]

As I finish this chapter and move on to the last requirement mentioned in 2 Chronicles 7:14, I will close with the priestly blessing God delivered to the Israelites through Moses when Aaron was the chief priest. The Israelites looked to Moses as their go-between because he had a face-to-face relationship with God. I want to challenge you not to settle for Moses, but to go up the mountain to seek God's face yourself. Be in the presence of God on your own, *daily* and *deeply*.

A few years ago, I designed some personal letterhead with this special priestly blessing printed at the top. Although modern readers tend to think of blessings in general terms, it is likely the Israelites in the wilderness would have understood blessings in terms of their day-to-day concerns: food, water, health, protection from enemies, family well-being, etc. As you receive this ancient blessing, I suspect the "favor" you most desire somehow relates to your children. Seeking God's face will bring you to a more peaceful place no matter what your concern.

> *The LORD bless you and keep you;*
> *the LORD make his face shine upon you*
> *and be gracious to you;*
> *the LORD turn his face toward you*
> *and give you peace.*[84]

Coaching Corner

1. Can you think of a person you know whose life demonstrates the priority of ruthlessly seeking God's face?

2. Do you remember your eagerness to see your baby's face for the first time? What was your reaction? Do you still light up when you see your offspring?

3. What would it take to match your eager anticipation to see your grandchild's newborn face with equal eagerness to see God's face and enjoy a love relationship with Him?

4. How important is possessing a heart at peace during this stage of your life?

5. On a scale of one to ten with ten being perfectly peaceful, how would you rate your level of peace today?

6. How does seeking God's face relate to increasing your peace quotient?

7. What one thing could you change this week to gain more peace?

CHAPTER 8

How Tight Is Your Turning Radius?

OUR CHILDREN HAVE a way of shining spotlights on our short-comings. One young adult who left the church and declared himself an atheist succinctly answered the interviewer's curious "Why?" with these heart-stopping words, "I was never good enough for my parents. How was I ever going to be good enough for God?"

Ouch!

Gradually during life's third trimester, an awareness of the consequences of our parental mistakes pierces our consciousnesses. In your pregnancy's third term, something similar occurred.

Parallel #8: Pregnant moms deal with regrets about choices made earlier in their lives (things such as alcohol and drug abuse, STDs, abortions, eating disorders, obesity, or putting off starting their family until their forties). These actions created extra risks endangering their baby's development. Third-tri moms also struggle with regrets over mothering mistakes.

We've arrived at the fourth requirement God gave us for healing in our land to occur. Let me remind you again of God's four criteria for restoration and the positive or negative consequences resulting from our choices:

"Then if my people who are called by my name will *humble* themselves and *pray* and *seek my face* and *turn* from their wicked ways, I will *hear* from heaven and will *forgive* their sins and *restore* their land. . . . But if you or your descendants *abandon* me and *disobey* the decrees and commands I have given you, and if you *serve and worship other gods,* then I will *uproot* the people from this land that I have given them."[85]

Guideline #13: Conduct a fearless inventory of your shortcomings, repent, and turn to God.

Consider the verbs in 2 Chronicles 7:14: The first four actions (*humble, pray, seek, turn*) are our responsibility, and the last three (*hear, forgive, restore*) comprise God's response. How we yearn for Him to hear, forgive, and restore! So what happens if we ignore our part and replace our four responsibilities with the God-defying verbs in 2 Chronicles 7:19 (*abandon, disobey, serve* and *worship other gods*)?

God's action in response to human decisions to abandon Him, disobey Him, and serve and worship other gods is corroborated by happenings throughout history. The frightening verb is *uproot.* Violating God's decrees and commands, discarding Him, and worshiping other gods—none of these turned out well. Like other biblical predictions, history confirms their validity—the Israelites disobeyed, and God responded by uprooting them.

Fortunately, the New Testament message of "another chance" begins with John the Baptist proclaiming, "People should be baptized to show that they had *repented* of their sins and *turned* to God to be forgiven."[86] Soon Jesus also began to preach, "*Repent* of your sins and *turn* to God, for the Kingdom of Heaven is near."[87]

When God bestowed the Holy Spirit on Pentecost, the awed onlookers asked, "What should we do?" Peter's reply? "Each of you must *repent* of your sins and *turn* to God, and be baptized in the name of Jesus Christ for the forgiveness of your sins."[88] In every case, this requirement of repentance and turning from sinful ways precedes forgiveness and restoration. Hurrah! Even if disobedience won out for a period of their lives, people now have another chance if they repent and turn to God.

I have no idea what particular offenses against God you may need to turn from, but I believe Paul speaks the truth, "*Everyone* has sinned; we *all* fall short of God's glorious standard."[89] Turning around and going in a God-honoring direction begins by acknowledging we've ignorantly or intentionally gotten off track.

I hit the rails with my overemphasis on rules. Sadly, I also now recognize I wasn't as full of unconditional love and grace as God is.

I admit it; I confess it; I repent of it; and I want to turn away from excessive emphasis on rules to God Himself and learn to love like He does. I am so grateful Jesus died for me so I can be forgiven, first by God and then by my children.

Secondly, I believed the lie that if I loved my sons and daughter passionately, spent fun times interacting with them, took them to church, disciplined consistently, taught them what the Bible says, and protected them from worldly influences, then they would love and honor God and their parents. There are obviously too many I's in that belief and not enough recognition that God is the only one with the power to accomplish those goals or draw hearts to Himself. I trusted my own abilities too much and trusted God's abilities too little.

From my observations of other moms and dads and from my own experience as an unintentionally legalistic parent myself, I recognize the sobering truth that we share far too many traits with the Pharisees and Sadducees. Those P & S religious leaders were the self-righteous folks who gave Jesus the biggest headaches. Jesus hammered the smugly moral crowd, yet welcomed every willing and humble sinner, loser, and outcast.

FYI: You don't have to be a rule-bound Christian to earn the "hypocritical" adjective. Hypocrisy is rampant in the secular world also. For example, politicians, celebrities, sports stars, corporate executives, and media figures extol helping poor and disadvantaged people while wastefully spending their immense personal fortunes almost entirely on their own pleasure. Proud announcements about gifts to kids with cancer or food banks or disaster relief bring adulation to celebrities and corporate moguls making no genuine personal sacrifices on behalf of anybody. I see few examples of rich folks voluntarily choosing to live frugally on 1 percent or even 10 percent of their massive incomes, while giving the rest to benefit the sick and poor in body or spirit.

What's more, some individuals with minimal incomes may be hypocritical too, arrogantly viewing themselves as more noble and righteous and virtuously committed to helping the poor and down-trodden than rich or religious people, while they are sometimes just coveting the rewards of others' hard work. What a mess! Hypocrisy stinks, and it clings to us all like lard to a pig.

Guideline #14: Take responsibility and admit your parenting mistakes to your offspring and ask for their forgiveness.

So many of us moms in the third trimester season of life have found ourselves saying "Ouch." Our legs feel knocked out from under us by an awareness that we weren't the ideal parent we wanted to be. After we make the adjustments—humbling ourselves, praying, seeking His face, repenting, and turning to God so He can forgive and restore—what's next?

At age thirty-five, Beverly Engel authored a book, *Divorcing a Parent,*[90] about her decision to "divorce" her mother after years of childhood emotional abuse. Unfortunately, in Beverly's adulthood, her mom continued to treat her daughter in hurtful ways. Beverly became so emotionally and physically stressed that she made the decision to completely cut off her mother, leading to a three-year total estrangement. In the book she published, Beverly urged hurting readers in similar situations with their mothers to consider doing the same.

"One day the phone rang, and Beverly heard her mom's voice say, 'I'm sorry.'

"These were the words I had been waiting to hear most of my life," Beverly admitted. "I could tell by the tone of her voice that she truly regretted the way she had treated me.... Although I believed her apology, I didn't yet know if her behavior toward me would be different. This I tested over time. But by apologizing, she had acknowledged that I had a reason to be hurt and angry, and that was extremely empowering for me. Apology changed my life."[91]

Beverly's mother only lived three more years, but the two of them grew closer than they'd ever been, and tremendous healing occurred.

In acknowledgment and celebration of those last good years together, Beverly Engel wrote a subsequent book, *The Power of Apology*.[92]

Admitting our mistakes and apologizing to the children we wounded can turn a strained relationship around. Not always, but many times. It is possible your child will be unwilling to give up resentments and forgive you no matter how sincerely you communicate your regret over past errors. However, more often than not, a person who felt wronged will feel relief when parents genuinely take responsibility for their actions. The door to forgiveness cracks open, especially when changes in parental behavior follow their admissions.

Beware of manipulations or self-excusing apologies that are no true apology at all. Manipulation for our own ends is out of order and will always backfire. Include the three essential ingredients of a genuine apology:

1. Communicate personal *regret* for having wounded your son or daughter. Convey your pain for how you hurt them.

2. Take *responsibility* for your hurtful actions without making excuses for what you did and without blaming anybody else. Explanations may be warranted; excuses are not.

3. State your intentions to *remedy* the situation to the extent possible. Sadly, what has happened in the past cannot be undone; it is set in stone. You can choose better options today and tomorrow, however. Convey your sincere intentions to not repeat the offending behaviors in the future.

I listened to Chuck Swindoll every morning on the radio as I was preparing to go to my therapy office. His wisdom on "Insights for Living" inspired me throughout my second and third trimesters of life.

However, I experienced Swindoll's most profound influence when he confessed his parenting struggles and described his efforts to deal with the "distance" he felt from his grown kids. In one sermon series, Dad Swindoll reported praying extensively with his wife and feeling led to try a new approach to break down the walls.

Chuck and his wife, Cynthia, each decided to write down a list of five or six behaviors they regretted because they now realized those particular actions and attitudes impacted their children negatively. As a couple, Chuck and Cynthia identified these offenses and helped each other prepare for a meeting with their adult kids. Only their children would be present, no spouses. In addition, the parents arranged for a trusted counselor to be with the family to process with their children whatever feelings emerged. Dad and Mom Swindoll planned to leave the group after they'd spoken their apologies, wanting to relieve any expectations for how the children were supposed to respond.

Each hurtful offense Mom and Dad humbly confessed was preceded with the phrase, "I have now come to realize . . ." Parents often have no idea how certain of our actions and attitudes will end up wounding a son or daughter. Only in hindsight do we see the pain we inflicted. After naming each negatively impacting behavior, the Swindoll parents individually conveyed, "I am very sorry, and I would ask you to forgive me. I hope you know how sincere I am." Tears flowed freely on all sides.

Swindoll and his wife resolved in their hearts not to bring these offenses up again unless a child opened the conversation, despite the temptation to say more later. They also determined not to have expectations for their kids to respond in any particular way. They knew it might take time for the children to process their parents' apologies. Recovery would occur in individual ways, depending on each child's temperament.

A few months before my children's father died, I helped Chuck prepare a similar list and their dad proceeded to talk to our kids one at a time when the opportunities arose. The phrase, "I have now come to realize" captured his sentiments exactly. He had acted in ignorance of how certain selfish priorities and ways of communicating would hurt his precious, sensitive kids.

I kept those scrawled yellow pad confessions, and wept when I re-read them recently. Those admissions truly were a case of "I have now come to realize . . ." Neither their dad nor I wanted to commit any of the hurtful mistakes we could only identify in retrospect. Then parents wait, resolve to exhibit changed behavior, and persistently pray and love.

After your conversation with your child when you admit acting in ways you now regret, it is time to let go of obsessive thoughts and enter a peaceful waiting period, minus all the angst and painful obsessing. You are committed to a new way of mothering now, and it is time to embrace a more serene outlook.

Accept the fact that you are incapable of fixing all relationship issues, even if you have humbled yourself, are praying and seeking God's face, have repented and turned to God, and have asked your child's forgiveness. The ball is in God's court and your child's court.

Guideline #15: God gave us all free will—your children included. Parents' mistakes are not responsible for all foolish or anti-God choices your children made, or continue to make, in adulthood.

While trudging on my elliptical in the basement of our lake cabin in Indiana, I often call friends to catch up with the latest developments in their lives, acknowledging I need a diversion to forget how much I would like to quit bicycling my legs and tugging on the arm bars.

Knowing I'm working on this book, one recent conversation went like this:

"Hey," I said, glad to be momentarily distracted from my exercise regimen. "What's new with the kids?" I was referring to my friend's daughter in her forties and her son in his fifties.

There was a pause, followed by a sigh. "Nothing new to report. They don't communicate much, and it feels awkward when we do talk or visit because of the underlying tension. I always feel like a cork is about to blow. I just don't understand what I did that caused them to resent me so much and to veer so far from how they were raised." (This mom had already made her moral inventory and had asked God and her kids for forgiveness for the infractions she'd identified.)

Putting on my reflective listening hat, I summed up her sentiments, "So another week of walking on eggshells and feeling perplexed as to why?"

"Exactly! What's going on with you?"

"I've been working on the chapters about adult children in my third-tri book. Do you know anyone I could interview about their later-in-life parenting challenges?"

The phone went silent so long I thought we'd been disconnected.

Finally, she choked out, "Charlotte, I've been trying to think of anyone not struggling with adult child problems. I think it's universal! And all of us wonder 'why' our grown kids act as they do."

The knee-jerk reflex in moms when their grown offspring continue to seethe with resentment or make foolish, life-damaging choices is to go back to asking *why* and blaming ourselves, even if we've supposedly done our part to make things right. We think, *I must have been a terrible mother to make them dislike me so much and choose such opposite paths in life.* The tape repeats endlessly: *Obviously, I have failed at the one thing I most wanted to do well—being their mother!*

Parents keep trying to figure out "why" their kids choose options mom and dad warned them about, all of which have damaging consequences. Those you birthed may be engaging in excessive drug or alcohol consumption, toying with the occult, opting for immoral lifestyles, and viewing God, the Bible, and the church as irrelevant. Other adult kids commit crimes, gamble recklessly, or live together without marrying. Financial irresponsibility, abortions, lazy work ethics, rage at authorities, and disdain for the Constitution and laws that have been in place since the country was founded, dismay us. You don't feel you taught or modeled any of those behaviors, but your child continues to choose contrary paths.

Lots of questions, few answers. We've been around this block before, but some of us are stuck in a bad Bill Murray *Ground Hog Day* loop.

Surely the Bible will give us the answers to "why?" Do you remember the promise you probably claimed, "Direct your children onto the right path, and when they are older, they will not leave it?"[93] And what about those parents whose kids have toed the line and never rebelled? Why does that happen? Did those kids have more flawless mothers who better modeled the way their child should go? Then you think about some admirable, God-honoring young adults you know who came from godless homes or had abusive, neglectful, selfish, or cruel parents. How could that be?

The entire chapter of Ezekiel 18 was written to people making the same knee-jerk reaction that modern-day mothers tend to make when perplexed about their kids' choices. In Ezekiel 18, the Lord *for-*

bids quoting a popular proverb in Israel, "The parents have eaten sour grapes, but their children's mouths pucker at the taste."[94]

The Lord proceeds to lay out a detailed account of the baffling cycle we often see: A good, loving, godly father may end up with a wonderful son who is just like him, but he might also raise a son who chooses to do a bunch of evil things his God-honoring dad would never do. Then, that rebellious offspring himself becomes a parent, but his son sees his father's wickedness and decides against that kind of life for himself. Therefore, this third-generation son lives an exemplary, moral, God-honoring life. The Lord declares, "All people are mine to judge—both parents and children alike. And this is my rule: The person who sins is the one who will die."[95]

These Scriptures don't comfort us much because we love our kids and are desperate for them not to *die*, but the Lord makes it clear He is equally loving and concerned for your prodigal's destiny. "Repent, and turn from your sins. Don't let them destroy you! Put all your rebellion behind you, and find yourselves a new heart and a new spirit . . . *I don't want you to die*, says the Sovereign Lord. Turn back and live!"[96] Isn't that the cry of your heart for your prodigals also?

Over and over throughout the history of Israel and Judah, you see noble kings whose sons do evil in God's eyes once they ascend their father's throne. More puzzling, a few horrific kings are followed by sons who reject their fathers' godless, idolatrous paths and faithfully follow God. I have searched for explanations embedded in 1 and 2 Kings and 1 and 2 Chronicles for clues about who is at fault when the next generation takes a bad turn and who gets the credit for good outcomes. I could find no instances where less than perfect parenting justified rejection of God, the embrace of pagan idols, and immoral behavior by offspring. Each generation is held responsible for its own choices to follow God, or not.

In case you wonder if this phenomenon of a godly mom and dad parenting a rebellious son or daughter is strictly an Old Testament occurrence, let me remind you of the familiar parable Jesus told about prodigal children. In Jesus' story, the son who came home after wasting his inheritance on wild living was met by a loving, compassionate father who'd been watching for eons for his lost son to return. There is no hint the prodigal's dad had been anything but a loving, kind father from the get-go.[97]

- Have we made mistakes, committed sins, and wounded our kids? Yes.

- Can we take credit for a good outcome in the next generation? No.

- Do we determine our child's ultimate destiny? No.

- Regardless of our offspring's good or bad choices, should we repent of our own mistakes and turn to God? Yes.

- If our children are wonderful chips off the old block and making us happy every day, or if they leave us heartbroken every day, is it still appropriate for us to humble ourselves, pray, seek God's face, and turn from wicked ways? Yes.

How do I know? James, the brother of Jesus, wrote the following words after he became convinced of Jesus' deity: "God opposes the proud, but gives grace to the humble. So humble yourselves before God.... Come close to God, and God will come close to you.... Purify your hearts, for *your loyalty is divided between God and the world.* Let there be tears for what you have done."[98]

If we want to achieve a good destiny for ourselves, James urges us to *turn away from our divided loyalties between God and the world.* The 2 Chronicles 7:14 passage about God's promise to heal Israel's land uses a slightly different terminology to describe the disobedience He won't tolerate: *If you serve and worship other gods.* In both cases, the Old and New Testaments are pointing us back to the first commandment, "I am the LORD your God . . . You shall have no other gods before me."[99] Not even your children.

Love your sons and daughters and trust God's Holy Spirit to draw them to their heavenly Father while you wait in faith. After you've done all God has told you to do, let go of blaming yourself and stop asking the "why" question.

As a result of this chapter's discussion about repenting and turning to God and apologizing to your children, I will close with an additional guideline that makes sense now.

Guideline #16: Never stop trying to be a godly example of kindness and goodness and faith and joy to your adult children and others. They are still watching to see how well the Bible works for you.

Coaching Corner

1. As you've read in this chapter about repenting and turning to God, what is your timetable for taking any necessary steps?

2. Do you have any reluctance about confessing your sins to God and forsaking sinful behaviors?

3. What would need to happen to reduce any resistance you have?

4. When could you read or reread chapter 18 of the book of Ezekiel?

5. How would you paraphrase the popular Israeli proverb God forbade people to use? "The parents have eaten sour grapes, but their children's mouths pucker at the taste."[100]

6. How does our tendency to blame our parenting mistakes for ungodly choices our children make stack up with God's declaration, "All people are mine to judge—both parents and children alike. And this is my rule: The person who sins is the one who will die."[101]

7. Have you already asked your adult kids' forgiveness for hurtful parenting mistakes? If not, do you want to make a plan for that to happen? When?

8. Can you approach giving your apology because you feel genuinely sorry for your children's pain and not because you want to manipulate them in any way? Why or why not?

9. What do you think about Chuck Swindoll's model of apology to adult children? Outline the various components Swindoll included.

10. Which of Swindoll's elements do you want to include in talking with your offspring?

11. Are you ready to move beyond asking, "*Why* do my son and daughter make such bewildering choices?" Instead of mulling over the *why* question endlessly, what one step could you take to instead concentrate your attention on interacting in healthy ways with your kids and grandkids from this point on and living in greater serenity?

CHAPTER 9

———— ♔ ————

Beyond Why

THIRD TRIMESTER MOTHER Syndrome often includes a paralysis keeping us stuck asking *why* when it's time to move on and ask ourselves *what, when,* and *how* questions. Randy Carlson, therapist extraordinaire, claims that asking the *right* questions, which are also often the *tough* questions, determines whether counselors, news journalists, and ESPN interviewers will become successful at their professions.[102] Third-tri mothers belong on that list of folks needing to broaden our repertoire to include additional *right* and *tough* questions beyond our knee-jerk *why*.

The first section of this book dealt with facing any maternal deficiencies, coming to terms with the need to correct our own shortcomings, and enlisting God's help in the process of healing our families. If you've interacted with the coaching questions at the end of each chapter, you are hopefully at a different place, a more tranquil place, than when you first picked up this book.

The third trimester of your pregnancy involved preparation for a new stage of life. Now in life's third tri, we shift into preparation mode as well. We are no longer going to languish asking "Why?" Instead, we will work to revise the way we conduct relationships with the grown kids we love and prepare for the end of our last trimester. The next few chapters will include guiding principles to keep us on track.

Parallel #9: The third trimester of pregnancy is a time of focused preparation. All is lived in the shadow of the coming event—the end of the pregnancy and the anticipation of new life. Similarly, third-tri moms shift into preparation mode as we approach life's finish line and anticipate eternal life.

The familiar Serenity Prayer, attributed to Reinhold Niebuhr, is a backbone of most recovery programs and is appropriate for our current situation as third-tri moms: "God, grant me the serenity to accept the things I cannot change, Courage to change the things I can, And Wisdom to know the difference. . . ."

We cannot change what's happened in the past, so we must accept our previous family history as unalterable. However, we can learn from our mistakes, and we can bravely create a different today and tomorrow with the Holy Spirit's help. I am urging all third-tri moms to courageously change the things we can so we finish well.

One of the realities we cannot change, as discussed in the last chapter, is the fact that God has no grandchildren. Each member of each generation makes his or her own choices, no matter how good or bad a mother we were. Acceptance of these hard truths ushers in serenity.

Once we've made peace with these certainties, we can move on to practical strategies aimed at building better relationships with the grown kids we think about so constantly and love so much. Armed with courage and wisdom, we can seek answers to questions like the following:

- *What* behaviors are turnoffs to my adult offspring, so I can avoid them?
- *How* can I break the silence of estrangement?
- *How* shall I interact with my atheist child or one living in an alternative lifestyle not matching my values?
- *What* steps could improve communication with my children?
- *When* do I provide financial or babysitting support or other help?
- *How can I* improve relationships with my kids' spouses?
- *What* is my purpose now and what new callings exist beyond motherhood?

Guideline #17: If you weren't as good of a parent as you wish you had been when your kids were younger, change now. Your offspring will notice and appreciate your trying.

My friend Ruth confided, "My mother has changed and doesn't put me on guilt trips like she used to do. She also tells me she loves me after years of withholding those words. Those two adjustments have helped me be less critical of her and also unlocked my ability to mean it when I say, 'I love you, Mom.' In fact, I've come to admire how strong she's been in her fight against chronic autoimmune conditions all these years."

So many of the walls between generations arise out of differing cultural messages emanating from our constantly changing society. Younger Americans often perceive their parents and grandparents as "on the wrong side of history." The change in attitudes toward sexual behaviors during my lifetime is commonly termed a *sexual revolution*. It is no wonder our children sometimes seem like inhabitants of another planet. Our world has transformed during the few short years of our lifespans into a foreign, nearly unrecognizable place.

The bedrock of our "old-fashioned" value system remains the Word of God. We read in Scripture about five thousand years of history characterized by younger generations supplanting older generations, with accompanying revolts and cultural alterations. These societal modifications have sped up in the past century, but the ebb and flow of history documents that struggles, wars, families with generational conflict, and heroic acts have occurred the entire time. Many issues once deemed important no longer matter, while many problems transformed into modern variations and continue to distress generation after generation.

Rather than stubbornly persisting in promoting our vision of "the good old days" to younger family members whose worldviews differ, *identify common ground.* As I've listened to individuals and couples in their twenties, thirties, and forties, I hear a universal desire. Their yearning to love and be loved by their parents surfaces over and over, as it has for centuries. That's the same thing we third-tri mothers want. Your adult children would like you to be proud of them, just as you wish they would be proud of you as their mom. The better we implement Jesus' Sermon on the Mount instruction, "Do to others whatever you would like them to do to you,"[103] the more likely the generations will develop warm feelings toward each other. Jesus described this simple Golden Rule concept as "the essence of all that is taught in the law and the prophets."[104]

Since Jesus calls us to love as our highest aim, why not consider how we might be garbling the love message through unintentional turnoffs? Consider the sentiments of thirty-six-year-old Trina: "It's not how my mom raised me as a kid that causes me pain; it's how she's behaved since I became an adult that makes our relationship so hurtful and shallow. She did mother-like things when I was a child, and Mom proudly reminds me of skills she taught me and activities we did together. It's almost as if she's building a case to convince herself and me that she was a good mother. I acknowledge our once-upon-a-time history and appreciate her long-ago efforts.

"When I finally grew up and went out on my own, however, I approached Mom with trepidation one day, trying to use "I feel . . ." statements to address how unloved I felt as an adult. My mother appears to lack any interest in what I think, do, or feel now as her grown-up daughter. Mom's total self-centeredness as she's aged and her lack of attempts to build an adult friendship with me hurt so deeply. Mom reacted to my careful "I feel" comments by denying, then pouting, then crying hysterically for hours. She successfully turned the whole discussion around to make me feel like a bad person for hurting *her*!

"Mom won't admit her self-absorbed focus during her empty-nest years and the way she immediately turns every conversation around to herself and her problems. She seems blind to how engrossed she is in her own activities and the lack of interest she shows in listening to any details about mine. I don't even try to share what's going on in my life anymore; I've concluded she's clearly not interested in a friendship, nor apparently in any significant relationship at all with an adult daughter she obviously doesn't care anything about."

Miscellaneous Turnoffs to Our Adult Children

Because I know both Trina and her mother and witness the suffering arising from opposite perspectives on their relationship problems, I want to offer a series of guidelines for moms who may be clueless to how certain behaviors trigger their offspring. Looking at Trina's case, both Trina and her mom feel sadly unloved by the other.

Several guidelines emerge after listening to your sons and daughters and to younger adults like Trina:

Guideline #18: Listen, and then listen some more. Seek to understand what is causing your child's reluctance to engage with you. You can't proceed to make good decisions about how to proceed without good information.

You probably are blind to what is upsetting your sons or daughters or their spouses. If they don't volunteer the source of their pain, ask about their pet peeves. What are you doing that is such a turnoff? Tell them you want to know so you can make adjustments that could make things better between the two of you.

By now, I hope you have apologized and asked forgiveness for misunderstandings and wounds you inflicted while raising your family. If your son or daughter persists in blaming you, recognize parents and children often possess divergent memories about long-ago or present-day events. Accept that your child may have built a case against you unfairly. But what about today? What could be improved now?

Guideline #19: Welcome the painful discussion. Don't be defensive and angry when accused of parental faults you displayed either before or after your children left home. Seriously consider whether your son or daughter might be revealing some blind spots.

Refuse the temptation to spout anger or sarcasm or dissolve in tears. Instead, tentatively paraphrase in a friendly tone what you hear your child saying. "It feels to you like I lost interest in your life once you flew the nest, is that right?" Wait for your son or daughter to correct your proposed paraphrase, and try a new paraphrase if the first one was flawed. You are hoping eventually to nail your paraphrase of their feelings, so they will agree, "Exactly!"

If this sounds similar to using the disarming technique I introduced in Chapter 5, you are correct—it is. Rather than rushing to tell accusative offspring they are wrong and starting to defend yourself, just keep listening and paraphrasing. Ask for examples if their complaints seem too general and confusing, such as "You're so self-centered, Mom." Show sincere curiosity as to what they are feeling and why. Ask what behaviors would better communicate love. Don't try to turn off their emotional spigot too soon.

Once your child is convinced his or her feelings of being unloved have been heard, demonstrate sorrow for any words or behaviors that have communicated such an unfortunate message. Thank them for helping you understand why they would have felt that way. Admit any blind spots you now regret.

Then express your wish to explain what was going on in your mind and heart—circumstances they might not have known about. Ask for permission to give them information to help them process those hurtful words or actions differently, but do not argue. This is a time for explanations, not excuses, which would only be another turnoff.

I still remember my mom insisting when my brother and I were fighting and loudly protesting the other's behavior, "It takes two to fight." I did not agree then, but I do now. There will be no argument, no "scene," unless you respond defensively, go on the offensive, or have an emotional meltdown.

Guideline #20: Simply put, don't talk about yourself all the time.

In your rush to fill your empty-nest life with activities to fill the hole left by departing children, don't become totally self-absorbed with your new interests and give the impression you're disinterested in their adult lives. Don't pry and pressure your adult child for information, but show interest and curiosity about details and developments. People drop friends who only want to talk about themselves all the time.

Trina was unhappy because her mother didn't foster a friendship with her daughter by showing more interest in the details of Trina's life. Other women from Trina's generation report the opposite problem. A frequent comment I hear is, "I wish my mom would 'get a life.' I don't have time to talk to her on the phone every day. I don't want to feel responsible for entertaining my mother with the details of my life. I'm too busy working and keeping up with my own kids."

Guideline #21: Build a life with a network of friends. A balanced third-trimester woman has abundant time and attention for her grown kids and grandkids, but also a vibrant personal life and additional hobbies, interests, and friendships. You will be more interesting to your adult children if you create a life not depending on them to entertain you.

The easiest time for me to build female friendships was when my kids were little. During the second-trimester life stage, I naturally gravitated to like-minded young moms going through child-rearing challenges like my own. It was a piece of cake to hang out while our kids played. Whether at church or the ballfield, I regularly found other young mothers with similar values and interests with whom to share my life.

My next effortless season for friendship development arrived as a natural part of the work world. Hours together laboring on common objectives, sharing personal tidbits at the office, hearing about coworkers' family lives, and participating in organized social or work-related events all helped us get close. When retirement happens, those friendships may drift. Still, for seventeen years, my mother met once a month for lunch with other retired teachers she'd worked alongside for the previous thirty years. Their gab fests became a highlight of her social life, although common interests changed from third grade students to husbands in decline, health problems, and reports about each other's grown kids and grandkids. My mother remained happily engaged with her retired schoolteacher friends at least twelve times a year for nearly two decades.

You may be surprised to learn another big spurt in friendship building can occur in the third trimester of life, especially when you are widowed. As married couples age, they often spend more and more time together, especially after retirement. It is common for older couples to enjoy a few close couple friends, but not much time is spent by wives solely with girlfriends during this stage.

Once Chuck's body died, a new friendship outlet opened for me. Many couple friends disappeared from my radar, but other widows and single women befriended me and invited me to join them in social outings. I needed people who understood the particular challenges of widowhood. Suddenly I had a more active social life than I'd enjoyed for years when caretaking and job responsibilities dominated. My single girlfriends brought zest to my schedule. Several were widowed or divorced women I'd known as acquaintances before, but now we became each other's playmates and lifelines.

As you take advantage of learning opportunities, travel to new places, explore new ventures, join small groups, and adopt new hobbies, you will meet even more like-minded women. Say "yes" when you are invited to participate in novel activities and soon you will feel in the mix of things, instead of lonely and bored. You will actually have some "news" of your own when you talk to your grown kids. Just don't overdo it. Listen to details about your sons' and daughters' lives first and foremost. You are not in a competition for who has the most exciting life!

Guideline #22: Adult children want to run in the other direction from parents who stay morose and depressed.

How to cope with a demanding, negative, complaining mother became the substance of many counseling sessions with young professional women. Stress from arduous jobs as pharmacists, dentists, or school principals paled in comparison to the frustration these young women experienced from interacting with guilt-tripping, negative-minded mothers. One nurse particularly dreaded her exhausting commute home at the end of each day because Mom demanded forty-minute "daily check-ins" laced with one complaint after another. Don't be that pity-partying mother!

Even if these young women recognized that their moms were depressed people, no amount of "availability" was enough to cure their mothers. If you feel overwhelmed, don't dump your negativity on your adult child. One of the hallmarks of depression is a sense that all of life centers around you and your troubles. Therefore, you appear to others as entirely self-absorbed. Ask your doctor or pastor for the name of a caring therapist to treat your depression and relieve the burden on your adult child.

If you tend toward this melancholy direction, I suggest you write down four things for which you are grateful during the day. Make one of them about your adult child and vary the list each day. This habit will keep you on the outlook for positive things to add to your daily gratitude lists. When your child asks, "How are you doing, Mom?" surprise them with a recitation of some items off your list, including one reason you are thankful for them being your son or daughter. Scientific research shows you will both feel better.[105]

Guideline #23: Stifle the urge to talk about your aches, pains, and hardships during every conversation. Be truthful when asked, but don't volunteer information about chronic health problems often. Adult children respect a mom who "never complained." Earn that high praise!

I often talk about the aging process with my group of friends. A number of pitfalls lurk, and we stumble into them so readily. One Christmas, Anna made framed copies of "The Nun's Prayer" for all of us as reminders of our resolves to avoid unnecessarily irritating our offspring. I have no idea which nun, if any, wrote this prayer. However, the author hits upon the folly of constantly complaining about health problems, along with numerous other turnoffs we want to avoid:

The Nun's Prayer

"Lord, You know better than I know myself that I am growing older and will someday be old. Keep me from the fatal habit of thinking I must say something on every subject and on every occasion. Release me from the craving to straighten out everybody's affairs. Make me thoughtful, but not moody. Helpful, but not bossy. With my vast store of wisdom, it seems a pity not to use it all, but You know, Lord, I want a few friends at the end.

"Keep my mind free from endless recital of details: give me wings to get to the point. Seal my lips on my aches and pains. They are increasing, and love of rehearsing them is becoming sweeter as the years go by. I dare not ask for grace enough to enjoy the tales of others' pains, but help me to endure them with patience.

"I dare not ask for improved memory, but for a growing humility and a lessening cocksureness when my memory seems to clash with the memories of others. Teach me the glorious lesson that occasionally, I may be mistaken.

"Keep me reasonably sweet. I do not want to be a saint—some of them are so hard to live with. But a sour old person is one of the crowning works of the devil. Give me the ability to see good things in unexpected places, and talents in unexpected people. And give me, Lord, the grace to tell them so. Amen."

Guideline #24: Adult children are interested in learning about your youth and the "old days" only in small doses. It's tiresome and annoying for you to talk about yourself and your memories all the time.

Remember our theme: Your adult kids want you to show interest in their current lives. That includes not switching the subject to yourself and your memories in every conversation. Don't live in the past. It's okay if they invite you to talk about some historical happenings, but everything in moderation. The younger generation may be fascinated by a bit of reminiscing, but be careful to balance those stories with adequate interest in what's presently going on in their lives.

Both the nun and I are cautious about repetitiously doing anything "all the time," whether complaining, pontificating, criticizing, recounting our aches and pains, or repeating childhood memories. Of course, none of us thinks we are guilty of constant obnoxiousness. However, I want to remind you of studies that show any behavior done as often as three times out of ten is perceived as your regular identity. If you complain, criticize, give unsolicited advice, or offer a strong opinion during three out of ten contacts with your child, he or she will label you in their mind as a constant complainer, relentless critic, perpetual controller, or incessantly opinionated. Considering the ratio, you don't have a lot of room for error in permitting yourself turnoff behaviors. One time of transgression out of ten is more than enough!

Guideline #25: Refuse to indulge in guilt trips.

This guideline is so important, I am going to mention it again even though I already warned you in Chapter 2 that manipulative, guilt-tripping comments will backfire. When you whine about how seldom your son calls or comes to visit, guess what? Your son will run in the opposite direction and find every excuse in the book to avoid exposing himself to more of your accusatory self-pity.

Instead, express genuine thanks for any attention bestowed on you. Don't ruin their small gifts of time by minimizing them. Terse reminders of duty and honoring father and mother need to be removed from your vocabulary.

Much better would be a simple, direct request such as, "Could you stop by sometime next week? I would just love to see your face."

Then listen without grimacing or voicing any sarcastic remarks if they say their schedule is too busy. Because you are pleasant and understanding about their busyness, they will be more motivated to make the time to connect soon.

Audrey was a conscientious daughter and generously offered to allow her aging, but still able-bodied mother to move in with her. To Audrey's dismay, her mom watched the clock like a hawk and accused her daughter of selfishness if Audrey didn't walk in the house within ten minutes after her shift ended. Mom vehemently protested if Audrey met up with a friend for lunch on the weekend or went to her book club meeting. Mom would accuse her daughter of not caring that her mother was lonely. When Audrey started dating, Mom routinely threw tantrums any time the hated suitor showed his face, calling him "that disgusting bald man." Audrey's mom sabotaged what could have been happy years living with her daughter with poisonous self-centered guilt trips.

Guideline #26: Get creative in finding alternative ways to manage your life and affairs without continually expecting your offspring to provide all the help you need with home maintenance, yard work, transportation, finances, etc.

We all know families where adult offspring cheerfully look in on their elders every day and volunteer to help. It may require personal sacrifice, but they honor their moms without any resentment whatsoever. They do it out of love and appreciation for all the years Mom devoted to raising them and because they consider it to be part of God's natural plan. Clearly love prevails. It is beautiful to behold the family rapport in these families.

We admire the multi-generational bonds in Italian or Amish families, where grandmas help with grandkids while parents are working. Later, Grandma becomes the recipient of affectionate care and elder-sitting herself. Unselfish multigenerational involvement remains a marvelous tradition in Italy and many other countries.

The emphasis on individualism and the feminist revolution fostered changes in many of those close multigenerational traditions in the USA. Children grow up and leave their home communities to pursue better educational, financial, and cultural opportunities. Some of us left our own mothers behind to move across the country decades ago. How can we be surprised when our offspring depart for distant places?

I have observed many of the most devoted sons and daughters in the younger generation had parents who modeled intergenerational caring when they were growing up. It seems natural to make sacrifices because their mom stayed in her home community and cared for her elderly mom, dad or mother-in-law when they needed help. When still kids, they caught the idea almost by osmosis that Grandma deserves to be a treasured part of the family's daily life. After all, Grandma sat at the supper table with them for years.

Throughout this book we've embraced the idea of gaining serenity by accepting the things we cannot change. We cannot go back and institute closer relationships with now-deceased parents. Our best option is to make ourselves pleasant to be around in our advancing years, so our adult offspring enjoy our cheerful company. Then we must find other ways to fill in the holes when our sons and daughters are not available for friendship or otherwise eager to help.

If you discern that your child doesn't welcome frequent phone calls, consider making a daily "check-in" call with a third-trimester friend instead, or ask if your child might find a daily text message less interruptive than a phone call. Consider resources in your church. Sisters and brothers in Christ can often help each other, particularly if you return the favor by baking them a pie, putting gas in their car, or babysitting to give them a child-free weekend. Within a group of widows, you can take turns ferrying each other to doctor appointments, as after cataract surgery, for example. Seek to give as much as you take from your helpers.

Other times we flat out just need to *hire* assistance or use low-cost community services to avoid prematurely wearing out our children with caretaking chores. Many of us hesitate to spend money on landscapers, painters, home nursing aides, tax preparers, plumbers, electricians, housecleaners, or Uber drivers because we are conserving our money in hopes of bequeathing a substantial inheritance when we die. Consider whether leaving a smaller estate along with a larger amount of consideration now might count for more in the end.

Some of us live on very tight budgets out of necessity, but others have always been frugal and struggle to loosen the purse strings. Pray for wisdom to know whether you are in actual danger of not having enough to survive or whether you are captive to an unwarranted fear of scarcity. Out of love for your overextended adult children, strive to be self-sufficient for as long as feasible. Take pride in your ingenuity and resourcefulness. Avoid expecting too much of others and expecting too little of yourself.

Do you remember the story of "Peter and the Wolf"? If you make every request for assistance more important than the activities your adult child had planned for her/his day, the time may come when your situation is truly dire. However, your sons or daughters are so worn out with your constant neediness that they eventually ignore your dramatic appeals. Give them a chance to admire your self-sufficiency, so they can rise to the occasion when you really do need help that only they can provide.

Coaching Corner

1. What turnoff behaviors discussed in this chapter might solicit a response of "That's just like my mom!" from one or more of your children?

2. Referring back to the Serenity Prayer, what items belong on your list of "things you cannot change"?

3. What strategies do you want to employ to achieve peace with unchangeable things?

4. Can you identify one or more things you need courage to change?

5. Where will you obtain that courage?

6. How do you relate to the sentiments in the "Nun's Prayer"? Which of the nun's petitions do you want to pray this week?

7. To which of the guidelines in this chapter do you want to direct special effort? How do you intend to implement that guideline this week? What will be your first step?

8. Whom could you tell about your intentions and then report to them your progress in making your change a reality?

9. When are you going to talk about your goals with that person?

CHAPTER 10

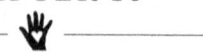

Communicating the Truth with Love

CONSIDER THE DIFFERENCE between two signs in a nearby neighborhood. One scrawled warning on a splintered board reads, "Beware the Dog." A few yards into the next block, a neatly stenciled signpost announces:

Home of

Samson the Dog,

A faithful

Co-protector of his family

Which dog owner would you choose to be your friendly next-door neighbor?

Conveying truth with love is a fine art—an art worth perfecting. The words you speak matter; the words you don't speak also matter. Social science research indicates your facial expressions and other nonverbal communication create an even more powerful message than the words you do or don't say. How we communicate sets the tone for our relationships.

If you haven't already implemented a third-tri decision to emphasize sensitive, kind words and a pleasant demeanor, your internal turmoil over children's baffling attitudes and behaviors may push you into angry, damaging outbursts. During pregnancy's third trimester, you fought similar battles.

Parallel #10: Emotional volatility occurs. Both pregnant moms-to-be and moms in the third tri of life must deal with hormonal fluctuations, unwanted stretch marks, and tendencies to lash out when tired and frustrated.

Before I started this chapter, I decided to give a longtime friend a call. I wanted to interview Rhonda before I revealed additional communication guidelines for life's third-trimester moms. Social scientists like Joshua Coleman[106] and Kathy McCoy[107] provide sensible frameworks, but I wanted to see how their concepts fare in my friend's family.

Rhonda and Roy parent ten adult children (half by birth and half by adoption), and Rhonda is another of my heroines among third-tri mothers. Her adopted children were added to her family at various ages and from assorted countries, usually not a great recipe for success. But it works—not perfectly, but impressively!

You will probably not be surprised to learn that Rhonda attributes the closeness in her large family (now including twenty-nine grandkids and an ever-increasing number of great grandchildren) to the modeling of her own mother and Rhonda's desire to follow biblical principles.

Rhonda describes her ninety-three-year-old mother as upbeat despite the ravages of advanced aging and her quarantined condition during the Covid-19 pandemic. "Mom always has a funny story to tell about the day's happenings," her daughter says.

As I contemplate the influence of Rhonda's mother, a pertinent guideline comes to mind. Rhonda's deliberately cheerful demeanor replicates her mom's positive outlook despite Rhonda's years of crutches, walkers, braces, frequent surgeries, a cancer diagnosis, and financial setbacks.

Guideline #27: Be fun to be around. Stay as active as you can. Seek ways to laugh and play together as often as possible.

Rhonda's beloved mama was shut off from family contact during Covid-19 restrictions. Rhonda suggested to several of her brood they might want to set a reminder timer on their phones to call Grandma once a week at their convenience, because total isolation for the elderly is "rough," and "everybody loves Grandma." Rhonda hasn't pushed or harangued, sermonized, or checked up to see if her offspring followed through with her request, but word has leaked back from Grandma that she's been thrilled to have several grandchildren touch base. "One suggestion and then drop it," says Rhonda. "Maybe give them some positive feedback, if Grandma reported how much she enjoyed their contact."

Guideline #28: Don't take it personally when adult children opt to act differently than you'd prefer.

As adults, your sons and daughters have their own lives, time pressures, and preferences. Be respectful and don't interpret their behavior as deliberately defying you when their plans don't coincide with yours. If you have an internal battle raging because you have personalized their decisions as spitting in your face, it will be hard to communicate affection and unconditional love.

You might yearn to eat Sunday dinner together every weekend, but some or all of your offspring might possess sound reasons to opt out. They might have another side of the family to consider or stressed-out kids needing a nap instead of more stimulation. Maybe they're vegans, and your home cooking emphasizes meat, eggs, and dairy products. Or perhaps they can't afford to gather at a restaurant every week. Could it be your expectations rob them of the right to choose how they want to spend their Sabbath in peace and rest? Let it go. Don't turn every move contrary to your ideas into a challenge to you or your family traditions.

Other times, chalk their conduct up to immaturity and lack of experience. Rhonda recommends, "You need to be an adult even if they're acting childish. Don't take things personally. They don't understand yet." Think about all you've learned about life since you were thirty. And you've learned a lot since fifty, and even more since sixty and seventy, so grant your grown children time to gain experience and wisdom as they mature.

Rhonda continued, "If they're pouting, it doesn't mean you have to pout too! If they've lost their cool, keep yours! If they want to be their own person and do things their own way, let them. You've given them roots; now give them wings!"

Guideline #29: Give advice only if adult children ask for it, and then cautiously.

Give your sons and daughters the gift of acknowledging that you recognize they are adults and believe them capable of making their own decisions. Consider advice-giving temptations as opportunities to validate your trust in their inner compasses. One wise mother usually responds to requests for advice with, "What do you think God wants you to do?" This mom has children professing to be Christians. Such a response would, of course, seem confrontational and insensitive if you know your child would check the "none" response on forms asking them to identify religious preference.

Rhonda remembers blowing her no-advice guideline but found a way to redeem her mistake. If the impulse to give your opinion overpowers you, consider her damage control remedy.

One of Rhonda's sons served in the military and was frequently deployed. He took his young wife with him whenever possible, and they would rent a small apartment with another military couple to conserve on expenses. When the husband in the other couple would deploy, her son would live with his wife plus his buddy's young, attractive wife until his own orders came. This pattern continued for several months, and Rhonda worried about potential problems.

One day, Rhonda opened her mouth and declared, "I don't think it's a good idea to put yourself in temptation's way. If your friend deploys first, you will be living with his pretty wife in your space. Then, there's the problem of your wife possibly living with another soldier, even if he's married. You need to figure out some other kind of living arrangements." The call ended abruptly.

Rhonda immediately recognized she'd overstepped her boundaries about advice-giving. Within minutes, Rhonda called and sincerely apologized, admitting she'd been wrong to impose her opinion and confessing she'd wrongly attempted to control their marital decisions.

The thread of apology and forgiveness weaves through the chapters of this book because it relates to so many aspects of a woman in her third-tri of life. All of us reading this book know Rhonda's heart was in the right place when she gave her opinion. Unfortunately, her advice was like "beware the dog." It was received as ugly and jarring and hurt their relationship.

Rhonda's apology mirrored a "Samson the Dog" communication, however. In recounting this incident, Rhonda marveled, "My son and his wife received my heartfelt words of confession as respectful and truly unexpected, especially by my daughter-in-law. My apology set the tone for them to forgive me and for us to have a wonderful relationship ever since."

Because Rhonda admires her mother and aspires to be like her, Mom's example helps Rhonda resist many urges to interfere. When discussing the importance of not imposing advice, Rhonda credits her mom's pattern of restraining from spouting unsolicited counsel. When Rhonda and her husband adopted child after child during the same time span when they were birthing five of their own, her mom said nothing. She now realizes how difficult it must have been for Mom not to express reservations about how Rhonda was building her family.

Not giving advice is one of mothers' hardest assignments after their nest empties. Jane Isay sums up her version of restraining from advice-giving as follows:

> "Don't give it.
> They don't like it.
> They don't want it.
> They resent it." [108]

Guideline #30: Take a lesson from Facebook. No matter how bizarre or negative or complaining some of the postings are, Facebook friends support, praise, console, and "like" what was written.

Adult children are far more likely to talk about their personal feelings if they feel confident of a listening ear and unconditional love instead of anticipating disapproval and judgment. Again, Rhonda's mom led the way. When one of Rhonda's brothers married, his bride was only fifteen years old. Never once did Rhonda hear her mom say anything but positive comments about this teenaged daughter-in-law. Instead, her mother praised the girl's housekeeping abilities and gardening skills and applauded her contributions to her son's happiness. Mama is still extolling the virtues of her daughter-in-law after forty years of their successful marriage.

Words of affirmation promote a friendly atmosphere and create positive changes in adult children better than critical comments. When our kids were little, most of us made it a point to "catch them being good." We commended their praiseworthy choices, instead of carping on objectionable behaviors incessantly. In hindsight, we only wish we'd focused even more on the positives and less on the negatives. Now's our chance to work on our ratio. According to Rhonda, her mom is a fifty to one kind of mother.

Lest you think I am promoting overly permissive parenting, I want to balance out the picture. When her children were young, Rhonda and her husband taught a lot of principles, especially the ones Jesus emphasized. They made a point of noticing when a child showed generosity, kindness, mercy, unselfishness, industriousness, truthfulness, compassion, self-control, moral virtue, loyalty, etc., and doled out appreciation and praise on those occasions.

Rhonda has never stopped her habit of appreciating the positive and ignoring most troubling traits. Several times a week I notice social media posts with Rhonda acknowledging praiseworthy aspects of a child or a grandchild with a birthday that week, or after visiting Grandma and Grandpa's house. Knowing some of Rhonda's children now as adults, I can say they are among the kindest, most caring and loving human beings I've ever met.

Much like she was raised, Rhonda used the child-rearing years to promote an understanding that sons' and daughters' actions and attitudes are ultimately between each child and God. In so doing, she moved her kids to see God as their ultimate judge, albeit a loving One who dispenses mercy, grace, forgiveness, and rewards for obedience, along with needed discipline.

Discipline for defiant disobedience was the standard, but not for childish mistakes. Rhonda described the process as "setting boundaries." Boundary setting remains the norm with her adult children. Anyone who is around Rhonda knows she's crazy in love with her kids and grandkids. Most of her Facebook posts include photos of intergenerational celebrations and grueling trips to visit kids in distant locations. She spotlights various kids and grandkids, applauding them for making her proud. Such harmony has not been without intentional effort.

Rhonda confided in my interview three strategies she shares with other mothers who ask to learn from her experiences raising a brood of ten. Rhonda's "secrets" will become my next three guidelines since they coincide with advice from many professional family experts.

Guideline #31: When grown kids hit a rough spot, consider setting boundaries around how long and under what conditions they will be allowed to live with you. Discuss the circumstances openly and make a contract.

Contracts may seem like "unnecessary overkill" to some mothers reading this guideline. In some well-functioning families, housing a loving and respectful son or daughter, possibly even with a congenial spouse and kids in tow, may not be a problem. For a temporary period while getting established in their career or in times of crisis, all three generations enjoy the arrangement and each other's company. However, most families are not "high-functioning" enough to weather prolonged shared living spaces without tension developing.

Lots of loving parents need help implementing boundary policies. In a desire to be supportive, many mothers inadvertently prolong irresponsibility and create relationship strains persisting for years. Lasting rifts may occur between parents and adult children because no one spelled out the expectations before they camped for extended periods in their parents' home.

Fractures may also occur between you and your husband over boomerang children. If your spouse is not on the same page about sharing the household with returning offspring, your marriage can be at risk!

Financial adviser Dave Ramsey adds his voice to Rhonda's in recommending parents communicate clearly defined understandings about roles and expectations from the beginning. Ramsey warns that house-sharing requires tough talks about tough issues like financial and labor contributions.

Even grandmas and grandpas with enormous love banks available to their kids and grandkids can wear thin when kids move back home.

Generational differences in child-rearing practices and housekeeping standards rear their ugly heads when a daughter or son returns to the nest with fledglings in tow. When our own hatchlings fought with each other, screeched for food, left their messes everywhere, whined about chores, and complained about going to bed, we took it in stride. However, we also exercised our authority and brought order to our chaotic household. Spell out with your returning chicks how much authority is appropriate when you are a grandma.

After a few years of marital solitude, most seniors become accustomed to peaceful and calm surroundings. High-decibel noise levels, food-stained furniture, and myriads of toys underfoot assault their senses, even if they were once accustomed to energetic youngsters twenty-four hours a day. What is delightful in small doses may stress us to the max, if prolonged.

"Don't fail to make a contract upfront," urged Rhonda. "Each situation requires unique adjustments, so sit down within the first few hours. Better yet, even before anyone moves in, discuss individual circumstances, needs, and expectations. Negotiate the length of time your family members are allowed to occupy space under your roof. Compassionately listen to their perceived needs for space sharing, but yes, you and your husband get to decide because it's your house. Make it clear you are creating the contract to *preserve* family unity and affection, not destroy it. Hurt feelings happen most often because the younger generation believes we love them and adore the grandkids (true), and also think we are happy to share life and our living space indefinitely (usually not true)."

After discussing quandaries such as how to share grocery shopping and storage, meal preparation, car usage, cleaning chores, TV viewing, bedtime and wakeup expectations, bathroom division, laundry access, use of technology, childcare (including disciplinary considerations), pet arrangements, financial expectations, and other potential conflictual areas, put the agreement into writing. "The most important part of all is the anticipated departure date," Rhonda emphasized. "All parties sign the document and receive copies."

Rhonda is a loving, generous, self-sacrificing mother, but she is also a wise mom who knows prolonged dependency is not helpful anywhere in the animal world. She compared her views to the habits of eagle parents attempting to launch their young into the scary world of adult eagle survival.

By Rhonda's account, mama eagles line massive nests made of sticks with their own feathers to soften the bed for the arrival of baby eaglets. Mom and dad endure twelve to thirteen wearying weeks of hunting for fish and waterfowl morsels to fill wide-open beaks while the babies grow. Some well-developed eaglets still don't attempt to fly despite sufficient maturation. They remain content to be fed by their parents indefinitely. They seem oblivious to the fact that they won't survive if they don't learn to fly.

At this juncture, Rhonda maintains that mama eagle housecleans by throwing the feathers overboard. The nest is not now so comfortable. If the youngsters still resist moving out, she may remove some of the smaller sticks supporting their bodies and then a few of the larger sticks, until her offspring fall through the riddled nest. The implications for human parents are obvious!

The information available on the Internet about bald eagles describes a little different process but leads to the same end. In reports I read, the exhausted mother eagle, worn out from feeding, lures any offspring who are disinclined to fly to step out and teeter on a branch by making her food supply hard to reach. One observer reported seeing a mother eagle tantalizing her reluctant youngster by repeatedly flying past while holding a favorite meal. The young eagle began losing weight, and mama seemed pretty cruel. In its effort to snag mama's bait, the fledgling lost its balance, plummeted, and hit the ground with only a few flaps of its wings to break its fall. Then the hovering mama bird dropped the delicious fish as a reward.

Usually, maturing eagles and adult children want to be independent and self-sufficient. For some, however, it's tempting to let their third-trimester mom do the work since it's easier and more comfortable to be fed. We are afraid boomerang kids will be offended by our boundaries. Occasionally they are, but feathering the nest beyond the point when they are capable of supporting themselves does them no favors, denies them the chance to achieve their fullest potential, and can lead to total estrangement.

I've observed numerous sad cases of ruptured relationships following prolonged efforts to house a grown child. The offspring's sense of entitlement, lack of work ethic, no appreciation, and zero contribution became unbearable. Unfortunately, there were no discussions upfront and no defined contract. The adult child is shocked and incensed when asked to leave, usually after repeated unenforced ultimatums, harsh words, and hurtful arguments. Those grown children may refuse to communicate with their parents for years, nor allow them to see grandchildren, remaining convinced their parents are mean and selfish people.

To repeat the truth: Boundaries protect loving relationships, so we don't end up alienated from each other. Rhonda had to give this exact message to one of her own who returned home with her husband and two little kids. Rhonda loves them dearly and had the utmost sympathy for their situation. After two months, however, they needed to find another place, even though it would be meager and not lined with any feathers. After reminding her houseguests of their contract and the love motivation behind their boundary, Rhonda and her husband were able to keep love flowing in their family.

Guideline #32: Don't compare children with each other. Kids are super-sensitive to parental favoritism growing up, and they still have their favoritism "antenna" up throughout their adulthoods.

Showing partiality creates major breaks in parental relationships with the less favored offspring, and sometimes even with the "favored" child. Rhonda has a "no comparisons" policy.

I still remember the sting when my mother appeared to favor my brother in childhood but also during decades of adulthood. It was particularly annoying to proudly describe achievements of my three youngsters, only to have Mother change the subject to tell me how stupendously my brother's children were succeeding. I'm sure she believed she was just innocently passing on family news, but it rubbed me the wrong way.

Getting everything right in life's third tri is hard! I occasionally blow it and make stupid remarks triggering my kids' favoritism antennas myself. Our best protection from this error is informed mindfulness. We don't want to tiptoe around for fear of offending at every turn, but recognizing how sensitive our sons and daughters are to sibling comparisons can make us think twice about our words and actions.

Rhonda also warns against sharing one offspring's confidences with other siblings. Talking on the phone can be tricky, especially if one child asks mom how a sibling is doing. Mom may know intimate details, but we jeopardize our status as sounding boards when we disclose what we know. At most, we may want to say, "Your sister is having a hard time. I think she'd appreciate you touching base" or, "I think she might have some interesting developments worth celebrating with her. I'm sure she'd love it if you texted her."

Encouraging sibling interaction in adulthood can be a delicate matter but has huge payoffs. Every mother wants her children to enjoy brothers and sisters and grow lasting adult friendships. Sometimes Mom is a hub, and all communication between siblings passes through her, with the kids seldom reaching out to each other. Rhonda thinks always playing the middleman role is a mistake, particularly since the hub will depart the earth one day, leaving the next generation adrift from each other. Rhonda is thrilled when she observes one of her kids offering to help a brother or sister by volunteering construction skills or technology acumen as they cooperate in changing out a water heater or setting up a computer system.

To navigate the sibling rivalry hazards effectively, it is worth contemplating the centrality of sibling relationships in identity formation and self-image. "Of all the factors that shape your personality—your genes, your parents, your peers—siblings are at the top, according to one major theory of human development. If you think about it, the relationships with your sisters and brothers will likely last longer than any others in your lifetime."[109]

Comparisons to siblings possess the potential to drive success or stifle initiative, thus promoting a path either similar to, or opposite from, those taken by brothers and sisters. No matter how intelligent, athletic, or world-travelled your child, if he or she has a sibling who's even smarter, a better athlete, or more of a globe-trotter, their behavior tends to be affected. Some rise to higher levels than they would have attained without the competition. Others decide to focus on entirely different arenas and carve out territory where they can excel and be admired. They seek recognition for musical or artistic accomplishments instead of math and science prowess, social idealism instead of financial achievement, for example.

Guideline #33: Continue to reach out to your adult sons and daughters even if it is rarely, if ever, reciprocated.

In a 2015 study conducted with over eight hundred people, researchers confirmed that *the adult child initiates most estrangements between parents and adult children.* A random survey of mothers (ages sixty-five to seventy-five) with two or more living adult children documented that 11 percent of moms were estranged from a child. A whopping 62 percent of moms reported less than once a month contact with at least one child.[110]

Don't give up too soon on grown children who greatly reduce contact with you or spitefully cut you out of their lives, even if it feels like your child has nastily discarded you. Dr. Josh Coleman, popular authority on parent-child estrangements, discusses common causes for these devastating outcomes in his chapter, "All Grown Up and Wants Nothing to Do with Me." Family wounds like abuse, alcohol, drug dependency, mental illness, parental divorces and remarriages, or rejection due to political, religious, and sexual lifestyle differences constitute a few of the reasons. "Parents who *don't* continue to reach out may be inadvertently sending the message that the child has no right to complain and should get over it, already."[111]

Other times it is obvious the rupture is caused by an exaggerated, distorted rendition of ancient or recent events. Coleman recommends limiting parental contrition to actual mistakes and sticking with fact-based truths. If your child accuses you of heinous generalizations such as, "You only cared about yourself throughout my whole childhood," Coleman suggests humble, truthful responses such as, "I certainly wasn't a perfect parent, but I was very, very devoted to you."[112] Making multiple defensive retorts may only cement the estrangement. Listen, paraphrase, agree with what you can, and apologize for grievances possessing any degree of validity. Stay calm despite the seeming unfairness and distortion of their memories.

Because things can change over time, Coleman urges parents not to give up and passively accept a no-contact policy. Once your children begin dealing with older kids themselves, they may come to understand that perfect parenting is an impossible expectation. At least until the age of thirty, continue to reach out often, maybe every couple of weeks, and send a card or small gift at birthdays and Christmas, assuming you have their address, and unless your offerings are returned to you refused and unopened.

Rhonda suggests upbeat texts to show you've been thinking of the one ignoring you. She recommends writing one or two sentences along the lines of "I thought of you today when I saw the daffodils blooming outside your bedroom window." A follow-up attempt could be, "I ran into your friend Billy at Walmart today. He hasn't changed a bit since high school." Rhonda has also used food-based connections such as "I made your favorite lasagna recipe for supper tonight. It reminded me of all the birthdays when you requested lasagna and death by chocolate for your cake." Let go of your disappointment and resentment if there are no replies.

Coleman finds strategies may need to change with offspring older than thirty. By that time, you will probably know whether your child considers your attempts to communicate as "harassing." After a decade of attempted communication, you may need to back off from your frequency, but continue to send an occasional text and wishes for a happy birthday and Christmas.

In her helpful book on dealing with family ruptures, *We Don't Talk Anymore*, Dr. Kathy McCoy admits that estrangement is uniquely painful during our age of instant communication. It may feel like you are emailing or texting into a void. Several of my friends have been forced to watch their grandchildren grow up solely via Facebook photos. The peeks available on Facebook only occur if adult children have not defriended their mother on social media, in which case, no photos, nothing.

McCoy emphasized five facts about breaking the silence of estrangement:

1. "The sooner the silence is broken, the better.
2. The person to break the silence will probably be the parent.
3. The parent will probably be the one to make concessions.
4. Remember this is about reconnection, not defending yourself.
5. The key to reconnection is listening . . . and love."[113]

The importance of trying to overcome alienations sooner rather than later is reinforced by findings of researcher Dorothy Herrome, who observed, "A striking feature of these cases was the tendency for estrangement to go on unchallenged. Assumptions were made, conclusions were drawn, and the ensuing stalemate could last for decades."[114]

The best time to reach out and seek resolution, even if you believe you've been unjustly demonized, is as soon as you can make contact without reigniting the conflict. Although you may feel you are owed an apology, you will likely need to take the step of starting the conversation by apologizing first—not groveling or overstating your failures, but apologizing in honest ways already discussed in a previous chapter. Otherwise, over time the viewpoints of both parties frequently harden into stone, making reconnection even less likely. No mother wants to pass from this life unreconciled with her children.

No matter how many years have passed since you were cut off, a humble apology can change the course of your family history. Tara Westover wrote in her memoir, _Educated_, "I know only this: that when my mother told me she had not been the mother to me that she wished she'd been, she became that mother for the first time."[115]

The Generational Stake Hypothesis

The "generational stake hypothesis" argues that parents retain a larger stake in sustaining close relationships with their grown children than their children feel. The offspring are focused on the next generation, on their own kids. With their emotional energy centered on their growing family, they don't feel as much need for closeness with mom as she craves with them. To put the generational stake hypothesis in stark terms of love, "Mom generally loves her adult children more than her adult children love Mom."

Because of the generational imbalance of power, based on the premise that the one who most wants a relationship has the least power, mothers will need to resolve to bite the bullet and make suitable concessions. However, concessions flying in the face of your convictions may make you resentful, so choose which concessions are possible for you without compromising your conscience. Maintaining a stubborn belief that life must be fair and withholding all concessions only torpedoes progress.

Researchers discovered that parents typically blame estrangement on causes apart from themselves—influence of daughters-in-law, brainwashing by a secular society, a child's addiction, or clashing worldviews. In contrast, adult children often attribute the schism to personal characteristics of Mom or Dad. They may view your behavior as toxic or believe you possess unchangeable noxious personality characteristics, or sometimes they simply feel unloved by you. Parents' long-standing offensive traits such as arrogance, narcissism, dictatorial attitudes, prejudices, self-centered monopolizing of conversations, or angry outbursts seem to them the obvious roots of the problems.[116]

Once you understand the cause of estrangement from their perspective, it is time to change your attitude and behavior or permanently lose your relationship. For example, "It can mean that helping him or her to feel loved does not include arguing that, of course, you always loved him. Instead, it can mean listening to what she is saying and finding new ways meaningful to her to show your love."[117]

For some long-suffering moms, despite working to implement steps to reverse estrangement, continuing rejection becomes a way of life. Your child may refuse to accept who you are and may not be amenable to loving compromises regarding your differences. So how do you handle continuing exclusion and the not-so-subtle message that your child can't stand you?

The choices you make at this juncture will make a huge difference in your quality of life. Decide to *accept the reality that you have no power to change another person and determine to surrender your child into God's care. Then change how you process your adult child's decision to separate from you.* The other alternatives—prolonged bitterness, self-pity, and depression—are ruinous.

Don't let your hurt define your life. Don't persistently ruminate about the painful mystery of "why." Don't let your grief steal all the good still available to you. Reinvent your life without your child at its center for now, or even permanently. Keep the door open for his or her return, but live your life to the fullest in the meantime.

Laura Perry, who spent twenty years in intentional rebellion against God and the way she was raised, now joyfully honors her Christian mother. Her mom's spiritual growth during the time Perry was pursuing multiple sex change surgeries spoke volumes. "I realized that the angry, stressed-out, exhausted legalistic mother I grew up with had been completely transformed, and her religion had been exchanged for real faith . . . And the moment I saw the complete regeneration in my mom, was the moment I knew that the gospel was true."[118]

In a more recent blog, Perry addresses mothers suffering from estrangement: "You might say, 'life isn't so fun without my children.' Let me ask you, if your prodigal child never comes home and you never see your grandchildren, what would define your life? If we continue to look at our lack in our circumstances, we will sink deeper and deeper into depression. The opposite of that is not positive thoughts or holding on to hope that they will return, but rather pursuing Jesus."[119] Perry watched her mother find peace through spiritual transformation and now Perry embraces the same journey for herself.

Coaching Corner

1. Do you suspect your grown children sometimes think of you as a "Beware of the Dog" communicator? Why?

2. What one improvement could you make this week to come across as a "Samson the Dog" communicator?

3. Which traits do you admire about Rhonda's ninety-two-year-old mother?

4. What behaviors of your adult child do you struggle not to take personally?

5. What would your children say about your record of advice-giving?

6. How can you come across as more of a cheerleader for your grown children, giving positive feedback about their strength areas?

7. What did you think about Rhonda's suggestions about setting boundaries when adult offspring want to live with you for a period of time?

8. Do you see evidence of sibling rivalry and parental favoritism creating problems between you and any of your kids or grandkids?

9. What steps could you take to reduce favoritism triggers?

10. Did you glean any new insights about overcoming estrangements from this chapter?

11. If you are experiencing estrangement from any of your grown children, what next step would God want you to take?

12. What is your reaction to the generational stake hypothesis?

CHAPTER 11

Thorny Dilemmas

USING THE RESOURCES we've gathered thus far, let's buckle up and discuss three particularly thorny dilemmas in more detail. We may need to exercise considerable self-compassion because of previous mistakes committed in these areas:

1. How do I deal with daughter-in-law or son-in-law difficulties?

2. How can I solve intergenerational money-related quandaries?

3. What if my offspring and I possess vastly different value systems?

Your Kids' Spouses

Mother-in-law jokes fuel comedy routines on YouTube, and interfering mothers-in-law supply ready villains in television and movie scripts. Most scenarios revolve around a propensity on the mother-in-law's part to "meddle."

Perhaps you got off on the wrong foot with your daughter-in-law by vocalizing opposition to your son's marriage to her. Your negative judgments about her not being suitable for your son filtered back to his fiancé, and your daughter-in-law has viewed you as the enemy from day one.

Your insistence on participating in planning the wedding and honeymoon, even if you paid for them, creates another common area of conflict with the bride. Also, rethink any plans to rearrange the contents of your daughter-in-law's cabinets as a gift you intend to improve her kitchen organization. Many in-law rifts had their origin in mother-in-law comments or behavior before or on the day of the wedding ceremony. Many brides report feeling steamrolled to add people to their guest list and conduct the wedding and reception in accord with their mother-in-law's wishes. They decided their mother-in-law was controlling and overbearing and have been collecting (or fabricating, in some cases) evidence for their opinion ever since.

Jim Burns, a popular author and seminar speaker who writes about building friendships with grown children, assigns the responsibility of the groom's mother at her son's wedding as follows: *Wear beige and keep your mouth shut.* His simple four-point list of rules for navigating a successful relationship with your son's or daughter's spouse emphasizes one essential ingredient:

- Don't criticize the in-law.
- Don't criticize the in-law's parenting.
- Don't criticize the in-law's treatment of your son or daughter.
- Don't criticize anything about the in-law. [120]

Guideline #34: Every human being craves love and approval from their parents and in-laws. Adult children, and especially their spouses, are super sensitive to criticism. It is not too late to withhold criticism and increase the doses of love and approval you dispense.

We all hate the sense that "whatever I do is never enough" to please certain people. If your adult children or their spouses believe their efforts will always be insufficient to earn your approval and respect, they develop an attitude of "Why try?" You may have that same knee-jerk reaction yourself because of their critical stance toward you.

In contrast, words of respect, admiration, affirmation, praise, encouragement, and appreciation increase the chances that your progeny, as well as their spouses, will be motivated to want involvement with you. When the younger generation helps you out, don't be critical of how they do things, and always express your gratitude. Be alert for opportunities to express approval in both verbal and nonverbal ways. You may be surprised how quickly prickly relationships can turn around when you become your daughter- or son-in-law's cheerleader.

In-law territory landmines are so plentiful that it is impossible to identify all the potential pitfalls. Mothers-in-law send disapproval messages innocently, with no intention of offending. Well-meaning suggestions about potential jobs your in-law could seek to add to the family income, or the opposite, suggesting ways to become a stay-at-home mom to your grandchildren, can come across as critical. Likewise, your verbalized agreement with an offspring's angry complaints about their spouse during a marital argument will eventually trickle back to their partner. Your son-in-law or daughter-in-law may forgive their spouse's criticism but will consider your agreement with the complaints unforgivable. Predictably, well-meaning parenting suggestions also sadly backfire unless they are *specifically requested*. As emphasized in Chapter 10, simply refuse to utter any comments that a super-sensitive in-law might interpret as *criticism*.

Guideline #35: Be aware how easy it is in close families for the daughter-in-law or son-in-law to feel excluded from the cozy family togetherness and shared history. Go out of your way to pull the newcomer into your circle, even if you would feel content spending time just with your son or daughter.

On special occasions, giving thoughtful gifts equal in value to those you give your offspring will be noticed and appreciated. Other times, spontaneously delivering something as inexpensive as two luscious chocolate-covered strawberries, or even an appropriate find from the thrift store, will carry a message that you care and were thinking about your son- or daughter-in-law.

Be mindful of diet or allergy restrictions and go the extra mile to prepare special foods suitable for your child's spouse. They may not relish the childhood delicacies you make for the children you raised. They will hold against you any negative comments about their adherence to paleo, vegan, fast food, or any other current trend.

Invite your daughter-in-law for lunch or an outing for just the two of you. Keep the conversation light and pleasant. Avoid any subject matter putting her in a defensive position. Ask her opinions about things, listen, and learn. Don't insist on talking by phone if she prefers to only text. Help her feel safe with you. Use the terms "daughter-in-love" and "son-in-love" when introducing your in-laws to others. These terms of endearment soften both your hearts and shine a good light on them in other people's eyes.

If your daughter-in-love has a mother she adores and with whom she spends lots of time, you may feel you can never measure up. Don't try to force what can never be equal. Be satisfied your son is happy, continue to treat her lovingly, and cheerfully look in other directions for the companionship you'd hoped to enjoy.

If your daughter-in-love has a mother of whom she's quite critical, she may be triggered by things you do that remind her of her mom. Knowing some of those trigger points, you will naturally try to avoid exhibiting those behaviors. However, she may keep you at arms' distance and remain unable to attach to you because mother figures are all tainted in her mind by painful past experiences with a maternal figure. Persistently reach out in love, but realize her faultfinding attitude toward you may be difficult to overcome. Nevertheless, keep trying to demonstrate affection and caring and interest in her life.

Jesus underscored the biblical injunction for sons to leave their fathers and mothers and cleave to their wives, becoming one flesh. Your son's wife may see you as a competitor for her husband's affection, especially if you enjoyed a warm, close relationship with your son before their marriage. Don't be surprised if he pulls back out of deference to his wife's feelings. Your daughter-in-law and son-in-law want to be certain they come first in their spouses' priorities. As a student of biblical teaching, you want to celebrate their leaving and cleaving, just as you and your husband once deliberately "left and cleft."

Avoid making your son feel he must choose between the two women in his life. If he picks loyalty to his mother above all, his wife will build a wall of resentment against both of you, endangering their marriage. If your son always sides with his wife, you must accept the normality of that hurtful posture. A wise mother-in-law acquiesces to her daughter-in-law's wishes without arguing, complaining, or attempted manipulations. Sometimes it is a son-in-law pulling your daughter away. Persistently work on forming a strong bond with your child's spouse, if s/he will let you.

Jane Isay maintains that two crucial elements determine the smoothness or difficulty of relationships with in-laws: (1) chemistry and (2) character.

The chemistry with some in-laws is inherently good and spending time together flows easily because you are naturally drawn to each other. Both parties feel warmth and natural affection. "When the chemistry is off, character may help to carry the day. Character shows up when we put our feelings on the back burner and make an effort to forge a strong relationship anyway."[121]

Carolyn took an instant dislike to the woman her eldest son brought home as a prospective bride. She seemed cold, bossy, and opinionated. She showed no appreciation for Carolyn's hospitality or the restaurant meals adding up on her credit card. Nevertheless, her son married his girlfriend, and soon there was a grandchild on the way. Carolyn knew she would need to work at being kind, generous, and forgiving of slights or lose access to grandchildren. Over time, her daughter-in-law matured, but her abrasive personality continued to chafe. Carolyn determined to demonstrate love and respect, even if it was not reciprocated. To her surprise, Carolyn found her daughter-in-law to be a doting mommy to her grandbaby and noticed homemaking talents and other qualities she could admire. The personality issues faded in importance as Carolyn's resolve to accept and love her daughter-in-law prevailed.

"Feelings" of love may be slow to materialize, but treating someone in loving ways is a decision of your will and should not be dependent on your feelings. I am not urging a grudging, frowning, "tolerance" kind of love for your son- or daughter-in-law. Instead, decide to treat your child's spouse in warm affectionate ways. Then wait expectantly for your heart, and theirs, to fall in line. I cited the familiar 1 Corinthians 13:4-7 scripture in Chapter 5, but I include it again because loving the spouses of your adult children well requires mastery of every one of these characteristics of love.

"Love is patient and kind. Love is not jealous or boastful or proud or rude. It does not demand its own way. It is not irritable, and it keeps no record of being wronged. It does not rejoice about injustice but rejoices whenever the truth wins out. Love never gives up, never loses faith, is always hopeful, and endures through every circumstance."[122]

Marie, a mother with a confrontive, self-centered, and competitive daughter-in-law, chose to memorize 1 Corinthians 13:4-7 because she knew she couldn't depend on good *chemistry* to make interactions with her daughter-in-law easy. Marie recognized the relationship would likely not improve unless she committed to exercising *character* to win the day. A lot of progress followed Marie's persistence in implementing love principles in all her relationships, but especially when she thought about or interacted with her daughter-in-law. Both parties softened due to Marie's tenacity in making 1 Corinthians 13:4-7 her daily guide.

Financial Dilemmas

Financial advisers and experts in family dynamics hotly debate questions about how much monetary assistance to bestow on adult offspring, and they generally answer with the qualifier, "It depends." Certainly, fears of "enabling" scare us. Our reluctance to remove incentives for sons and daughters to work hard and gain satisfaction through their own accomplishments plays into the equation. On the other side of the issue is the reality that gifts are the primary love language of some people and withholding monetary assistance may leave your child feeling distinctly unloved.

There may be generational expectations based on cultural norms. For example, Italian families routinely purchase homes for their sons when they marry. It's expected and planned in advance. Even in America, grown children may insinuate you are a stingy, selfish soul if you don't provide financial help for a house down payment. Guilt trips emanating from either generation do damage to relationships. Forgive them and focus on how good it feels to give generously to those you love.

Parents struggle with giving when they currently possess enough to share but aren't sure what their future circumstances might require. The pain of seeing their grown offspring "do without" often motivates decisions impoverishing parents as they age. Fear of the unwanted consequence of becoming financially dependent on our grown kids someday should fuel caution about giving away too much too soon.

Moms and dads who went through a lot of lean days themselves, but gradually attained a level of comfort by working long hours over long years, may not be eager to fund a young couple's desires to possess homes, cars, and entertainment experiences equivalent to what their parents only acquired late in life. Also, they don't want to rob their grown kids of the satisfaction achieved through hard work and determination.

Most of us in the latter decades of our third-tri era received very little financial help from the older generation, except possibly in the form of eventual inheritances. Our parents either didn't have it to give, or believed each generation should make their own way unless physically incapable. Knowing we were "on our own," without government or parental handouts on the horizon, stimulated strong work ethics. Frugality, saving to buy a house or car, avoiding debt, rarely eating out in restaurants, foregoing expensive entertainment, and eschewing costly travel and lavish vacations were not only all required, but seemed "normal." These sacrifices may seem ridiculous to those who grew up during more prosperous times.

When so many circumstances, contingencies, histories, and expectations collide, solving intergenerational financial quandaries requires immense wisdom and flexibility. Hurt feelings abound. Still, some general principles that *usually* hold true may be helpful.

Guideline #36: Helping adult children financially is a slippery slope. Every case is unique. Do not let yourself become hostage to entitlement mindsets. However, judicious financial help can convey love and caring better than any words in specific situations. Pray and seek counsel. Don't allow yourself to be emotionally manipulated, blackmailed, or impoverished because you are trying to buy your offspring's favor.

Jim Burns, an insightful expert on family issues, warns, "Parents who make a habit of bailing their adult children out of bad financial choices only stifle their children's ability to develop healthy financial muscles and to become responsible and independent with their finances."[123] Continued dependency tends to foster resentment and control issues, frustrating both the parents and grown offspring. Conversations about money rarely feel good to either party and often create yet another wedge between the generations.

Studies show that during the second trimester of life, the child-bearing and child-rearing years, mothers' life satisfaction scores rank higher than those of non-mothers, only to reverse when their children launch into adulthood. By age forty and beyond, childless counterparts chalk up higher life satisfaction scores than mothers of adult offspring.[124]

Researchers found 54 percent of mothers had "mixed feelings" about their grown children. "The strongest predictor of ambivalence toward an adult child was *whether their mother continued to financially support them*. And the biggest predictor of interpersonal stress between adult child and mother was her affirmative answer to the question 'Do you feel that you give more than you receive in this relationship?'"[125]

Most mothers are hoping for on-going gratitude, kindness toward their benefactor, and willingness to work hard from any recipients they help. The sheer joy derived from being a generous parent diminishes when mom gives to an ungrateful, entitled adult child who demonstrates scant affection, appreciation, attention, or esteem in return for his/her mother's financial help.

Parents who have the resources and desire to be generous can invent ways to bless their beloved offspring without feeling "forced" by guilt trips. The right kind of receivers receive and remember such gifts with joy and thankfulness.

Mothers who possess enough cash might consider the option to make a generous vacation gesture. Mom arranges for the family to get together for a vacation week at a beach house, mountain chalet, dude ranch, or international location. You are investing in making new, fun memories with the kids you raised and with your grandchildren. You may need to subsidize or pay all the expenses for some or all family members. Work the numbers before you issue invitations. Making yourself part of the party gives you a chance to relate in a relaxed environment.

Offering a week at your farm or in the hometown where your children grew up won't cost nearly as much. It can turn into just as much fun and offer as many bonding experiences as exotic locations. Experiment with planting a garden, fishing in the pond, picking apples, making apple pie from scratch, swinging on a tire, riding on the tractor, exploring the creek, sharing root beer floats at the hometown diner, and visiting the county fair or festival. Other options include attending a local high school theatre production, going to country church services, taking walks in the woods, playing in the barn, milking a cow, and identifying different birds and wildlife.

Life lessons abound for grandkids raised in the city. Getting your adult children and grandchildren out of their regular routines and away from their tech devices often leads to priceless conversations, shared learning experiences, and treasured memories.

Guideline #37: It is okay to say *No*. Do not create a culture of entitlement to your money or your time. Do not enable children who pursue destructive lifestyles or engage in addictions. Use actions more than words. Release your adult kids to the financial consequences of their choices. When you decide it is in the best interests of all concerned to refuse financial relief, speak the truth lovingly, not *angrily*. Sermonizing along with your financial refusal only fans the flames. Saying *no* becomes even more difficult when compassionate moms fear a son or daughter will end up living on the streets or worry that an innocent grandchild may suffer deprivation. In those situations, determine to link any financial help to maintaining steady employment or going into rehab. If they don't abide by your conditions, keep your word to turn off the money flow, but don't yell at them. Closing your check-book speaks louder than words.

Other possibilities include funding education or training opportunities aimed at preparing for a better job. Be aware your attached strings may rankle sons or daughters who would prefer to prematurely live the lifestyle of a financially secure retired person. Some offspring choose not to work hard enough to improve their situations. They refuse to invest the years before sixty-five in a targeted effort to achieve financial security. If your children want to do only what they feel like doing every day, that is their choice. Love them, pray for them, listen, offer emotional support, be sad for their meager circumstances, but do not stand in the way of their opportunity to learn that "those unwilling to work will not get to eat."[126]

Sometimes offspring are laboring long, hard hours, perhaps following David Ramsey financial principles, and living exemplary lives, but an accident, illness, or other tragedy derails them. If you are financially able, give an outright gift, offer a no-interest loan, or pay some rent or utility bills for a specified time period. Watch this industrious type of son or daughter express copious gratitude and do everything in their power to be on their own again as soon as possible.

What if your adult child repeatedly comes back to you for bail-outs because of making foolish life choices? Some offspring persist in running up credit card debts they can't pay. Some believe they should be exempt from working a forty-hour workweek. Others decide against marriage and choose unstable romantic relationships, or succumb to alcohol or drug addiction. As mentioned earlier, financial help is predicated on the qualifier, *It depends*. In the case of repeat offenders, the answer should probably be, "No, I can't." Our inability lies not in our *bank* account, but in our *love* account. Our love will not let us cripple those we love by standing between them and the chance to learn from their mistakes and proudly grow financially independent.

Guideline #38: Be helpful! Adult children notice if we are self-absorbed and selfish. Be a grandma who willingly babysits and sacrifices her time and energy. Some adult kids complain they feel like an interruption in their parents' lives. Consequently, those we raised may believe they are no longer a priority, and some even feel abandoned.

Many grandmas live for the opportunity to babysit their grandsons and granddaughters and are mesmerized by their grandkids' puppy-like adorability. Others treasure the chance to mentor and teach. They can't imagine a more satisfying way to spend their days than interacting with their precious grandchildren.

A chemistry factor exists with grandchildren as well as with in-laws, however. If relationships with your grandkids don't flow naturally, exercise your character muscles and try to love and connect as well as you can. Some women are naturally playful people and are wired to relate well to almost every child, while others struggle with certain personalities or ages.

Because many women in our age group remember fondly the love and influence shared with their own grandmothers, most are motivated to undertake babysitting opportunities, exhausting though they may be as grandmas age. Entertaining youngsters might not come naturally, but a trip to the library to collect some ideas for age-appropriate crafts, homemade games, and other fun activities may help you prepare for enjoyable hours together. Since your grandkids probably already own almost every toy ever invented, giving the gift of *time* to play hide and seek, bake cookies, enter into imaginary worlds, or master board games their parents once played may be the ticket to their hearts. Many grand-kids spell their main love language "t-i-m-e" and they never get enough of it from the grownups in their lives.

When we were little and visited our grandparents, Grandma let us tag along and participate in whatever work needed to be accomplished, with an occasional special activity thrown in. Modern kids have higher expectations for stimulation. Telling them they can play with a sack of clothes pins or help us in the kitchen sounds distinctly boring. Likewise, a small box of crayons and scrap paper may not seem very exciting com-pared to their own home's elaborate craft spaces filled with expensive art supplies and tech devices. Your most valuable contribution can be the absence of so many options and the availability of your time to enter into their imaginary worlds together. Open your heart to them and let them teach you how to play again! Tackle the assignment of inventing creative play opportunities without all the store-bought plastic usually cluttering their rooms. Even playing with clothespins can be fun if done together!

I've talked to third-trimester women who say, "I raised my kids and now it's their turn to parent. My adult kids take advantage of me as a babysitter, so they can have fun going places and doing adult things. No one took the kids off my hands for multiple hours every week, so why should they expect me to wear myself out now while they partici-pate in adult playtimes?"

Some third-trimester moms are reluctant to give up their yoga classes, bridge parties, Bible study groups, bicycle treks, food pantry volunteer days, lunch outings, and book clubs to free their grown offspring from childcare duties. They conclude their adult sons and daughters want to participate in similar fun pursuits at the expense of Mom's canceled plans.

Alternatively, grandmas may process requests for babysitting as attempts to avoid childcare expenses. Grandma suspects sons and daughters want to save their salaries to fund the purchase of luxury vehicles, extravagant houses, and Rhine River cruises, despite being fully aware that their mother's house is modest, her car is old, and her only trips are to visit relatives.

It is certainly understandable how each generation can end up with hurt feelings. The "*it depends*" phrase applies to helping adult children in nonmonetary ways as well as when dollars are concerned. If you don't prioritize personal sacrifices to spend time with your kids and grandkids, it is nearly guaranteed you will have little positive impact on their lives, and you will also put additional distance between you and the younger generations. For most of us, the more time we invest in being together, the more love flows.

Looking back, we remember sacrifices dating back to our pregnancy days. You readily gave up indulgences like cigarettes, wine, and risky athletic competitions because you wanted to protect the development of the one growing within. You made your sacrifices out of love for the one you carried close to your heart.

Parallel #11: During pregnancy's third trimester and in life's third tri, mothers are committed to personal sacrifice for the well-being of their offspring.

Balance is important. Balance not allowing selfish exploitation by your grown children with dispensing unselfish love! If your grown kids don't express much appreciation when you help out, or if they try to shame you for not doing more, kindly set boundaries and resist their manipulations. If, however, you can parlay gifts of babysitting into delightful interactions with the young crowd, throw yourself into this uniquely wonderful stage of life, one that can benefit every generation. The long-term rewards of closeness and intergenerational affection last a lifetime.

Statistics on geographical separation in the U.S. indicate the majority of adult children live in close enough proximity to see their parents frequently, if that's their desire. "Overall, the median distance that Americans live from their mother is eighteen miles, and only 20 percent live more than a couple hours' drive from parents."[127] It may be a shock and an impetus toward self-pity if you are a long-distance parent and grandma reading these stats. How disheartening to know that half of all adult children reside only eighteen miles or less from their mother, while your kids may live in distant states or on another continent. Highly educated offspring with professional degrees are the most likely to move far from home.[128]

Do not despair. After several years in distant locales, a yearning for hometowns and time with their families of origin often grows. Those fresh out of college may crave the excitement and entertainment available in big cities, but eventually realize they miss the people from whom they once sought to flee. Some start to work on plans to diminish the noise and crush of their big-city life and find ways to support themselves back in the vicinity of their hometowns. However, your offspring may choose to relocate near the other in-laws instead of near you, and you will once again need to fight disappointment and jealousy. Coping with disappointments and banishing jealousy are lifelong assignments.

Focus on discovering new ways to find fun and fulfillment and invest in building family-like relationships with others in the same boat. Accept your situation and make the best of it. No one gets everything the way they'd like in life. Concentrate on the blessings you have instead of obsessing over what you are missing. Your level of happiness is ultimately your choice.

Family life definitely offers more options when easy access exists between the generations. Geographically nearby families more easily stay united, since frequent involvement in each other's lives is practical and possible. Parents with children living far away struggle to make once-a-year holiday visits sustain the kind of closeness they crave. If you are an outlier mother with no grown children or grandchildren anywhere around, accept your circumstances and pour energy into keeping communication flowing long distance. Don't give up if you are a grandma living far from your grandchildren. Be present in every way you can!

Perhaps you will decide to join the crowd of retired folks relocating across the country to become a hands-on grandma. Moving nearby makes it possible to attend grandkids' school and extra-curricular events and enjoy more togetherness. Helping each other out across the generations and doing more things together is finally feasible.

Geographical distance impedes in-person connection, and even more so when the world is fighting a plague such as Covid. Use your creativity to become like Gretchen who texted a joke every day to her nine-year-old grandson during the Covid-forced isolation. Make the most of opportunities to celebrate your kids' and your grandkids' successes and milestones from afar. Covid has thrown a monkey wrench in the works whether you live close or far away.

Value Differences

In my introduction to this book, I quoted Jane Isay, "It's almost impossible to stop loving your parents, and even more difficult to stop loving your children. Given this obvious truth, what's the matter with us? Why can't we find a way to be easy with our grown kids, and just be close and relaxed?[129] Dare I suggest value differences may be the interfering culprit for some families?

Recently, on Valentine's Day, my husband and I viewed the 1971 award-winning movie *Fiddler on the Roof*, an annual tradition for us. This heartwarming and heart-wrenching musical portrays the love flowing in a poor Jewish family in Russia during the historical period when persecution of the Jews was ratcheting up. The conflicts between beloved traditions, religious convictions, family loyalties, and a changing society play out in ways that make us laugh and then reach for the tissues. The love of Tevye for his daughters, and their love for their father as they reach adulthood, are tested in ways familiar in America today. Out of love for his daughters, Tevye bends from his traditions and gradually accepts changes. Despite his girls' willful picks of life partners he would never have chosen, he incorporates their alien modern ideas. Only when one daughter pushes the limits of her father's belief system beyond his capacity to bend, does the family break. Yet the movie's ending leaves a glimmer of hope.

Hard as they are to talk about, differences in morality, religion, and values loom large, and an authentic book about mothers who love their adult children cannot ignore the topic. Some of you may have purchased this book specifically because you seek wisdom to keep your heart and your family from breaking. You may wonder, *How shall I interact with my atheist child or one living in an alternative lifestyle not matching my values and beliefs? How can I possess peace when my child is incarcerated or living the life of a junkie on the streets or engaging in immoral behavior or participating in a cult?* While I do not possess an exact cookie-cutter answer for such daunting value quandaries, I want to provide a glimmer of hope.

Guideline #39: Face the reality that your Christian beliefs may be the main wedge between you and your adult children.

Perceptive author and family expert Gary Thomas reminds us Jesus predicted He would become a "sword of division" between parents and children. "From now on families will be split apart, three in favor of me, and two against—or two in favor and three against. Father will be divided against son and son against father; mother against daughter and daughter against mother; and mother-in-law against daughter-in-law and daughter-in-law against mother-in-law."[130] Why are we so surprised when divisions play out in our families precisely as Jesus foretold? We just never expected it to happen in *our* families![131]

Your offspring may resent you, believing you were hypocritical and pushed Christianity down their throats. They may feel helpless to gain your approval. What you consider to be the "Good News" may offend them to the core. Paul addressed the issue head-on when he wrote, "Our lives are a Christ-like fragrance rising up to God. But this fragrance is perceived differently by those who are being saved and by those who are perishing. To those who are perishing, we are a dreadful smell of death and doom."[132]

Parallel #12: As the third trimester drags on, pregnant moms-to-be get impatient with waiting and find it difficult to trust God's timing. Third-tri moms likewise grow impatient.

Reflect how you felt as a pregnant mom-to-be when the last days before your delivery date seemed to drag on and on. The waiting seemed interminable. For many Christian third-tri mothers, it seems as if they've been waiting forever for God to answer their prayers for beloved grown children to choose God-honoring paths.

Many mystified mothers I surveyed point to comparable timelines in their family histories. Kids went to church, youth groups, Christian concerts, and camps. They often made sincere professions of faith and were baptized. Some were homeschooled or attended private schools. Many were bright, affectionate, high-achieving, talented, obedient children and close to their parents.

During high school, some sons and daughters began to question whether their church youth group was filled with hypocrites and whether Jesus was who He claimed to be. Besides, their Christian parents seemed so obviously flawed. Conversations ensued, sometimes heated ones, as parents attempted to defend the Gospel and biblical teachings, but the kids were listening to different voices now.

Skeptical peers, idolized musicians, irreverent comedians, persuasive authors, Hollywood celebrities, and some teachers challenged what their children had once believed wholeheartedly. Then came college. One mom described her fruitless efforts to convince her university offspring to remain open and investigate the evidence for Christianity from an adult perspective as "attempting to hold on to oil as it dripped uncontrollably through my fingers."

For decades now, universities have made it a mission to get students to think for themselves, question former assumptions, and not blindly accept what they previously considered to be true. Sounds good, right? Unfortunately, in their quest to enlighten students, many brilliant, respected, and likable professors present contradictory "truths" that have little relevance to their subject matter, and students swallow their profs' political and religious views hook, line, and sinker. Christianity is rarely presented in a secular university classroom as a viable worldview worthy of consideration and honest investigation.

I have heard story after sad story from discouraged mothers who regret skimping and saving for years to finance their child's "higher education." To their dismay, some of their children's professors *subtly or overtly* denigrated Christianity, promoted humanism, secularism, socialism, sometimes Marxism, and tolerance for every worldview except Christianity. In our current climate, the pressure on faculty to perpetuate politically correct views affects teachers from kindergarten all the way through graduate and professional levels.

Outside of Christian universities, faculty members championing the evidence for Christianity struggle to survive. Professors who are outspoken believers and openly espouse traditional biblical principles in their classrooms are often accused of being patriarchal, sexist, intolerant, xenophobic, homophobic, racist, or bigoted. In today's culture, religion has been sadly politicized, and adherence to traditional biblical teachings generally equates to "wrong politics." Unfortunately, devout professors who personally hold biblically-based worldviews must often teach with gags in their mouths or face punitive consequence

Adding to your college offspring's confusion during such a critical life phase is a desire to be liked and respected by fellow students. Your sons and daughters discover some of the friends they admire are agnostic or atheist and skilled debaters. Beer-infused discussions with equally misguided peers begin to make a lot of sense and further the process of chipping away at the Bible as a credible authority.

Way back in the 1960s, when I started college, popular atheist professors teaching in the honors program weakened my previously held beliefs the very first semester of my freshman year. They ridiculed biblically-based faith as naïve and unintelligent. Of course, I wanted to be sophisticated and smart! Within months, I didn't know what I believed about God anymore and stopped attending church. If Bill Bright, founder of Cru, had not spoken on the University of Kansas campus and offered a rational, scholarly, historically persuasive alternative and presented a way to know God personally, I would probably be embracing anti-Christianity rhetoric today.

The upside of having childhood faith demolished in young adulthood is the reality that many kids need to transition from blindly accepting their parents' faith to choosing for themselves as an informed, mature person to follow Christ. If they haven't been "silenced," caring Christian faculty members can assist questioning students seeking truth. Also, organizations like Cru are a lifeline to young adults who need someone to come alongside and help them move from a child's unexamined faith to a mature love relationship with God Himself. Like-minded peers involved in Cru discipleship activities give them courage to grow and stand against opposing forces.

By the time my children entered college, even more professors had jumped on the secular bandwagon. A person from my children's generation described how a professor's words affected her during her impressionable years when she was crystalizing what she believed. The nagging doubts she brought with her to college were inflamed by an introductory anthropology class at a regional state university.

Meghan's professor asserted with great authority on the first day of class, "You students will never be the same people you were when you entered this classroom. You will know something very few people know. You will know that all religions were created by people. Be-

cause you know what everyone else doesn't know, you will be an outcast because of your special knowledge. You will never be able to go
back to having faith in God because studying anthropology will convince you any belief you now have in God is intellectually incompat-
ible with knowing mankind's history. All religions will be eliminated
because you will learn they were all created by people and, therefore,
have no validity."

Sadly, no intellectually convincing voice was there to inform
Meghan that establishing a mature love relationship with Christ is
desirable for many reasons and exists as an intelligent option to explore. Sunday school level Christianity is no match for an articulate,
revered professor.

Because anthropology studies also show the propensity for human
civilizations to seek spiritual meaning in their lives, a long list of substi-
tutes for Christianity get a free pass. For example, many professors treat
Buddhism, Hinduism, Islamism, Humanism, Spiritism, Paganism,
Wicca, Marxism, and New Age practices with more respect than biblical Christianity. A wide range of "acceptable" world religions, cults,
and pagan practices attract spirituality seekers because people are wired
to seek meaning, purpose, and fulfillment.

At the same time as professors are pontificating, hormones are
flowing. Sexual experiences beckon and prove to be abundantly available if young persons can rid themselves of Christian morality principles. Temptations often win. *Cognitive dissonance* then takes over.
Dissonance is what you experience when an orchestra is warming up—
unpleasant discordant sounds occurring when there is no harmony between the parts. Cognitive dissonance is likewise distinctly uncomfortable when one's beliefs and one's actions don't match. To rid themselves

of the painful mental and emotional dissonance, university students must either change what they believe or change how they behave. Typically, they change what they believe, so their sexual behaviors and those of their friends don't feel so wrong.

If you want something for your grown offspring more than they want it for themselves, you will rarely be successful in turning them to your point of view. As discussed earlier in this book, realize that their baffling choices are between your grown kids and God. If you stop viewing value differences as parent-dishonoring decisions, then you can let go of your anger, stop being their warden, and become their friend.

Keep your own God-honoring values intact and remain available to discuss why you believe as you do, if your kids are willing to hear your viewpoints. Often, they don't welcome the conversations. Many times, it will be someone other than Dad or Mom who touches their hearts to find faith in God later in life. Sometimes we fear our grown kids' belief systems are immovable objects. However, remember that love is an irresistible force. Ask God for love and the Holy Spirit to prevail.

Giving up addictions, choosing biblical marriage standards, embracing traditional Christian teachings about the cross, creation, sexual morality, and the sanctity of life are all confounded in young people's minds with "science" and their "rights." Over the years, however, as idealistic young adults must live with the consequences of their choices, their certainty about what is scientific and right may begin to crumble.

Science is a work in progress, with new discoveries eventually replacing previously sacrosanct "science-based" theories and dogmas. Even though contradictory viewpoints may currently prevail in the scientific community, we can confidently trust that honest scientific scrutiny over time will eventually confirm what Scripture teaches. Consequences from basing choices on what seems right in humans' own eyes can be severe. Charles Swindoll puts it this way, "Pain plants the flag of reality in the fortress of a rebel heart."[133]

Parents would spare the ones we love from pain if we could, whether it's the eventual calamities in the country from voting for certain candidates, disintegrating physical or mental health, relationship disasters, or separation from God. We need to keep our relationships as strong as possible, so we can be there to help beloved sons and daughters pick up the pieces once the flag of reality pierces their consciousness. We can also pray, love, wait in faith, and keep working on ourselves.

Coaching Corner

1. How would you describe your relationship with each of your children's spouses? Which ones have easy chemistry, and which ones require character effort on your part?

2. Can you think of any ways your daughters-in-law or sons-in-law would like you to be different?

3. What stands in the way of improving your in-law relationships? What can you do about those barriers?

4. Write 1 Corinthians 13:4-7 on a piece of paper, giving a line to each component of love named in the passage. Evaluate how well you live out the characteristics of love with each of your grown children and each of their partners. Give yourself a grade from A to F for each characteristic and each person.

Your grades should reflect how well you've mastered these important components of loving.

5. Considering the grade card you produced in response to coaching point #4, how willing are you to memorize 1 Corinthians 13:4-7 and review those verses every day?

6. What thorny issues exist between the generations in your family?

7. How do you think God would want you to deal with those dilemmas?

8. What specific value differences, if any, threaten your family's future?

9. What options exist for dealing with those value differences? Which of those options do you want to implement? When will you move in that direction?

10. The last sentence in this chapter reads, *We can also pray, love, wait in faith, and keep working on ourselves.* In practical terms, what would those four actions look like in your life on a daily basis?

CHAPTER 12

Necessary Adjustments

UNTIL TWO MONTHS ago, I always felt "young." When required to reveal my age, currently seventy-five, I customarily felt stunned to confess such a large number. My body parts mostly worked well. My mind felt relatively sharp. People often reacted with surprise when discovering my World War II-era birthdate, often maintaining I looked younger than my birth certificate declares. On May 20, 2020, I had exercised as usual, including logging miles on our home treadmill. No problem!

Suddenly, during my first-ever episode of disorienting vertigo, while wiping off the kitchen island, I slammed down on the concrete floor. All my weight landed sharply on my left hip, followed by the thud of my skull against the rock-hard surface. My husband called an ambulance to transport my broken body to the university hospital thirty miles away. Covid-19 visitor restrictions were in full swing. Tooger had no choice but to tearfully kiss me goodbye as I lay on a gurney in the ambulance outside our front door, and off I sped all alone to deal with my broken hip ordeal.

Seven other people with broken hips arrived at Indiana University Hospital that night, according to the orthopedic surgeon who "pinned" me back together two days later after I'd passed the required Covid test. My osteoporotic fracture was a common injury in life's third era. Surgeries for hip replacements, knee replacements, and painful back, foot, and shoulder reconstruction are commonplace among elders. Likewise, cancers, heart problems, diabetes, and countless debilitating diseases stalk those in the Third-Trimester Club. When I hit the floor, a piercing spotlight illuminated seven more of the forty parallels I'd identified between the third trimester of pregnancy and the third trimester of life.

Parallel #13: An encumbered body often makes life physically uncomfortable and inconvenient for extended periods. There may even be excruciatingly painful stages that feel all-consuming and unbearable. Frequent urination, disturbed sleep, aching backs, and swollen ankles go with the territory, both for pregnant moms-to-be and for third-tri grandmas.

Health problems are no fun at any age, but the likelihood of incapacitating diseases and disabling conditions increases with age. However, the more we keep our ailments in perspective and retain our sense of humor, the better we will manage what life throws our way.

An interesting piece of data about Covid-19 arrived in my mailbox today. According to statistics from the CDC, those aged sixty-five or over comprise only 16 percent of the U.S. population, but 80 percent of Covid deaths occur in that age group. Those fortunate to survive to seventy-five or older constitute just 6.7 percent of the total U.S. population, but account for 57.6 percent of the Covid-19 deaths.

Covid-19 obviously discriminates on the basis of age, killing those in life's third season disproportionately. Many of us have developed other health problems complicating recovery from the virus.

Yet most of us won't succumb; 95 percent of those over seventy-five survive the virus.

Additional good news: Preeclampsia, a life-threatening disorder afflicting some moms-to-be with spikes of high blood pressure and protein in their urine, won't kill a single one of us older folks because it targets young pregnant women. Doctors recommend strategies for avoiding Covid-19, and they advise young moms-to-be how to avoid preeclampsia. It makes sense to follow your doctor's instructions whether in pregnancy's third trimester or life's third era.

Along with trying to rehabilitate from my broken hip this summer, I suffered from two large kidney stones requiring surgery, along with a bunch of persistent kidney/bladder-related discomforts and the onset of glaucoma. Frankly, my symptoms reminded me of the ninth month of pregnancy—no way to get comfortable in bed, distressingly frequent trips to the bathroom, "kicks" to the bladder, trouble getting in and out of the bathtub, and I waddle when I walk. My surgical recoveries were prolonged, but the pain level was similar to the first week after a C-section. I made it through three pregnancies, and I'm determined to make it through life's third-trimester annoyances too!

Love As a Motivator in Every Trimester

Love was the main motivation for your pursuit of a healthy lifestyle when you were pregnant. Likewise, you want to avoid forcing unnecessary caretaking burdens on your spouse or adult children in your current life season because you love them.

It is not news that your physical abilities fall in the category of use-it-or-lose-it capacities. Many empty-nest moms successfully stay fit and lean during the first decades of life's third tri. However, as we accumulate more birthdays, we may find our older bodies can't handle high-impact exercises like jogging or Zumba, the kinds of activities that kept us moving when we were younger. We need to find alternative ways to exercise instead of passively sitting just because we can't do what we once did.

Some buy a pedometer or Fitbit exercise tracker and set a goal for ten thousand steps a day. I recently invested in an adjustable stand-up desk and padded floormat for burning more calories and varying my positions when reading and writing, thus decreasing aches and pains from sitting too much.

Depending on where you live, investing in a treadmill, elliptical machine, basic weights, or a stationary bike may be the ticket, especially when the weather is not conducive to outdoor activity. Still others take up gardening, mall walking, or attend Senior Sneakers classes paid for by many Medicare alternative plans. Others bike in their neighborhoods and on biking trails. Some join the gym and use the walking track, swimming pool, or various strength-building machines.

Perhaps you have the money to hire a trainer or physical therapist. Older couples may rediscover dancing or sign up for dance lessons to learn a skill they've longed to possess all their lives. When Covid-19 risks make options fewer, consider exercise videos available on YouTube or purchase DVDs you can use in the convenience of your home.

Developing flexibility in the mode of exercise is not enough, however. Persistence is the key. Yard sales and thrift stores offer bargain exercise equipment because would-be exercisers rarely stick with it. Desire for comfort can soon win out over love. However, the rewards for maintaining a commitment to exercising regularly and eating healthy foods are enormous, both for you personally and for those you love. My dentist quips, "Only brush and floss the teeth you want to keep." A variation on that advice would be, "Only exercise the body you want to keep."

I concede that many better models of long-term successful exercisers exist than the author of this book! However, I will offer a few tips serving me well so far in my third trimester of life.

Apply the Premack Principle to build an automatic reward for your exercise efforts. Dr. David Premack famously suggested linking an activity you want to perform because it is good for you with a satisfying activity you are already doing. Thus, the original enjoyable habit becomes a reinforcing, rewarding consequence for implementing a new healthy behavior that was previously not occurring.[134]

Some of the activities women naturally enjoy in the morning include drinking coffee, eating breakfast, perusing Facebook or emails, reading the newspaper, calling friends or family on the phone, checking up on the news, or watching HGTV. Why not pair a morning walk with eating breakfast or checking Facebook? Determine not to eat that yummy toast with almond butter until you've finished your forty-minute walk. Resist the impulse to check Facebook or your newsfeed until you complete your exercise video. Your breakfast or the social media time then serve as your reward for a virtuous workout. Soon you will be so high on exercise that persisting with your routine comes more easily. You'll probably miss your three-mile walk terribly when something interferes.

Your cellphone is a wonderful device to promote walking on the treadmill or in the park. Stick earbuds in your ears or turn on the speaker function and slide your phone into your pocket or fanny pack. Then chat with a girlfriend or family member while striding on your machine or marching through the neighborhood. Since I treasure my relationships, I get caught up in my conversations and forget how exhausted my legs feel. As a result, I can exercise twice as long while keeping in touch with treasured people. When someone calls, let it serve as a trigger to grab your walking shoes, head out the door, or flip on the elliptical or treadmill.

When no one is available for a phone conversation, I open interesting apps like *Family Talk* or *Focus on the Family,* thought-provoking podcasts, or favorite music groups to combat exercise tedium. I simultaneously take in positive content and hike the trails near my house. There is no excuse for sitting when I could just as well be moving.

Recently I dug out my old Italian language learning tapes. They occupy my mind and prepare me for the trip I want to take next summer. Learning a new language is good exercise for the brain and helps ward off Alzheimer's, some doctors think. Therefore, I plop in a tape and stride on the treadmill for half an hour some mornings, repeating the words and phrases when the cheery Italian teacher prompts my responses.

Choose to eat mostly whole unprocessed plant foods like greens, beans and other legumes, fruits and vegetables, grains, nuts, and seeds. Abundant unprocessed whole plant foods supply our bodies with necessary nutrients to prevent, delay, or reduce the severity of diseases like diabetes, cancer, and heart disease. What you eat now is as important as when you were pregnant. Then you sought to eat a diet rich in vitamins and minerals. You abstained from drugs and alcohol and watched your weight for the good of your baby. Similarly, exercise and a plant-rich diet may help save your loved ones from needing to assume overwhelming caretaking responsibilities for you because you were too stubborn to alter bad habits. Make your choices for the sake of the body you want to keep and out of love for your dearest ones.

The Mediterranean Diet is endorsed by many doctors. I also highly recommend Dr. Michael Greger's remarkable book, *How Not to Die*.[135] Its contents and Dr. Greger's website, NutritionFacts.org, educate me and simultaneously motivate me to improve my dietary choices. Dr. Greger's book brilliantly lays out compelling, highly researched advice about how to avoid diseases brought about by unwise eating choices and sedentary lifestyles. Dr. Greger makes it clear that more deaths in America result from the long-term effects of eating animal products and processed food than from any other cause. Dr. Kim Williams, 2015 president of the American College of Cardiology, was asked why he ate a strictly plant-based diet. "I don't mind dying," Dr. Williams said. "I just don't want it to be my fault."[136]

Parallel #14: Body limitations affect work, recreational, and travel possibilities. Choices to "go and do" are restricted in the last weeks of pregnancy and also late in life's third trimester.

A dozen years ago, when I became aware my empty nest life could leave me increasingly on the sidelines, I considered my options. All my children lived in distant locations, and my husband, Chuck, suffered from serious health conditions and was no longer able to travel. I put on paper some of my dilemmas and my options for solving them, intending to share my conclusions with my third-tri clients and potential readers of the book I wanted to write "someday."

As I flew from Lexington toward the Pacific Ocean, I began to write on the clipboard I'd stowed in my carry-on. My viewpoints about traveling when I was more than a decade younger than today haven't changed much. Part of my commentary from an earlier period of my third tri follows:

Traveling in the Third Trimester

"As I sit scribbling in my notebook propped on my tray table today, I notice that the brave flier in front of me, probably near eighty-five, is attached to an oxygen device and sports clear plastic tubes delivering air to her nostrils. Her frail husband has rummaged in the overhead bins a dozen times since our flight commenced five hours ago, burrowing into their carry-on bags for sweaters and water bottles and prescription vials. Several teenagers are rooting through their backpacks also. Needing something from one's luggage mid-flight is not the exclusive province of the senior adult. The lady on oxygen support is flying to visit her grandchildren, she told me, when I queried her over the plane seatback.

"As I boarded, I stood in the Jetway while a steward pushed a wheelchair transporting a lady about my age to the airplane door. I watched as her helper cheerfully offered his arm for support and patiently escorted her the last few steps to her seat. I counted numerous gray heads in almost every row as I made my way back to the bathroom mid-flight.

"Already it's a bit harder than it used to be to travel. I had to borrow a young woman's husband to hoist my carry-on into the bin above my head today. Admittedly, I was never adept at lifting heavy objects over my head, but it wasn't so noticeable when my strong husband was at my side. He was proud to demonstrate his muscles and help his bride as long as he could. I notice the young man who helped me today got an approving glance from his wife for exercising his strength and his gentlemanly manners. Her admiration and my appreciation constituted his reward.

"I'm flying today, albeit alone, and so are many other passengers in the age bracket of sixty to ninety. Unfortunately, many others remain on the ground because they are too intimidated to tackle the friendly skies. I'm all for following a doctor's orders if health realities contraindicate leaving home, just as in my pregnancy's third trimester. However, travel beckons and is possible for most of the third tri for many of us. When we were younger, it was hard to get time off from our jobs, and money was scarcer when we were raising and educating our kids. When we are in life's third trimester, mission trips and journeys to connect with our offspring in distant places and exploring God's creation need to be considered from a now-or-never framework."

Parallel #15: You fight worries about health problems, and the hyper-awareness of bodily sensations dogs you. During pregnancy's third trimester and life's third tri, you gather a team of medical experts around you.

A late-stage expectant mom stays closely attuned to her baby's movements, and anxiety creeps in when she hasn't felt an internal jab recently. Similarly, the inability to recall a once-familiar name or failure to remember why we entered a room set off "senior moments" alarm bells. The inability to thread a needle, read small print, decipher a street sign, or experiencing sudden flashes of light in our field of vision prompt anxious calls to the eye doctor. A family physician becomes a gateway to specialists of all sorts. The week's calendar may leave room for little else in addition to various doctor appointments and all the accompanying tests and treatments.

If we think back to long-ago pregnancy inconveniences, we remember our prenatal visits dominated our schedule then too. Assembling a list of trustworthy doctors adds confidence to an otherwise precarious time. It's a common part of this season of life to have more health challenges to treat as you age.

During your first- and second-trimester years, you may have successfully avoided spending much time in doctors' offices. That was also true during the early stages of pregnancy, but once-a-month obstetrician visits eventually turned into once-a-week appointments when delivery dates loomed. Serenity increases as we accept the rhythm of life. We want to maximize our health-promoting habits like daily walks and plant-based eating, but also find peace with the inevitable body challenges of encroaching age.

Parallel #16: Your physical appearance changes in ways you don't like.

When I was a young mom in my twenties, I remember a stooped elderly woman who was being interviewed on television, and she said the most astonishing thing. She declared, "I'm still the young woman I've always been, but now I'm trapped in an old person's body." Before that surprising revelation, I had considered old people as a totally different species from me. Having transformed into that aged person myself now, I resonate with her and a recent Facebook quote, author unknown, "The sad part about getting old is you stay young on the inside, but nobody can tell anymore."

The sideways profiles of pregnant mamas in their third trimesters don't meet societal standards for beauty that our culture foists upon women today. Yet their unique pregnancy glow overshadows waistline expansion, and good husbands view their wives' baby bumps as beautiful, fascinating, and endearing. Stretch marks from weight gain and awkward gaits are to be expected.

The choice to lighten up about our aging bodies, our foibles, and our eccentricities, to laugh at ourselves, and to allow others to tease us good-naturedly will lubricate otherwise sensitive subjects. We can glide through the changes still smiling. Make fun of yourself a bit when your body parts droop, your hair thins, your face wrinkles, your knees hurt, your eyesight or hearing fades. Instead of living in denial or acting irritable and easily offended because people don't speak loudly enough for you to hear, accept the aging process and the effects of gravity on your body with grace and humor.

My new husband, Tooger, lovingly called me a "Shar-Pei" this week. Have you seen any photos of the folded wrinkles characteristic of the Chinese dog breed named Shar-Pei? Now mind you, I know my underarms are dimpled and, to my distress, flap a bit. That's why you won't catch me wearing the cute sleeveless dresses that look like dynamite on celebrities and firm-bodied younger women. But as Tooger wrapped his arms around me, naturally feeling my softness, he affectionately dubbed me a "Shar-Pei." I had to make up my mind whether to be insulted or collapse in laughter.

No secrets remain about our bodies once we're married, and we disguise less than we think even when fully clothed. Tooger knows I inherited my body type from my mother and grandmother, just like a purebred Shar-Pei resembles its doggy mommy and daddy. However, I believe Tooger when he sings the lyrics from John Legend's "All of Me" and professes to love my flaws and imperfections, including my Shar-Pei parts. As I'm writing this, I'm thinking I want to google "dog breeds" and come up with a canine that reminds me of Tooger. I know already it will have to be a playful puppy instead of a stodgy old-timer dog!

Guideline #40: Cultivate your sense of humor.

My lifelong friend, Liz, and I were catching up on the phone this week. She filled me in on the latest developments with her dear husband's health. Larry suffers from Parkinson's disease but hardly gives his Parkinson symptoms a thought because he is so distracted by a dreadful internal abscess located in the most unfortunate place you can imagine. Liz described herself as "naive" for thinking Larry's first surgery would remedy the situation. After eight months, surgery #6 was performed this week, with every operation requiring mind-boggling aftercare and wound packing from Liz, who previously was downright queasy around blood and body excretions. I noted Liz's cheerfulness and upbeat demeanor while describing distinctly distasteful medical procedures she must perform.

"Larry and I laugh a lot," Liz said, "especially at each other's quirks and how aging accentuates those traits. Humor helps us take it all in stride. We're doing well!"

Some of us never displayed much of a funny side in our first and second trimesters of life. Perhaps you are naturally serious-minded like me. My professional training required me to take many standardized tests as part of my psychology classwork. I am embarrassed to admit I took life so seriously in my younger years that a personality test at age thirty-nine showed me at the first percentile on the "playfulness scale." That means, out of every hundred people who took this test, ninety-nine scored as more "playful" than I did.

My appalling test score functioned as a huge wake-up call. I wanted to blame my nose-to-the-grindstone, no-nonsense mother as the culprit for shaping me by her example and contribution to my genetic makeup. Perhaps you also suffered with a frowning lid on the merriment and frivolity in your life's first-trimester home. I value the strong work ethic my mother bequeathed me, but I realize it came with side effects. Because my autopilot was set on responsibilities and hard work, I often didn't appreciate my husband's quirky sense of humor. All work and no play made me a serious, successful, but not dependably fun woman.

In my shock, I found myself asking the question, "What must it be like to live with someone so deadly serious?" Sure, eternal issues are at stake, but will anyone be attracted to my God if I radiate no joy? I asked family members for joke books for Christmas that year and have intentionally increased my play-appreciating side ever since. The first time I memorized a joke and related it at the dinner table, my husband and three children put down their silverware and clapped. Now I'm twenty-eight years past the emptying of my nest and far along in my third tri, and as life's challenges get tougher, I value humor, lightheartedness, and joy as God-given coping mechanisms more than ever.

Cleverly teasing about our defects and shortcomings brings people closer when it's done in a spirit of acceptance, fun, and playfulness. No mean-spiritedness allowed and no thin skins permitted. Be discerning. Don't overstep and hurt supersensitive people by joking at their expense. Mostly poke fun at yourself instead. Self-deprecating humor allows others to laugh with you, and everybody wins the humor prize.

Two of the first questions I always asked couples seeking marital counseling from me were "What character qualities caused you to fall in love with your spouse?" and "What made you want to spend the rest of your life with this person?" Their answers included being able to talk easily to their partners and possessing common values and interests. The number one response, however, especially from women, was "He made me laugh."

Although you might value humor, perhaps your husband has broken his funny bone after years of marriage, or you are divorced, widowed, or live alone. No need to despair if you have no partner or your spouse has become a sourpuss. A study found, "Individuals *laughed more frequently* following something *they themselves said* than following something said by their conversational partner anyway."[137]

The research on laughter also indicates we are *thirty times* more likely to laugh when we are *with others than alone*—one more reason to not isolate as the years pass.[138] Since laughter is essentially a social behavior, seek to rediscover humor with your husband. Be as playful as you once were when first dating. Likewise, lighten up with friends and try joking a bit with strangers such as grocery store clerks, medical personnel, landscape or cleaning helpers, and business contacts.

In addition to affectionate marital mirth, enjoy sidesplitting, uproarious times with friends, family, and strangers. Instead of always playing the same old card or board games, be brave and turn up your humor quotient by trying out some of the hilarious new games for sale online or in big box stores. Entertaining games effectively connect people across the generations.

Seek out funny movies and search for clean comedians on YouTube sites like Dry Bar Comedy. As professional funny guys and gals point out the comical side of everyday life, prime your own humor pump. Let their witty perspectives be contagious and assist you in becoming a more amusing person yourself.

We're shocked when we hear of hospital operating room hilarity, but humor works to defuse tension in even dire situations. Laughing at yourself and life's absurdities works to relieve stressful situations. Simply decide you will become a less uptight person. Laugh instead of agonizing or complaining. Who wants to play the role of a grouch or be around a grouch? Your choice!

Parallel #17: You become more aware of potential dangers, resist risk-taking, and become more cautious in the third trimester of pregnancy and in the third trimester of life.

Similar to when you were pregnant, you correctly desire to protect your precious cargo. However, you may be confused as to when risk avoidance is appropriate and when steering clear of all risks could backfire and negatively affect the mother's marriage or the one growing inside. I can think of formidable obstacles to risk-taking in life's third trimester, so let's consider their validity.

Health Reasons

Absolutely, there's legitimacy to some of the limitations we accept because of health conditions. However, work at being supremely flexible even with your health concerns. Be creative in finding ways to deal with your health problems away from home.

One of my friends has a severely diabetic spouse with a fragile heart. He needs certain routines to manage his diseases and was refusing to travel anymore. Rosalie swallowed big and pushed herself to learn how to drive a large comfortable RV, even though the thought at first seemed overwhelming. Having all his supplies available was the encouragement her husband needed to hit the road with her. A creative "can do" attitude leads to remarkable accomplishments.

Although my first husband was completely homebound with numerous insurmountable body restrictions, when my son, Daniel, called on the Fourth of July and asked, "What did you do to celebrate Independence Day?" I replied, "We went to Brazil." To be exact, Netflix streamed an episode of "1000 Places to See Before You Die" into our living room on that occasion. Chuck and I glided down the Amazon, swam with pink dolphins, drummed with stone-age tribesmen, vicariously experienced the thrills of hang gliding in Rio, hiked through snake-infested jungles, and danced the Salsa.

Since we'd traveled internationally in our first and second trimesters and during the earlier years of our third trimester, we could imagine the smells, tastes, nature sounds, and skin sensations. We basked in the adventure of discovery. Don't give up enjoying our incredible planet even if your body can't physically traverse it anymore. You can explore virtually with Planet Earth videography. You will benefit from spending time with your neighbors all over the world by watching educational and geographical programs. Instead of routinely dulling your mind with too many violent detective shows, endless Andy Griffith reruns, discouraging news programs, or sex-infested dramas, use some of your television time for nature exploration and education.

Pride

Some remain in isolation at home because they're too proud to be wheeled through an airport in a wheelchair by an airline employee. If walking long distances in concourses is no longer feasible, swallow your pride and be thankful for the wheelchair service. See the attendant as God's provision, allowing you to participate in family gatherings where you get to love and be loved.

For some proud souls, arriving at church in a wheelchair or leaning on a walker feels embarrassing. You'd rather stay home than deal with your shame about "looking old and feeble." Be creative in finding ways to cope with your health problems away from home, and decide to attend family and community events. Your participation and example will encourage others.

I Can't Do It Alone Mentality

Since statistics show many third-tri women will enjoy good health longer than their husbands, we must consider another deterrent. We must tackle the erroneous belief that we can't possibly travel "alone."

My widowed mother could have continued to enjoy time with her children and grandchildren for several more years if she hadn't believed she couldn't get on a plane by herself. She insisted she wouldn't fly unless I accompanied her. That meant paying for two extra round-trip tickets for me and reserving two rental cars. One expensive ticket and rental car was required to reach small-town Kansas where Mom lived. After reaching the Wichita or Kansas City airport, I needed to drive 200 or more miles to pick Mom up, drive back to the airport, drop off the car, and accompany her on the plane to the family destination. A second equally expensive ticket was required to accomplish the reverse journey, flying with Mom back to Kansas, dropping her off, returning to the airport, and flying home—a total of three expensive round-trip tickets and two rental cars to accomplish her visit. Money was scarce, so despite travel agents' reassurances that Mom would receive an assigned escort from plane to plane, Mother quit flying after my dad died, and she spent many lonesome hours feeling unnecessarily isolated and deserted.

Because I didn't want to duplicate my mom's travel restrictions, I was determined to fly alone if necessary, especially to visit loved ones. When I first started writing this book on my flight to Seattle years ago, I gazed down on spectacular Mt. Rainier poking through the clouds as our plane made its approach to the Seattle-Tacoma airport. I felt so blessed to anticipate a reunion with my daughter and granddaughter despite making all my family trips by myself.

Mission trips and vacation trips also possess potential for flying with friends, if your spouse can't or won't accompany you. Entities like the Smithsonian Institute, Road Scholar, Adventures Abroad, and numerous others offer fascinating travel experiences for people of all ages. Check with a travel agent or search on your computer for guided tours for seniors. Unfortunately, as the years fly past, friendship networks can fray if we don't put in the work to keep them vital, and if we don't keep adding new sisters to the mix.

My Friends Are Gone!

Like other widows who remarry and relocate, I was forced to build entirely new friendship networks. My late-in-life remarriage took me away from familiar Lexington linkages. It buoyed me during this challenging time to remember back to my first trimester of life when I'd faced my first days at summer camps. Although I initially knew no one, I soon felt accepted by brand-new pals.

A few years later, after my parents unloaded my meager belongings, kissed me goodbye, and pulled away from Kansas University, the butterflies in my stomach fluttered as I blinked back tears. My unknown roommate hadn't yet arrived on campus, and the university looked baffling in its vastness. However, I quickly created lifelong connections with former strangers, and the campus converted into a familiar and welcoming place. First-trimester friendships worked out wonderfully! Why not expect the same in a new place and stage of life now?

My daughter forged an important lasting link with another mom-to-be during the course of her childbirth classes. Those pre-baby friendships persist even though both women have recently transitioned from their second to their third trimesters of life when their daughters left for college. Do you recall involvement in social clubs or special interest groups or spiritual retreats that led to the blossoming of valued relationships when you were younger?

Identical tactics still apply when yearning to connect with people who start as strangers on your path. Don't believe secluding yourself is compulsory as you age; you needn't succumb to isolation. Take heart from remembering how previous connections developed and use loneliness-depleting strategies like the following:

- Push yourself to take the *initiative* to meet people and spend time together. Be friendly.
- Listen and express interest in others' life stories.
- Join special interest groups where you will meet like-minded people.
- Be vulnerable and open about your own journey.
- Recognize similarities.
- Take risks, knowing your invitations might be rejected.
- Celebrate and build on commonalities.
- Genuinely care, help, encourage, and seek the best for those you meet.
- Be spontaneous and get outside your comfort zone.
- If getting out of the house is not possible for you, join special interest forums on social media sites and make cyber-friends based on common hobbies and interests.

Within the friendship network you are building, adopt an enthusiastic, adventurous mindset. Let the interests of your friends expand your own activity possibilities. Authors of *Refire! Don't Retire*[139] suggest surrounding yourself with a group of friends, whether singles or couples, who have signed on to a unique agreement. Everyone in the "Last-Minute Gang" consents to join the fun if someone in the group calls and invites them at the last minute to do something. Unless you're already scheduled elsewhere, you say "Yes," get off the couch, and join them.

If your Last-Minute Gang includes individuals with diverse interests, celebrate the novelty. The academic might agree to spend an evening at a dog or garden show, while the diehard sports fan might accompany friends to a museum exhibition. Opening yourself to a variety of entertainment options exposes you to new parts of the world around you, and the shared experiences foster laughter, bonding, and the acquisition of new knowledge.[140]

Coaching Corner

1. Can you think of ways you've handled the bodily challenges of aging with grace and humor?

2. Which body changes cause you the most distress at this point in your third trimester?

3. Which suggestions from this chapter could you use this week for lessening the negative impact of your changing appearance or personal health issues?

4. Using the Premack Principle discussed in this chapter, what health-enhancing habit do you want to link to an enjoyable part of your day?

5. What could you do this week to celebrate your aging triumphs?

6. Do you remember reading in this chapter about a research study showing individuals laughed more frequently following something humorous they themselves said than following a witty comment made by their conversational partner? Will you give yourself permission to look for the comical side of life this week and entertain yourself by deliberately voicing a funny comment or two?

7. Can you identify any genuine limitations (unrelated to Covid-19) restricting your current activity level?

8. How does travel fit in your vision for your third trimester? What mindset changes or tweaks could make trips more possible for you?

9. Is there a destination you would like to add to your list of places to go and activities to enjoy? Why not schedule the first step required to embark on your future journey? If not this week, when?

10. What gathering place for potential friends are you going to commit to investigating? When?

11. Have you already met some women you would like to get to know better? How are you going to fast-forward that friendship-building process?

12. Can you think of any friends to invite to join you in a "Last Minute Gang?" What are their names? When are you going to call each one to discuss establishing this new group?

CHAPTER 13

Practice Flexibility

ONE OF THE disdainful descriptions frequently used by younger generations to put down elders is "They are so set in their ways." This description is not a compliment. Adaptability is an essential mindset mothers need to adopt as part of their identity as they age. Once you allow yourself to become inflexible, your options to enter into youth-promoting and mind-developing experiences diminish.

Guideline #41: Avoid set-in-your-ways behavior.

When grumbling grown children complain about their parents' set-in-their-ways mindsets, they are often describing a mom or dad unwilling to make the effort to travel and visit. Because their parents refuse to flex and endure some discomforts in order to get together, they leave adult offspring feeling abandoned and unloved. One example is rigidity about always sleeping in your own bed, believing you are unable to make the transition to a softer, harder, or smaller mattress because you are accustomed to a king-sized one.

Are you *stubbornly insisting* on any of the following? Check any applying to you.

- A preferred noise level (quiet guests and calm grandchildren).
- Your ideal room temperatures.
- Your partiality for particular foods or drinks to be honored.
- No one else to occupy your favorite chair.
- Your taste in music to be accepted by all generations.
- Rigid schedules for meals and bedtimes. No exceptions to bedtime at 9 p.m.
- One Bible translation only.
- Attendance at no other church but yours for even one Sunday.
- Travel to exclude airplanes or boats. You're scared of flying and won't consider a cruise, sure you'd be miserable.
- Arbitrary standards of neatness and cleanliness. (Isn't cleanliness next to godliness?)
- Always the same TV news, sports, and weather channels.
- Communication only in person or by phone (no texting, Facebook, Twitter, WhatsApp, etc.).

Rigid stances irritate people in the younger generation who must put up with set-in-their-ways family members, and rigidity also robs you of joy-filled novel experiences. Add a little spice to your life by deliberately introducing variety. Once you set your mind to it, you will be impressed with your adaptability and will start feeling more youthful. We've been adhering to laws not existing except in our own minds. I'm not advocating sin. Notice, however, the rigid stances listed above do not constitute sin-avoidance attempts. We are simply creatures of habit and elevate comfort and familiarity to higher priorities than they deserve.

Set-in-our-ways behavior and thinking tend to be more prevalent as we age. When young, most of us went with the flow and adapted easily. Arthritic aches and pains and other chronic health conditions justify some of the inflexibility, but much is in our minds. I found out I can sleep on a different pillow and with less clothes and covers and without my noise conditioner in a room that is not totally dark. I'm able to snooze with a ceiling fan whirling and the windows wide open and lying on the opposite side of the bed from where I slept for the past fifty years. I just thought I couldn't because dealing with my first husband's many health problems contributed to a set-in-our-ways mindset. Even before I was widowed, I determined to practice being more flexible and adaptable. When we move outside our comfort zones, our lives grow bigger and more fun.

Some adjustments in our third trimesters of life are due to genuine limitations. Remember, you also dealt with some real constraints and drawbacks when pregnant, especially as you moved into the last month or so. Your doctor probably restricted travel when your due date approached—no plane trips or fourteen-hour cross-country drives at Christmas that year. So how did you cope?

- You accepted the limitations as logical, even though you didn't like them.

- You found alternative ways to celebrate occasions you missed.

- You refused to feel sorry for yourself.

- You kept your eyes focused on the importance of the momentous future event to come.

- Although sometimes uncomfortable and physically miserable, you were a good sport and laughed as much as you could about some of the ridiculous situations you encountered.

- Out of love for the baby depending on you, you concentrated on the importance of staying safe and healthy.

- You coped by flexing!

Flexing remains your assignment as you now manage some genuine third-tri limitations. I can guarantee that people are depending on you to be their inspiring example as you age.

1. Accept your limitations as logical, even though you wish the constraints didn't exist.

2. Find creative ways to make up for what is restricted. Cheerfully celebrate in whatever alternative means are available to you.

3. Replace lurking self-pity with gratitude for your blessings.

4. Keep your eyes focused on Jesus, His promises, and the eternal rewards awaiting you when He calls you home on your appointed day.

5. Cultivate a keen sense of humor about your challenges.

6. Out of love, accept your limitations and practice flexibility so you can spare others from caretaking chores. Do it for the sake of those depending on you.

Unfortunately, it is possible to be a third-trimester dropout. Some pregnant teenagers quit high school and never continue their education. Akin to school dropouts, third-tri women can restrict themselves to limited mind-dumbing home environments devoid of learning opportunities. If learning and adapting to change remain top priorities, the third era of life offers thirty to fifty years of continuous development mentally, spiritually, socially, and even physically,

I admitted several sad truths as I wrote on my clipboard while flying back home from Seattle. "For thirty years, Chuck and I slept with white noise machines blocking sleep-disturbing sounds. But now, in my third trimester when I want to travel as lightly as possible and not check bags, I've discovered I'm not a slave to an anti-noise device after all. In fact, I loved the quiet peacefulness in my granddaughter's bed last night as I slept on a verdant island in Puget Sound, far from home. I could pick up the faint slap of waves on the beach and soothing insect noises, the very sounds that sleep-enhancing machines attempt to imitate.

"Another condition I used to think I couldn't abide was sleeping with light beaming through windows and shining in my eyes. I prefer a dark sleeping room with tight shutters. In earlier days, I packed safety pins to fasten motel room drapes if they allowed a sliver of light to disturb our sleep. However, in recent years I've slept staring straight up into a five-foot square skylight in Oxford, England, and in curtainless lofts in Moscow, Russia.

"Last night I slept in my granddaughter's room, adorned with iridescent stars and moons glinting from the ceiling. Her decorations reflected light shining through the open windows as the sun set near 11 p.m. and arose again at 4 a.m. during Solstice season in the Pacific Northwest. I realize it was fretting about light that kept me awake, not the light itself. As soon as I learned to relax by believing I could handle whatever brightness existed, I dozed right off.

"We can actually flow against the tide and become less stuck in our ways as we age. Every small step in the direction of flexibility, novelty, spontaneity, and adaptability is a step toward freedom and a youthful mindset. Too easily, we become the elephant still tethered by a flimsy rope to a minuscule stake. Somewhere earlier in our life journeys we became convinced we couldn't move freely and grew into prisoners of those certainties."

When I was sixty-four and writing down the lessons I was learning during my long-duration marriage to Chuck, my college sweetheart, I couldn't have predicted the number of adjustments ahead. None of us know what our future holds. After Chuck's body died, I entered a new stage of widowhood with all its accompanying alterations. Then, to my surprise, God brought an amazing widower into my life and led me to marry again, bringing yet another set of challenging changes.

Just as the early weeks of pregnancy set the stage for developments in the last trimester, our required adjustments at ages fifty, sixty, seventy, eighty, and ninety have seeds in our youth. Many shifts in geography, relationships, and lifestyles feel more manageable when we recognize how early life experiences prepared us. My recent transition to becoming a bride again, after two years of widowhood, hammer home this point.

Not that long ago, or so it seems, I was still in my first trimester of life and graduating from high school, heady with valedictorian status in my rural high school class of twenty-five kids. Looking to the future, I hungered for new adventures in a larger more sophisticated world. How eager I felt to escape the confines of my Kansas farm and upbringing. I foolishly vowed that I would never return to the "boring" existence suffered by people stuck all their lives in small towns and rural areas. Regrettably, at that pride-filled juncture, I valued little I'd experienced during my first seventeen years. Like most young folks, I had a lot to learn in the years ahead!

Jumping forward fifty-five years, I abruptly retired and closed my psychotherapy practice just two weeks before my second wedding at age seventy-two. Immediately I moved to Florida, an appealing location to most people with its mild winters amid palm trees. Unfortunately,

I despise sand, sunburns, and wearing a bathing suit. I associated the word misery with every day at the beach I'd ever endured. How would I survive the Florida lifestyle? I had no doubt my new husband was a gift from God, but concerns about sudden retirement and seashore living persisted as part of a package I still needed to unwrap and figure out.

All my previous adult life, I lived in affluent urban centers with powerful universities influencing culture and worldviews. I worked in a professional capacity for thirty years, so I grew accustomed to receiving respect as an "expert." People routinely addressed me and introduced me as Dr. Melcher. Alas, who would I be when no one called me "Doctor" and no one knew either my old or new last name nor appreciated my accomplishments? How would I fill my time when I no longer scheduled clients daily and immersed myself in their fascinating life stories?

To further complicate a world full of challenging modifications, my new husband came from Louisiana Cajun territory, a background so different from mine that passports should be required to visit. I discovered delightful, lovable sisters-in-law in Louisiana, but flooded fields full of squirming crawfish and swampy bayous bore little resemblance to familiar Kansas wheatfields or Kentucky bluegrass.

Then, after only one month of marriage, Tooger transported me to rural Indiana to dwell during the summer and fall months in a rustic hand-hewn cabin he'd expertly crafted. Our cabin overlooked the thirty-acre lake he'd built with his bulldozer on his forested farm. The spectacular scenery reminded me of vacation weeks I'd enjoyed as a child in the Ozarks and later in the Smoky Mountains of Tennessee. However, my new surroundings weren't an isolated holiday retreat. The little cabin in the big woods was to be my new home for six months every year. I had prayed to be flexible and able to adapt despite my advancing years. How would God answer such prayers?

The first inkling that God's providence extended to the adjustments I was facing came with a strong sense of déjà vu. It was as though I'd been here before—the same lightning bugs at night flashing brilliantly to attract a mate, the identical birdsongs and frog croaks, the matching hay bales in freshly mown fields that typified my childhood environment. It felt natural to mount the tractor with its huge wheels and slowly back it up, guided by Tooger's patient directions, so he could connect the tiller and turn over the garden soil for us to plant tomatoes, beans, squash, and cucumbers. The reluctant midwestern farm girl who'd arrogantly turned her back on everything rural fifty-five years prior, was now "coming home" to her beginnings. Yes, my first trimester had prepared me for my third tri.

Knowledge and skills garnered in the previous two trimesters definitely serve us well today. Maybe you find yourself a widow missing your handyman husband, but once upon a time, you served as Daddy's little helper. You know how to wield a wrench, screwdriver, drill, or hammer when circumstances require those talents. Perhaps you can look back gratefully to years shaped by 4-H or Girl Scouts, parental or other educational training. Possibly all you learned earlier in life was to call a professional. Instead of complaining, punch in the plumber's or computer geek's number! As a side benefit, you'll be performing a good deed by helping working people support their families.

Knowing you've successfully been there and done that before leads to a positive attitude toward this new season of life. I don't want you to forget a pervading theme of this book: You successfully traversed your third trimester of pregnancy. The lessons you learned, the challenges you surmounted, and the strategies you employed are available for re-cycling as you navigate similar terrain now.

Parallel #18: In both pregnancy's and life's third trimesters, fears and anxiety threaten your peace as you anticipate the unknown. Life chang-es seem unpredictable, frequently unwanted, and often ominous.

To reduce my fears about the dangers and pain of childbirth when I first anticipated Deborah's arrival on the scene fifty years ago, I got in the habit of looking at every person in my field of vision as someone whose mother had successfully given birth. As I drove down a busy highway, I told myself each of those drivers and passengers had a mother, so what I was anticipating was a common and survivable process. Yes, anxieties stalked us once upon a time when facing the reality that our baby must eventually exit our bodies.

Likewise, in life's third trimester, the reality that our bodies must exit this world looms large. We must face the truth that death happens to everyone. At every age, we seek coping mechanisms to deal with our fears. What we say to ourselves matters. Gratitude can come to our res-cue. Therefore, we will start with more on that important topic.

Embrace Gratitude

For seventy-two years, dread crept into my heart in early August be-cause the summer would soon end. The arrival of fall, usually nature's most beautiful season, was tainted because I knew winter inevitably followed. Growing up in a drafty, uninsulated farmhouse with no heat in my frigid upstairs bedroom, I shivered at night under heavy stacks of homemade quilts. Frozen daytime landscapes resulted in disastrous falls and vehicle accidents on lurking ice, taking the life of my father-in-law, maiming my mother, and causing excruciating spinal injuries plaguing my first husband for nearly forty years until the day he died. Yes, I admit to possessing winter phobia.

The broiling nature of sultry Kansas summers also left its mark on my psyche and fair-skinned body. I never tan; I only burn and peel like a snake shedding its skin.

Surges of gratitude for my new winter home in southern Florida flooded me. In formerly bone-chilling December through March, I could now safely drive to the gym, run errands, go shopping, and take my customary early morning walks. I harbored no concerns about frozen streets and slippery sidewalks ruining my plans or creating life-altering accidents. Then I'd hunker down with "inside stuff" like writing books while the sun blazed outside. No sunburns that way!

If I had not suffered with winter phobia and blistering summer sunburns in my youth, I could never have appreciated my winter and summer reprieves so fully. Comparisons with past hardships enhance our delight in the present. Because my Cajun husband's family did not possess an indoor bathroom, the privilege of using his college dorm's indoor plumbing ushered Tooger early into a valuable lifetime habit of appreciation for blessings others take for granted. A consistently grateful heart during our advancing years dovetails with peaceful acceptance of new surroundings and unforeseen circumstances.

Getting outside my comfort zone led to all kinds of satisfying discoveries and relationships through the years. Why not again now? Our third trimesters offer an abundance of changes, some unnerving, but why not decide to view change as mostly advantageous?

There may be fewer fine-dining venues, not as many glitzy entertainment opportunities, less glamorous attire, and hardly any familiar faces initially in rural Indiana, but trade-offs exist. The privilege of marveling at twinkling stars piercing the night sky over our lake and interacting with my delightful husband, spending time with my endearing new daughter-in-love and son-in-love, and meeting the new family of God around me make losses shrink in importance. Once I laid down my childhood prejudices and foolish vows, I discovered that rural life fascinates me. Abraham Lincoln is credited with observing, "Most people are about as happy as they decide to be." Even if we didn't learn that truth earlier, we're not too old to embrace it now! I recommend intentionally choosing optimism and gratitude as your new norm.

Guideline #42: Deliberately incorporate habits of gratitude daily. Reduce complaining and choose to be a thankful person instead.

Most of us avoid the unpleasant company of complainers. Unfortunately, we may be blind to the frequency of complaints spouting from our own mouths. One of the main things third-tri women gripe about is dissatisfaction with aspects of their adult kids, totally forgetting momentarily what a colossal gift each son or daughter is. Finding ways to stay focused on the blessings embedded in each child, rather than on what we'd like to be different, results in significant improvements in our outlook and in our relationships. If we manage to suppress complaining out loud, we may still be an internal complainer. Eradicating complaining is both an external and an internal battle.

Are you aware that God is offended by complainers? Moses faced a major problem as he led the Israelites toward the Promised Land. Ungrateful former slaves persistently griped about their conditions, spreading discontent and rebellion in the camp. The disgruntled Israelites claimed they would rather live as oppressed mistreated slaves in Egypt where they could eat cucumbers, leeks, and meat instead of life-sustaining manna. They repeatedly whined and groused to each other about Moses and complained to God about His choice of leaders.

God eventually had enough of their griping and lack of appreciation. They ignored the miraculous ways He had orchestrated their escape from slavery and provided for them in the wilderness. In his anger, God sent quail to the tune of fifty bushels per person. As the Israelites gorged on the meat they'd insisted upon, a plague broke out, killing thousands who had complained the loudest.

Positive psychology researcher Robert Emmons, in his outstanding book, *Thanks: How the New Science of Gratitude Can Make You Happier,* found people reported 40 percent more personal well-being if they simply wrote down four things for which they were grateful each day.[141] As I recommended in Chapter 9, try embracing Emmons' prescription to record four unique thanks-worthy occurrences every day, and make one expression of gratitude relevant to an aspect of your offspring, and then add one pertaining to your spouse. Your sense of contentment in motherhood and marriage will both benefit from replacing a complaining mindset with gratitude.

A thankfulness habit, resulting in the reduction of complaints and an increase in gratitude to God and other benefactors, serves women well during all three trimesters. During several seasons of my life, I've made intentional efforts to foster gratitude. I remember commandeering a two-by-three-foot piece of poster board left over from one of my kids' school projects. I taped it to the inside of the door shutting off the master bedroom commode from the rest of the bathroom. I attached the poster board to the bathroom door at a time in my second trimester when I knew I needed to focus on my blessings, not my trials. When I privately made use of that tiny room, I often scribbled something wor-thy of gratitude on the large cardboard canvas. I discovered it was im-possible to feel sorry for myself when staring at a whole poster board covered with thanks-worthy items.

More recently in my third trimester of life, I purchased a lined diary to create a *Perpetual Gratitude Journal*. I reserve this book for recording ordinary and extraordinary occurrences in my life for which I choose to be thankful. Several days of the month, I jot down three or four happenings, circumstances, or blessings, numbering them sequen-tially as I add each new grateful thought.

Soon my continually expanding list numbered in the hundreds, and room exists for thousands. This gratitude list can reflect your indi-vidual personality. Mine is uniquely idiosyncratic and eccentric. Don't just write, *I'm grateful for my daughter*. Be specific on fifty different days this year about fifty different ways she's a blessing.

Parallel #19: Whether during pregnancy or during life's third tri, physical challenges make you more dependent on your spouse, your children, and your community, resulting in diminished self-esteem and feelings of being misunderstood or harshly judged.

A few weeks of reduced contributions to the family workload, such as happen during pregnancy's brief last trimester, pale compared to long-du-ration or permanent handicaps sometimes occurring during the third tri-mester of life. We've prayed we could keep our independence and not need caretaking from our spouse, family, or friends. We hate it when we discover we are not exempt from bodily trials. Somehow it seems surreal.

Recently, while my third-trimester friend Judy was stopped at a traffic light, she was rear-ended by an unlicensed driver in a car careening at fifty mph. Judy and her husband were leadership types, committed go-getters, busily working to change public policy to benefit families in the state of Kentucky. I use the past tense "were" because Judy no longer possesses the same capabilities after the car crash to speak eloquently before state lawmakers or travel the state lobbying for pro-family legislation. What a huge adjustment to lose part of your talents from brain and spinal trauma! The high-level executive function required for Judy to be effective at The Family Foundation diminished in a second. Fortunately, Judy retains her caring, lovable personality and continues to pursue new ways to glorify God.

Recovering from accidents and dealing with medical interventions required by accidents, illnesses, or surgeries is frequently hard, painful, exhausting work. It can seem the only one applauding your diligent efforts is your physical therapist. Most people in your circle go on with their lives, leaving you behind. They may even subtly convey you are a nuisance if you require their time, assistance, or attention. Self-esteem plummets because you no longer show evidence of being the achiever you once were, and you sense you aren't worth as much to other people because you have less to contribute.

Relationship aspects frequently complicate the physical pain and psychological aftermath of life-altering accidents or illnesses. None of us would choose to be physically diminished by diseases or accidents. We certainly don't want to burden folks we love.

Most hurtful are the judgments. Some think you could be getting better faster if you would work on your physical therapy exercises harder. Others maintain you should try a different approach, a different physician, take more or less supplements, consume a different diet, etc. It is possible they are correct. Still, you know you are doing the best you can with the body you inhabit and with the information you possess right now. Reduced to its ugly core, you feel judged and unfairly criticized for being old and ill and for interfering with others' busy lives. The healthy younger generations and judgmental peers who haven't walked in your house slippers yet will eventually get their turn, but how can we handle their critical spirits and lack of caring and remain peaceful?

Guideline #43: Employ strategies to keep yourself serene when feeling misunderstood and unjustly judged because of your age and body limitations.

- Sometimes we get stuck with critical family members. However, if possible, avoid judgmental folks and seek out encouragers.

- Consider saying "Ouch," when a person stabs your heart with a critical comment. Just utter that one word. Most folks are not intending to cause pain, but they are prone to perfectionism and critical spirits. "Ouch" is a low-offense way to get your message across to them when their implied or direct criticism stings.

- If you feel neglected by folks you thought would care about your physical challenges, send a text and show interest in their lives and activities. In this day and time, Americans are generally a self-absorbed bunch and your attempt to connect will remind them you are alive and care about them. Perhaps they will respond in kind.

- Don't spend your time pining away for some specific person to treat you differently and miss seeing the caring, thoughtful ones under your nose. They are God's gifts to you.

- Avoid being a copycat. Don't let the criticism of others turn you into a person critical of them. Be an encourager, even to your critics.

- Determine to reduce your own tendencies to be judgmental of others, both inward thoughts about particular people in your life and voiced comments about individuals. Sometimes a critical spirit manifests itself in gossipy tidbits shared with others. Like you, most people are doing about the best they can with what they know at the time.

- Repent of your own neglectful and judgmental attitudes toward sick or elderly people in the past. Ask God for forgiveness. If possible, ask individuals you handled poorly in their time of need to forgive you.

- Go to God's book to get assurance you are a beloved and worthy person, whether sick or well, young or old.

Little did I know when I chose my life verse in 2020, how much I would need its serene perspective to handle the Covid-19 pandemic, a broken hip, kidney stones, eight months of urinary tract infections, cataract surgery, political upheaval, divisions, and violence. How reassuring to repeat verses from a psalm sung on the Sabbath, going clear back to the time of King David, "Even in old age they will still produce fruit; they will remain vital and green. They will declare, 'The Lord is just! He is my rock! There is no evil in him!'"[142]

Adopt peaceful self-talk. Listen to Paul's advice, "Fix your thoughts on what is true, and honorable, and right, and pure, and lovely, and admirable. Think about things that are excellent and worthy of praise. Keep putting into practice all you learned and received from me—everything you heard from me and saw me doing. Then the God of peace will be with you."[143]

Express abundant gratitude to all the people giving you support and encouragement. Most of us are blessed with one or more compassionate family members or friends. Tell them often and clearly how grateful you are for their generosity, caring, and helping. Pray for God to bless them. See if you can find ways to "give back" in small, meaningful ways.

Coaching Corner

1. Would your adult children consider you "set in your ways?" What evidence do they have for their opinion?

2. Would you like to give up some of your requirements that confine you to a "set in your ways" lifestyle?

3. What is one of those rigid limitations you want to practice letting go of this week?

4. This chapter emphasizes the advantages of flexibility as you age. Which areas of your life would benefit from more flexibility?

5. Can you recall instances in previous life trimesters when you successfully adjusted to major changes in your life? Could you use any of the same strategies to make adjustments now?

6. Considering that some of your limitations may be unavoidable, which of the six coping methods in this chapter might help you deal with them better?

7. Do you allow yourself to complain internally or externally re: your adult children? Do you desire to eradicate your

complaining tendencies? What would it take on your part to do so?

8. Do you have any tendencies toward self-pity? If yes, what one strategy from this chapter will you employ to turn yourself into a more thankful person?

9. What would be required for you to start keeping a Perpetual Gratitude Journal? Will you do it this week? Why or why not?

10. Do you feel judged by younger members of your family for your age and physical limitations? Do you think they understand and care about your challenges?

11. What strategies can you use when you feel criticized and misunderstood by your critics? Circle two in the list of strategies in Chapter 13 that you intend to use to deal with this problem, beginning today.

CHAPTER 14

❧

What's Next?

WHILE MY THOUGHTS were first percolating about the empty nest era of life, I happened to be viewing early episodes of "The Bible" mini-series on TV. Because I was newly sensitized to life stages, I noticed the surprising maturity of many significant biblical characters when they were playing important roles in God's plan. These were no spring chickens.

– Sarah was ninety years old, and Abraham was a hundred when the Lord delivered the news that Sarah would bear a son. Sarah couldn't keep herself from laughing at the preposterousness of such a prediction.

– Noah worked for a hundred twenty years building the ark and was six hundred years old when the flood came.

– Moses was eighty when he began leading the Israelites out of Egypt.

– After Daniel was deported to Babylon as a teenager, he lived during the reigns of three powerful kings. Daniel was probably between sixty and eighty years old when King Darius threw him in the lion's den.

As discussed back in Chapter 2, cultural myths about the superiority of youth and the mandatory marginalization of anyone past age sixty or seventy proliferate in American society. In contrast, God seems to have reserved some of His meatiest assignments for selected seasoned individuals who have lived long enough to accumulate extensive life experience.

It tickled me to hear Benedictine nun Joan Chittister confess in her perceptive book, *The Gift of Years*, what she considers to be her most likely flaw as an author. "I may be too young to write it. I am, after all, only seventy."[144] Chittister's insightful views on aging grow out of her belief that each season of life has its own purpose. "This later one gives me the time to assimilate all the others. The task of this period . . . is to come alive in ways I have never been alive before."[145] Chittister urges her readers to resist the temptation to succumb prematurely to "enforced uselessness," and instead to probe for ways to make these the "capstone" years.

Gail Sheehy, a prolific researcher and best-selling author of books on life's passages, declares, "*As we grow older, we become less and less alike.* The consequences of genes, gender, race, class, marital status, income, and preventive health care (or carelessness) all pile up. But while our genes largely determine our health status and longevity, this holds true only until we reach sixty or sixty-five. After that . . . *it is our psychological attitude and behavior that more likely determine the quality and duration of our third age.* . . . Successful aging must be a *conscious choice* with a commitment to continuing self-education and the development of a whole set of strategies."[146]

Yes, life is about the choices we make all along the way. Fortunately, our past years of experience provide equipping value as we contemplate lessons learned from good and bad choices we've made and observed others make. How lovely to be able to rejoice that we are "older and wiser" now. We want to assimilate all we've learned and come alive in new ways, successfully turning our remaining years into our "capstone" years, as Chittister urges.[147]

All the mothers you've met in this book are ordinary fallible women, but they possess extraordinary potential to be far more "fertile" than a youth-worshipping culture would predict. Even after the nest empties, God calls us to be fruitful and multiply in continuing ways. Since traveling through this third era of life is not optional, it makes sense to continually recommit to "self-education and the development of a whole set of strategies."[148]

Parallel #20: Pregnant women clearly recognize they are "called" to motherhood. In life's third trimester, we seek clarity as God calls us to new chapters and revised identities. We long to know, "What's next?"

The "What's next?" question burns in the heart of every empty-nest mother until a clear direction emerges. For almost four hundred years, the Westminster Catechism has provided a concise answer to the purpose part of the conundrum. The Catechism asserts, "Man's chief end is to glorify God and to enjoy Him forever."[149]

"Glorify" is a puzzling concept to many people. Rick Warren captures the essence of the word in the opening sentence of his blockbuster book, *The Purpose Driven Life,* when he clarifies, "It's not about you."[150] Rather, our purpose is to fulfill God's purposes. That's how we glorify Him.

Johann Sebastian Bach, the genius master musician who wrote music that flowed so eloquently from his soul, composed 256 cantatas. Mark and Parker Batterson, inspirational authors of *All In,* identify the all-consuming purpose motivating Bach, "When he would finish a composition, he wrote three letters in the margin of his music: SDG. Those three letters stood for the Latin phrase, *Soli Deo Gloria—to the glory of God alone.* His life was a unique translation of that singular intention to give only God glory. So is yours. No one can glorify God *like you* or *for you.* Your life is an original score!"[151]

A coaching textbook uses secular terminology to describe purpose. "Life purpose is the reason we are on this planet. . . . When clients are 'on purpose' they are fulfilled. They are contributing and making a difference. When they are not on purpose, they feel discontented and unfulfilled."[152]

How can we accomplish our purpose and identify new callings once our children are grown and gone? So much of our time and attention have been directed toward fulfilling the call on our lives as mothers, but suddenly there is a vacuum. It nags at us. We don't want to fritter away the rest of our lives in superficial ways. We want meaning. We want our lives to count for something. We were passionate about parenting. However, just when we feel we've learned a few things and accumulated a bit of wisdom, we see no outlet for our passions.

Why has God arranged for so many of us to survive for extra decades beyond what has occurred ever before in history? Is it possible God wants to call a multitude of empty-nest mothers to eternally important service? Statisticians believe "More than half of all people who have ever lived to the age of sixty-five or more are alive on the earth today."[153] The majority of these are female. I can't help but think God is up to something requiring mature women.

It is common to think of pastors as having been *called* to the ministry. We assume some sort of encounter with God helped them know they should follow a path toward the pastorate. Has it occurred to you that God has been orchestrating encounters with you and calling you to distinct work during this third-tri season? Your mission may be related to how you fulfilled your purpose in your first and second trimesters, or it could be an expanded, revised, or an entirely new calling. He may call you to different aspects in each of the decades comprising your third trimester. In the following paragraphs, I will lay out how God has fine-tuned my own callings over many decades.

My clients internalize insights they embrace in my counseling room far better when a picture or object anchors their self-discoveries. This "a picture is worth a thousand words" concept fueled my decision to enlarge and frame a photograph I found while looking through an old family scrapbook. Since I was born during World War II when the government was rationing film, hardly any photos exist from my pre-school years. However, I discovered a tiny three by three-inch square depicting me sitting on the overgrown lawn in front of our farmhouse, smiling broadly in a striped pinafore. Underneath the photo, my mother had scrawled "Eighteen months." I am sitting with the spread-eagle

stance of a toddler teetering precariously. The unusual feature was my pudgy right arm lifted straight up toward the sky. My index finger pointed determinedly toward the heavens. Mother said I was singing "This Little Light of Mine."

When gazing at that minuscule photo, I realized the snapshot captured the essence of who God made me to be. From my earliest days, God designed me to be a little light pointing to Him. Illuminating His existence is the distinctive work God assigned to me. Years of hiding His light under a bushel basket followed, and Satan has certainly tried to "whoof it out!" However, my Father's plan has always been to let His light shine through me, pointing others to God and bringing attention to Him.

I not only know my purpose; I have pictures of it! When I was still a practicing therapist, I hung a framed enlargement of my old scrapbook photo on my counseling room wall, visible to me over the heads of my hurting clients. Now I display an identical copy on my Indiana desk near my computer where I am writing this book. Another enlargement is perched on my office desk in Florida, where I also write and blog. The framed photos serve as reminders of the "point and shine" mindset I need to keep during the many hours I spend in those spaces fulfilling my purpose and pursuing my callings.

You will notice I differentiate between my *purpose* and my *callings*. My eighteen-month-old index finger pointing heavenward defines my purpose, but I have lived out that lifelong *purpose* differently in various stages of my life as my *callings* changed.

When I was still a college student in my first trimester of life, God "called" me to involvement with college students as a staff member of Cru, working to fulfill Jesus' Great Commission[154] with Cru's "win, build and send" strategy.

During the nineteen years I worked with women on university campuses and in churches, one specific biblical passage addressed to "older women" remained on my bulletin board. Because I internalized Titus 2:3-5, I sought to implement Paul's instructions to me as an older woman to honor God myself, but also to teach and train young wives and mothers to honor God, love their children, and respect their husbands. These verses have served as a scriptural "call on my life" for over fifty years now.

I was only twenty-one years old when I embraced my calling as an "older" woman, although I actually was just slightly older than the college girls I mentored. As I look back on years of ministry, I gravitated toward teaching women going through a phase of life I had just completed or one I was simultaneously experiencing. I qualified as an "older woman" when I was twenty-one, and I still occupy that designation at age seventy-six.

The opportunity to fulfill my purpose (pointing people to Jesus) continued into my second trimester when I added "mother to Deborah, David, and Daniel" as my primary calling. I envisioned motherhood as most important of all my callings; I intensely desired to be a loving, nurturing light pointing my own three to Jesus.

Midway through my child-rearing years, I felt drawn by the Holy Spirit to equip myself for an additional calling. I enrolled in the University of Kentucky graduate program to prepare myself to help people with mental health problems and family relationship issues. I desired to provide a Christian perspective in a generally secular field. My calling was fueled by all the life stories I heard from discouraged young adults on university campuses, from women in Bible studies I taught, from couples struggling to make their marriages work, and from moms desiring to parent well.

My new calling required seven years of postgraduate studies and internships before earning my dual licensure as a psychologist and a marriage and family therapist. Once my nest completely emptied, I threw myself fully into my calling as a Christian counselor. For thirty years, I relished serving as Clinical Director of Focus on Relationships, Inc., a nonprofit counseling center my husband and I founded.

As I moved through my sixties, I experienced yet another shift. I increasingly focused on training to become a life coach and spiritual director. I felt less drawn to work with people suffering from mental health disorders and diagnoses associated with the medical model. The people I now most wanted to help were not mentally ill, but they were going through transitions and struggling with ordinary life challenges. As the years passed, my heart for women with family-of-origin issues, spiritual confusion, marital discord, and adult child dilemmas grew. The best substance abuse counselors have usually struggled to overcome addictions themselves. Similarly, I found myself assisting women just a step or two behind me in their relationship recoveries.

Way back in my thirties, when I started work on my Ph.D., I felt God wanted me to be a writer "someday." I'd majored in Language Arts as an undergraduate, but I believed I might attract more readers if I possessed a few alphabet letters of endorsement after my name. God knew I also needed to go through the crucible of life experiences to acquire enough wisdom to be able to help anyone else. I view writing this book as a third-tri fulfilment of my life purpose and early life callings.

Marc Freeman, founder and CEO of Encore.org, a nonprofit focused on mobilizing the talents and experiences of older people, says, "Life can have multiple chapters, and it's possible to do the work that we're proudest of in a period that used to be the left-over years."[155]

Encore.org offers monetary "purpose prizes" to people using their senior years to benefit their communities and beyond. Laurie Ahern, a former journalist, age sixty-one, received one of the awards. Ahern spent her last decade exposing inhumane treatment of young people, particularly disabled ones in orphanages, and she exposed the outrage of autistic children kept in cages. As a professional journalist in her younger years, Ahern possessed the necessary report-writing expertise to spur the U.N. to deem such abuses as torture.[156]

Another among the more than five hundred Purpose Prize honorees is Belle Mickelson (sixty-seven), a one-time science teacher who followed her later-in-life calling to become an Episcopal priest. As Mickelson aged, she enlisted Native Alaskan elders to join her efforts to lower rates of suicide, domestic violence, and sexual assault among isolated Alaskan young people through launching a "Dancing with the Spirit" program.[157]

Still another prize winner, Patricia Hinnen, sixty-two, spearheaded endeavors in her venture capital group, Capital Sisters International, to raise $15 million and generate one hundred fifty thousand microloans to women in developing countries.[158]

On a much smaller scale, I felt called in 2020 to commission an orphan home to be built in Tanzania. A Tanzanian young couple, Emmanuel and Peris, recently moved into the now completed "Melcher House" as parents. This development gives me a second chance to be an adoptive "grandmother" of sorts. I provide funds and encouragement from America while Emmanuel and Peris love and nurture ten orphan children, along with their biological toddler son. The kids were rescued from the streets and from abject poverty. Now they are incorporated into a loving family. They will be taught to sing songs like "This Little Light of Mine," just as I once did. I pray these "sons and daughters" will mature into men and women of God, following God's common purpose for all of our lives to glorify Him.

Emmanuel and Peris made commitments to work together in this African compound with nine other families raising orphans in nine similarly well-equipped houses. The ten parents in this community will nurture 120 children until these adopted sons and daughters are eventually grown, educated, and ready to start their own families.

The next building project will be a school for the kids living in the compound and nearby villages. In America, the sponsoring non-profit group is incorporated as "Remember the Children." In Tanzania, the sponsoring organization is called "Eternal Families." This venture, my newest calling, is a chance to shine my tiny light and pass the faith baton to another generation (in Africa this time), while enlarging my own eternal family.

Many third-trimester women who hear God's later-in-life callings discover that their natural gifts, previous training, and enjoyable hobbies coincide with needs locally and globally. My two widowed sisters-in-law, ages eighty and eighty-seven, transformed an unused section of their church's educational wing into a sewing center, well-stocked with sewing machines, a giant cutting table, fabric, and notions. Five widows meet there four days a week to sew clothing for Tanzanian and Haitian orphans supported by the many Smith family brothers and sisters.

Sometimes the widows quilt beautiful baby comforters to delight expectant moms who've made the choice to forego abortions. Their creations win blue ribbons at the county fair and then are shipped from Louisiana to children all around the world. In the process, these fun-loving widows live out their Dorcas-like callings, support each other emotionally after their bereavements, and build bonds of love.

Some third-tri women, like newly divorced and nearly bankrupt Carol Gardner, start new businesses. Because money was scarce at age fifty-two, Carol seized a chance to win free dog food for Zelda, her English bulldog, by entering a local pet store's Christmas card contest.

She submitted a photo of her pet in a Santa hat and beard. Winning the contest spurred Carol to begin sewing costumes for Zelda, snapping photos, and writing clever captions to put on greeting cards and posters. Carol's pet-themed creations propelled her appearance on "Good Morning America," resulting in nationwide exposure. Twenty-five years later, "Zelda Wisdom" has become a global multimillion-dollar brand selling calendars, books, clothing, jewelry, and household accessories for eighty-two-year-old Carol Gardner. "If I can accomplish all this just by dressing my dog," she quips, "imagine what *you* can do."[159]

Most of us will earn no earthly prizes nor accrue big financial returns for answering later-in-life calls to join the Lord in His work. On a personal and community level, however, the impact can be substantial. I watched Leslie (age sixty-seven) recycle her years spent caring for ailing family members into a new direction once her parents died. She parlayed her hard-earned knowledge into becoming a caring hospital chaplain and empathic grief counselor to mourning families in her church.

Tracy (age sixty-nine), a physical therapist and cancer survivor, offers free nutritional counseling to church members and to those ravaged by debilitating diseases. She recognizes suffering people are killing themselves consuming the standard American diet (SAD). Her extensive research during her own recovery from breast cancer provided information she now uses to educate others. Her support and encouragement help others learn to feed their bodies with the best fuel to successfully heal.

Kate (age seventy-one), a former homeschooling mom and county home extension agent, volunteers three mornings a week to patiently teach underprivileged children how to read and understand basic math concepts. Then, using her landscaping skills as a Master Gardener, Kate goes home and tends to an arboretum she created out of her postage

WHAT'S NEXT? | 267

stamp-sized backyard. The porch overlooking her garden provides the perfect setting for chatting with friends she's met through various community groups. In Kate's backyard oasis, women talk together about life issues, including worries about adult children.

In my circle of third-tri sisters, creative implementation of late-life callings abounds:

- Supporting and encouraging orphans, missionaries, and native evangelists
- Using talents to promote worthy political candidates and causes
- Staffing charity thrift shops
- Feeding the hungry through community kitchens and food pantries
- Renting out unused rooms to struggling college, seminary, or medical students
- Teaching English as a second language
- Hosting or mentoring refugee families
- Knitting shawls and lap blankets for the ill
- Assisting Cru staff members on American or foreign campuses
- Becoming foster parents

- Offering rides to doctor appointments
- Bringing meals to post-operative patients
- Mentoring young couples in the church
- Hosting neighborhood book clubs to discuss inspirational books
- Providing respite breaks for caretakers
- Developing blogs to share wisdom in personal areas of expertise
- Playing hymns on the piano and singing at local nursing homes
- Authoring novels with thought-provoking themes
- Bringing pets to visit children in hospitals or lonely nursing home residents

- Volunteering at pregnancy help centers
- Inviting international students for holiday meals
- Raising grandchildren when their parents are unable
- Walking alongside those recovering from substance abuse
- Leading Bible studies with female jail inmates
- Housing pregnant teenagers
- Fighting human trafficking
- Tutoring struggling students
- Engaging in political action that promotes family values

So many opportunities exist to participate in meaningful ways. Maybe you mainly feel called to dedicate yourself to large-scale involvement with your grandchildren. What a blessing and privilege for adults and kids alike! Other third-tri moms live out their purpose by finding and pursuing God-glorifying endeavors unconnected to their relatives. Discovering your calling at each stage of your third trimester journey becomes an exhilarating adventure. Authors such as Rick Warren, author of *The Purpose Driven Life: What on Earth Am I Here For*, allude to common elements that come together in most callings.[160]

- God speaking to your heart persistently
- A need in the world
- Life experience preparation and gifting
- A recognition that we aren't able to accomplish the call without God's help
- A willingness to respond in faith
- The Holy Spirit pours in and empowers us.
- Others are enlisted and become part of fulfilling your calling.

This chapter's Coaching Corner will include exercises to help you ascertain your unique purpose and how God may be calling you to fulfill that purpose. As you undertake adventurous new callings today and tomorrow, you develop a clearer grasp of your life legacy.

Coaching Corner

1. Do you agree or disagree with Rick Warren's portrayal of purpose as "not about you." Why or why not?

2. Have you considered the possibility that your third trimester can usher in your *capstone* years, as Joan Chittister maintains? What would it take for you to believe that?

3. What conscious choices, as described by Gail Sheehy, would aid you in aging successfully?

4. Have you already made any choices that fall into the category of *doing the work you're proudest of in a period that used to be the leftover years?* (Marc Freeman) What are some of those choices?

5. What resources, skills, hobbies, and life experiences could you invest in fulfilling new callings during your third tri?

6. Below are A to Z examples of life purpose statements inspired by *Co-Active Coaching: New Skills for Coaching People Toward Success in Work and Life*.[161] You will notice these are similar to my revelation that I am a little light pointing to Jesus. Which ones resonate with you most?

   a. I am a hand to hold when little/old/grieving/sick people are lonely, scared, or lost.

b. I am dynamite that shakes people up and transforms their lives.

c. I am a rock in the shoe that causes people to notice suffering in the world.

d. I am an alarm clock that awakens people to their need for Christ.

e. I am a lighthouse that guides people to their dreams.

f. I am a soup pot that feeds the poor and hungry.

g. I am a thumbtack that gets people out of their comfortable seats and happily serving God and others.

h. I am a warrior who battles and intercedes for God's mercy and healing and for His will to be done.

i. I am a golden retriever who provides unconditional love, hugs, snuggles, and giggles.

j. I am a trumpet announcing the need to be ready for Christ's return.

k. I am a lap for children to climb onto and feel loved.

l. I am a follower walking in the footprints of the Rabbi, teaching what He teaches me to those who follow me.

m. I am Jesus' checkbook to support the spread of the Gospel throughout the world.

n. I am a mirror reflecting the love, compassion, and forgiveness of God.

o. I am an open door welcoming strangers into warm hospitality and belonging.

p. I am a paperclip connecting people to each other.

q. I am an artist who opens people's eyes to see evidence of the Creator.

r. I am a middleman passing on God's resources to those who need them.

s. I am a dispenser of trophies to survivors of trauma.

t. I am a tree to lean against as I provide shade to people from life's scorching rays.

u. I am an escape hatch providing a way out for people imprisoned by addictions.

v. I am a hearing aid listening to people tell their stories without fear of judgment.

w. I am a pitcher pouring out water for the thirsty.

x. I am a tambourine leading people to thank and praise the Lord.

y. I am a warm blanket when people are shivering in the damp cold dark night.

z. I am a bullhorn broadcasting danger and announcing the way to safety.

7. Jesus used many metaphors to describe Himself in the New Testament. For example, Christ referred to Himself as the gate to a sheepfold, the bread of life, the lamb of God, the light of the world, the good shepherd, a grapevine, and living water. John the Baptist called himself a voice crying in the wilderness. Jesus challenged Peter, Andrew, James, and John to be "fishers of men." What would it take to get alone with God this week and ask Him to reveal your personal life met-

aphor and create your own unique purpose statement? You can use the following general format suggested in *Co-Active Coaching*[162] or phrase your purpose in any way God lays on your heart.

8. I am a _____

_____ (metaphor)

so that people _____

_____ (impact statement).

9. Which photo, piece of artwork, song lyrics, or Scripture passage could anchor God's purpose for you? Where can you look for more anchors to inspire you?

10. Construct a timeline identifying the life callings that you now recognize have characterized your life? Add any present-day callings you have not yet acted upon, but still anticipate. Where do they fit on your timeline?

11. The last of the seven elements listed as coming together in a person's call is as follows: "Others are enlisted and become part of fulfilling your calling." What names come to mind when you think about discussing your life purpose and callings with others? Whom could you enlist to join you in answering God's call?

CHAPTER 15

Your Choice: Celebration or Mourning

SINCE I AM writing a book for women, and we all grew up enjoying fairy tales and love stories, I hope you let yourself identify with the protagonist, Princess Promise, in the allegory that follows. Whether framing the "Greatest Story Ever Told" as a groom heartsick for his bride or picturing a heartbroken father yearning for his prodigal child to come home, the Bible is, at its essence, a love story. Unconditional love is also at the core of this fable about Princess Promise.

The Tale of Princess Promise

Once upon a time, there was a beautiful princess named Promise born in the faraway kingdom of Desire Land. The wide Desire River undulated throughout the empire, irrigating the crops and watering the glorious realm. Lush meadows, flourishing animals, and gorgeous multicolored flowers surrounded the sweet young princess.

From her earliest days, Princess Promise heard stories from her parents, the king and queen, about the brave handsome prince they hoped she would meet someday and then marry. Arrangements had been made, they said, and on an appointed day in the future, noble Prince Perfect would arrive astride a powerful stallion to carry Princess Promise away to live happily ever after.

As a child, Promise was fascinated by these stories and imagined her hero riding a black charger like the one pictured in her treasured *Black Beauty* book. In Promise's mind, the prince's eyes flashed with fire and his muscles rippled with strength and virility. His long blond hair blew in the wind and contrasted with the purple princely robe she envisioned him wearing as a symbol of his future kingship.

Unfortunately, after a few years passed, Desire Land experienced a terrible drought and famine, reducing the royal family to poverty. Desire River dried up. Princess Promise no longer daydreamed about the dashing hero, the one her parents claimed was destined to love and rescue their young damsel in distress. Promise didn't want to depend on a someday prince. Instead, she was determined to make her life better by satisfying her desires right now.

Despite the king's and queen's objections, Promise occupied herself scrounging in garbage heaps for extra morsels of food. Then she began to sell her body to lust-filled men for a few trinkets or money to spend on luxuries. Later, when the drought abated, Promise gave her attention to rebuilding the castle's food stores and acquiring extravagant furnishings. More and more, the princess focused on accumulating a splendid wardrobe to replace her tattered gowns.

Promise was determined to resume her elevated princess status, so she pressured the aging king to increase taxes on his overburdened subjects. The princess delighted in parading down the streets while onlookers admired her beauty and fabulous frocks. She dedicated all her time to satisfying her desires and impressing others.

Unfortunately, Promise was embarrassed now, after tarnishing her reputation in the earlier drought years with choices she wished she had not made. In her pursuit of redemption and marital happiness, Princess Promise spent endless hours managing her image and appearing desirable to the eligible men in the land. No flirtation, no possession, no civic involvement, no ball gown, no sumptuous food, no sparkling wine, no bank account seemed enough to satisfy, however. The princess desired more!

In desperation, Promise agreed to accept the marriage proposal of a wealthy man in faraway Lost Land, even though her suitor was thirty years her senior and repugnant in multiple ways. She knew the prince of Lost Land was ugly and corrupt, but he was also very, very rich. He promised she would one day be the queen of Lost Land!

It had been years since Promise had believed, or even thought about, her parents' stories describing the noble prince to whom she had been betrothed since birth. Princess Promise traded her childhood dreams of a someday prince for a life marked by moral compromise, accumulation of things, self-reliance, and self-promotion.

While trudging glumly in her shimmering wedding dress down the rose-strewn path in the castle garden to exchange vows with a man she did not love or respect, Promise felt regret welling up. Because her weeping father, the king, had refused to give his daughter's hand in marriage to such a wicked man as the evil prince of Lost Land, Promise took each hesitating step alone. While she slowly marched toward her waiting groom, troubling thoughts plagued her mind. Swept by conflicting emotions, Promise faced the disturbing reality that her compromises and self-centered choices had been foolish, awful mistakes. Was it too late to reverse her course and flee in the opposite direction, away from the evil master of Lost Land, away from living unhappily ever after with a vile, corrupt husband?

Although she felt trapped and afraid, Promise recognized with piercing clarity that she must make the right choice then and there. While the orchestra continued to play the wedding march, Promise hesitated in her promenade. Then she deliberately turned around and ran in the opposite direction from the waiting Lost Land prince.

Suddenly, Princess Promise heard deafening, thundering hoofbeats. Peeking out from under her veil, Promise was shocked to behold the most magnificent man she'd ever seen. To her amazement, a glistening jeweled crown topped his mass of chocolate-brown curls, and a gold-trimmed dazzling white robe reflected the sun. Tall, lean, and muscular, this splendid man was mounted on a powerful white stallion. Forcefully reining in his steed, Prince Perfect jumped to the ground, kneeled before Promise, and held out a magnificent diamond-encrusted tiara.

His words were earnest and tender. "I've come for you, my darling. I want you to be my beautiful beloved bride, to have and to hold forever. Will you marry me today?"

Promise stammered, "But I was expecting a black horse and purple robes and blond hair. I've scarcely thought about you since I was a young girl when I first imagined you looking splendid and noble. As time went by, I dismissed my attraction to you as childish and rejected my parents' stories about your perfection as mere fairy tales. I embraced the dark path and never even explored the path of light once I became an adult. I gave my body to other men and squandered my affection on material things. I've been so foolish! How could someone as flawless and faithful as you want me after I've ignored your existence and pursued the dark side?"

Falling face down, Princess Promise wept until her tears trickled on the prince's nail-pierced feet. She said, "I am so ashamed. How could you possibly forgive and love someone like me?"

"Rise, my darling," he whispered. The dazzling white-robed prince lifted the tear-streaked repentant princess to her feet, embracing her with his strong protective arms. Then gazing deeply into her soul with His piercing dark eyes, the prince gently removed her veil and tenderly positioned the glittering crown atop her long wavy locks.

"You don't understand, my dear Princess Promise," Prince Perfect assured his bride. "I knew all along you would need to be rescued from the dark path, from tainted desires, and from the evil prince of Lost Land. I have been preparing for this moment, the instant when you would turn from darkness and accept me as your lover and future King so I could save you from a life of everlasting regret and mourning. Now we both can be clothed in light and white. You must know, my beloved, I will always keep my promise."

And they lived happily ever after!

Contemplating the Inevitable

My purpose in composing the allegory, "The Tale of Princess Promise," is to highlight a groom's devotion and faithful love for his bride as we consider two more similarities:

Parallel #21: Whether in pregnancy or in life, the third trimester ends in either celebration or mourning.

For many of you, the happiest most love-filled moment of your life occurred when your newborn was laid in your arms. The rigors of pregnancy and the agony of childbirth faded when you held your infant son or daughter close to your chest and love exploded in your heart. What a joyful, awe-filled celebration of your pregnancy's termination!

Sadly, not every pregnancy's third trimester ends with celebrating a healthy baby, nor even an alive one. Only those who have experienced a miscarriage or late-term stillbirth, or those who have held tiny ones for only minutes before their immature lungs or hearts gave out, fully understand the pain and inconsolable grief of losing a baby when you so much wanted life together. My heart breaks writing this because the grieving never stops for bereaved mothers. No one wants that kind of devastating ending to their third trimester of pregnancy. Neither do women in life's third trimester want everlasting mourning to follow their body's eventual death.

Mothers-to-be anticipating their baby's first breath, and folks of any age taking their last breath, desperately want their third trimesters to "end well." Just as all pregnancies eventually conclude, women in life's third tri will all cross the finish line. Preparing for that juncture, we yearn to hear Christ's commendation, "Well done, my good and faithful servant."[163] But what does it take to "finish well"?

The Bible says each of us has been assigned a delivery date. Under the inspiration of the Holy Spirit, David wrote to his Lord, "You saw me before I was born. Every day of my life was recorded in your book. Every moment was laid out before a single day had passed."[164]

Complicating life's third trimester is a realization that we cannot know precisely when our third trimester will conclude, just as when we were pregnant. God has appointed when it will occur. In both circumstances, we appropriately wait in anticipation and with earnest preparation for the momentous event. Yet it is hard to wrap our minds around the fact that these years of our third tri will end in an instant when God decrees.

Parallel #22: Your delivery date is uncertain, so getting ready becomes critical. The timing of the culmination of your pregnancy and the culmination of your life are both unpredictable.

My tombstone was carved at the same time as my first husband's. Both our names are listed, and our two sides look exactly alike, except Chuck's birthdate and death date are etched into the stone, but only my birthdate so far. The end date is a mystery.

Those in their last months of pregnancy logically know their baby will be born soon, just as we third-tri women know the majority of our years are behind us. Even so, an expectant mother's water seems to break all of a sudden, and birth pangs surprise her without warning. Likewise, our earthly departure at a particular moment in time seems abrupt, even if we've been terminally ill.

With tears cascading, I texted family and friends before dawn April 5, 2015, with the words, "Chuck was called home today, early on this Easter Sunday morning, to celebrate Easter forever with his risen Lord face to face." Hospice had informed me that Chuck had only days to live, but it didn't seem real until his breathing suddenly stopped.

The Ultimate True Love Story

On the first anniversary of Chuck's passing, a friend told me about a novel sermon she'd heard on Easter Sunday. Her pastor described four funerals attended by Jesus. All ministers preach countless funeral messages and spend a lot of time preparing just the right words for each situation. However, Jesus preached *no* sermons on the occasions when He was present with grief-stricken mourners at funerals. Jesus did something unexpected: He made one astonishing pronouncement at each graveside. Let me explain.

Occasion number one describes a pitiful funeral procession coming out of the small village of Nain. The only son of a widow had died, and anguished mourners accompanied the heartbroken mother behind her son's coffin. Jesus tenderly comforted the despairing widow, touched the coffin, and directed, "Young man, I tell you *get up*!" Dr. Luke completes the story, "Then the dead boy sat up and began to talk."[165] The essence of Jesus' compassionate command was "*Rise!*"

Dr. Luke also records the second occurrence. Death arrived unexpectedly for an adored twelve-year old girl, the only child of a synagogue leader. Devastated people gathered, weeping and wailing. Jesus gently grasped the hand of the lifeless young girl and ordered, "My child, *get up*! And at that moment her life returned, and she immediately stood up!"[166] Again, no eulogy or sermon was delivered, only Jesus' order to *rise*!

The next story relates events surrounding the death of Jesus' good friend Lazarus. The sisters of Lazarus were distraught, and the crowd was wailing. To the spectators' astonishment, Jesus stood outside the tomb and shouted, "'Lazarus, *come out*!' And the dead man came out, his hands and feet bound in graveclothes, his face wrapped in a headcloth."[167] Yes, Jesus' shocking directive for the third time, in its essence, was "*Rise.*"

The fourth funeral in which Jesus participated was His *own*. Mary Magdalene and other women came to the burial chamber to embalm Jesus' body with spices, only to find the massive stone already rolled away. A white-robed angel announced to the bewildered and frightened women the stunning news: "Don't be alarmed. You are looking for Jesus of Nazareth, who was crucified. He isn't here! He is *risen* from the dead!"[168]

Jesus' body was not in the tomb, so Mary ran to tell Peter and John, who were sequestered and miserable in their grief. After seeing Jesus' empty deflated linen wrappings in the cave, Peter and John realized for the first time that what the Scriptures had predicted about the Messiah *rising* from the dead had now happened.

Yes, Jesus attended a number of funerals, but He never preached a single funeral sermon. Instead, Jesus each time decreed, *"Rise,"* and demonstrated His power over death by Himself *rising* from His own tomb, leaving His grave wrappings collapsed in a heap. Then Jesus *rose* to heaven to sit at the right hand of His Father's throne and to prepare mansions for beloved believers around the world who will one day *rise*.

Jesus revealed the future scenario to Paul. "The Lord himself will come down from heaven with a commanding shout, with the voice of the archangel, and with the trumpet call of God. First, the believers who have died will *rise* from their graves. Then, together with them, we who are still alive and remain on the earth will be *caught up in the clouds to meet the Lord in the air*. Then we will be with the Lord forever. So *encourage* each other with these words."[169]

Your Choice: Celebration or Mourning

Rising indeed sounds like an immensely encouraging prospect worth celebrating! However, what about verses such as, "Each person is destined to die once and after that comes judgment."[170] How can we be "encouraged" about "rising" when judgment is involved? Judgment sounds so ominous and foreboding. No wonder most people don't want to think about the inevitability of their lives coming to a screeching halt! Some prefer to believe they will simply cease to exist or be reincarnated in another form—anything to avoid the idea of a judgment. What's that all about anyway?

People say nice things about the deceased at memorial services and celebrate their lives. However, the way Jesus behaved at gravesides had nothing to do with eulogizing and praising the dead person's earthly accomplishments. A life marked by good deeds and commendable rule-keeping doesn't guarantee a heavenly party.

Remarkably, Jesus prompts jubilant celebration without any eulogies about exemplary accomplishments. By His miraculous resurrection, Christ proved God's promise that people could *rise*, but not to face a fearful dreadful judgment. Rather they can receive rewards and happiness beyond anything experienced on earth. Let me put Hebrews 9:27 into the context in which it is written, "Just as each person is destined to die once and after that comes judgment, so also Christ was offered once for all time as a sacrifice to take away the sins of many people. He will come again, not to deal with our sins, but to bring salvation to all who are eagerly waiting for him."[171]

What change would need to occur in order for you to be in the group "eagerly waiting" for Christ's return and confident of salvation instead of dreading judgment? It sounds like the criteria have something to do with forgiven sins and a love relationship with Christ, not how good you've been.

Along with names, dates, and other details on Chuck's and my tombstone, we ordered engraved the following personalized excerpt from Paul's second letter to Timothy: *"We have fought the good fight; we have finished the race; we have kept the faith."*[172] We chose that inscription because there was a day during our college years when we, just like Princess Promise, reconsidered our sinful, conflict-ridden lives marked by self-reliance, self-promotion, moral compromise, and accumulation of things. We turned and took a step in a different direction, the direction of trusting and following God. We chose *faith* in Christ as our new way of life.

Once we understood Jesus loved us, died to pay our sin penalty, and desired a relationship with us, we decided to spend the rest of our lives following Him. Although never perfectly accomplished, we grew in our ability to love God and other people over time.

With Paul, therefore, we can rejoice: "Now the prize awaits me—the *crown* of righteousness, which the Lord, the righteous Judge, will give me on the day of his return. And the prize is not just for me, but for *all* who eagerly look forward to his appearing."[173] Coronation Day lies ahead!

Just as the third trimester of pregnancy cannot continue indefinitely, no human possesses the option to avoid an earthly expiration date. However, while reading this book, you do still retain a choice about the outcome you will face some unknown-to-you future day. Your choice can make your delivery day one of tremendous celebration or horrendous regret and mourning.

In my fable, Princess Promise possessed a skewed view of Prince Perfect. I wonder, is your image of the flawless King of the Universe accurate?

Many of us maintain distorted views about God based on toxic church experiences in our past, or because imperfect fathers and mothers turned us off to the whole idea of a heavenly Father. Perhaps the hurtful words and behaviors of hypocritical Christians disillusioned you.

For others, early exposure to shame-producing teaching may have resulted in your imagining God to be harsh and angry at you. Some of you suffered painful traumas that scarred you and hindered you from trusting God's love. You may be mad at the God you maintain doesn't exist because you think He should have protected you.

Still others were swayed by peers, professors, and other influencers who subtly or overtly ridiculed your faith and created confusion. Has intellectual pride prevailed? You may believe yourself to be too educated, sophisticated, and science-savvy to believe in "biblical myths." You may think Christianity is on the decline and no longer relevant to modern life. You've dismissed God the Father, Son, and Holy Spirit as fairytale gods who are figments of people's imaginations.

People disappointed us. In our confusion, we end up making God in humanity's image instead of vice versa, and we feel afraid of Him or disappointed with Him. We wonder, "Is God really good if there is so much suffering in the world?"

Some of you got caught up in teenage curiosity and experimentation or caved in to peer pressure and the promise of love during hormonally charged moments. What psychologists say is people's greatest emotional need, to love and be loved, led you to look in all kinds of wrong places. You may think you aren't "good enough" now to be loved by Christ.

Perhaps you pour energy into good causes, but responding to God's love doesn't appear on that list. Countless first-trimester, second-trimester, and third-trimester individuals are sincerely following what the world defines as "being a good person," without awareness of, or respect for, the God of the universe's plan for their lives.

There are many in both younger and older generations today who don't think about much beyond their personal desires for delicious food and copious drinks, pleasurable entertainment, adventurous travel, enjoyment of nature's wonders, amusement available on the latest tech devices, fun times with friends and family, and pursuing beauty, success, and riches. Once we remove God from the equation, getting what we want, fitting in with our peers, and elevating human knowledge above the ancient wisdom of the Bible dictate attitudes and actions.

For the first time in American history, many people are growing up without much exposure to the Bible and its depictions of God's love. It seems irrelevant whether God exists or not, what with all the other world religions out there.

Some know enough to secretly desire a Christ-honoring life and a heart at peace. Perhaps they long to know they will go to heaven when they die, but no one has ever clearly explained how to get started in that direction. The Christians they know use a confusing foreign vocabulary that muddies the waters.

Now, in your third trimester, is it time to sort through all those roadblocks and get to know God as He really is? Did you find yourself in any of the descriptions of those confused about the path of light?

Dr. Tim Keller, a keen observer of people, writes in his book, *Making Sense of God: An Invitation to the Skeptical*, "The reality is that every person embraces his or her worldview for a variety of rational, emotional, cultural and social factors"[174] Pure logic simply does not prevail when it comes to religious beliefs and disbeliefs. If you feel stuck in skepticism about Christianity, I recommend Dr. Keller's book as a sensitive, intelligent response to questions keeping many wandering in the dark.

For those of you desiring to examine the evidence, profound arguments for God's existence can be found on YouTube videos by J. Warner Wallace, a Dateline-featured cold-case detective. He is also the author of several fascinating books, including *Cold-Case Christianity: A Homicide Detective Investigates the Claims of the Gospels.*[175]

In our maturity, it makes sense to revisit our view of God and consider whether we may be holding on to misconceptions having roots in the distant past. A relationship with Christ may be very different from what you've imagined. Is now the time to admit your questions and reasons for avoiding Christ may have rational answers?

"When I was a child, I spoke and thought and reasoned as a child. But when I grew up, I put away childish things. . . . All that I know now is partial and incomplete, but then I will know everything completely, just as God now knows me completely. Three things will last forever—faith, hope, and love—and the greatest of these is *love*. Let *love* be your highest goal."[176]

Responding to God's Love

The most well-known verse in the Bible places *love*, our foremost goal, within our reach. "For this is how God *loved* the world: He gave his one and only Son, so that *everyone who believes in him will not perish but have eternal life*. God sent his Son into the world not to judge the world, but to save the world through him. There is *no judgment against anyone who believes in him*."[177] The choice to believe that Jesus is the only Son of God and to *trust His love* is obviously a very big deal!

Despite any previous skepticism, do you now want to believe in the Son of God and look forward to His return and His call to *rise*? Do you desire now in your more mature years to trust that Jesus died for *your* sins, forever taking away the fear of judgment and assuring you of eternal celebration? Do you crave assurance that you will spend eternity in heaven with the Eternal One who died and rose to save you from judgment?

Guideline #44: Consider responding to God's love by accepting His Son as your personal risen Lord and Savior.

Following is a simple prayer similar to what I prayed to change my direction and turn my heart over to the risen Son of God. Many readers have already made their choice for or against this path, but I suggest everyone read the prayer anyway. Whether for the first time or as a step of renewed commitment, scrutinize its sentiments and then consider whispering this prayer to the One who hears your every word.

Father in heaven, I choose now to believe in You and Jesus, Your Son, and to trust Your love. Thank You, Jesus, for loving me enough to die on the cross as payment for my sins, so I don't have to fear judgment. I regret the foolish, selfish, and God-ignoring paths I've taken. Thank You for your willingness to forgive me and wash me clean. My heart's door is open to You, the only Son of God. Please live in my heart and help me become the person You want me to be. What's more, I trust you to say, "Rise," when you return so we can enjoy each other forever. Amen.

You've done it! Your prayer responding to God's love propelled you in the direction of light. It's okay if you want to tell somebody you think will understand and celebrate with you! It will be crucial in the coming days to find like-minded people who can help you grow as you follow Jesus on your path toward serenity and peace.

You know now that thriving in your third trimester of life goes beyond achieving great relationships with a husband, adult children, and grand-children, wonderful and satisfying as they can be. Of course, we desire harmony and closeness, and we've considered guidelines to help us mend and maximize relationships. However, there's an even more crucial issue.

Thriving goes beyond attendance and sacrificial service in a church or generosity to the poor. It goes beyond community involvement and intellectual or career achievement. Thriving goes beyond accumulating professional honors and leaving an inheritance for kids and grandkids. It goes beyond achieving good health and outliving your peers. Thriving goes beyond enjoyment of pleasurable entertainment, comfortable houses, gourmet meals, and adventurous vacations, desirable as all those things are.

Thriving includes getting to know the Creator of the universe better and developing increasing intimacy with Him. Thriving includes having a heart at peace because you believe the Son of God died for your sins and *rose*, so you might look forward to *rising* and living forever with Him. To truly thrive is to spend your remaining days trusting, loving, following, and obeying Him, so your third tri ends not in judgment and everlasting mourning, but in never-ceasing celebration when Jesus calls your name, and you *rise*!

"It will happen in a moment, in the blink of an eye. . . . For when the trumpet sounds, those who have died will be *raised* to live forever. . . . Death is swallowed up in victory."[178]

People of any age and stage are eligible to carry a living being, Christ Himself, to term. If you prayed the prayer responding to God's love for you, He dwells inside you. Paul urged, "Through the power of the Holy Spirit who lives within us, carefully guard the precious truth that has been entrusted to you."[179]

I will close this chapter with one more commonality between the third trimester of pregnancy and the third trimester of life.

Parallel #23: In pregnancy's third trimester and in life's third tri, you feel the Precious One moving inside you more than ever before. You find yourself wanting to sing and communicate with the Treasured One indwelling you. You want the Cherished One to know your voice as you become attuned to His voice and movements.

Coaching Corner

1. What do you have in common with Princess Promise?

2. Why could the Easter story be considered a love story?

3. Which roadblocks to accepting Jesus' death as payment for your sins seem most relevant? What do you want to do about those roadblocks?

4. If you need help believing Christianity is true and more than fairy tales, would you be willing to listen to J. Warner Wallace's YouTube videos or read his book on *Cold-Case Christianity* or read Tim Keller's *Making Sense of God*? Why or why not? When will you do your investigation?

5. If you prayed the prayer to invite Jesus to forgive you and live in you, with whom could you share this life-changing decision?

6. Think of a Christian you admire. Could you go to that person and tell her/him you'd like their help in learning how to grow in your love relationship with Jesus? When will you contact them?

7. How will expecting Jesus' call to "rise" impact the rest of your third tri?

8. How do loving your grown children and loving God relate to each other?

9. In what specific ways do you want Parallel #23 to play out in your life?

CHAPTER 16

Grand Finale

I RELATED DORIS'S challenging third-tri circumstances in the introduction to this book. We've covered a lot of territory since then, but I want to tell you the rest of Doris's story. Her life's most recent chapters illustrate how a mother's enduring love and "mom-prints" impact third-tri outcomes.

When I dialed Doris, I caught her in the waiting room of her physical therapist. Numerous medical problems have plagued Doris over the years, but she refuses to let them distract from her life purpose and callings.

Doris bubbled over as she started to describe the latest shift in her life callings since we last talked. She has discovered an agency serving pregnant girls in her area. Lifeline Family Center combines elements dear to her heart. The nonprofit assists pregnant women who need help rebuilding their lives, offering to house them for up to two years while providing classes to develop computer and tech skills, cooking, sewing, financial management, homemaking, and parenting proficiencies. Classes prepare the participants for entering the workforce and help the moms-to-be make good homes for their children because many do not want to abort their son or daughter or give them up for adoption.

As a retired teacher, Doris looks forward to teaching these young mamas essential life skills. Doris's first college degree was in Home Economics, and then she went back to school at age forty-six to become an elementary teacher, specializing in students with reading and math problems. A few years into her life's third trimester, Doris began working with prostitutes on the streets of Chicago. Even though these women were often homeless and dealing with all kinds of problems, Doris saw firsthand how the ability to read and manage a household could be a ticket out of poverty and prostitution.

Doris recently started volunteering, acting like an excited grandma, as she performs nonmedical ultrasound imaging to reveal tiny babies in utero to their pregnant moms. Having lost one grandchild to an abortion and knowing how difficult pregnancy was for her unmarried daughters, Doris has recycled her life experiences into a meaningful mission. Every morning, she wakes up praising God for the chance to interact with young women needing support, smiling encouragement, direction, and a helping hand.

Doris remembers being a softhearted child searching trash heaps for discarded baby dolls to rescue. She felt so sad for their unkempt condition. By the second grade, Doris recognized a boy in her class as "poor" and begged her father for money to help him open a savings account like the teacher had set up for the other students to learn money management.

Doris mused, "It's really quite amazing when you're able to look back and see all of the things in your life coming together for one grand finale!"

Life trajectories for the three daughters crashing at her home during their pregnancies have all taken stunning upturns. One of them eventually revealed she had been a victim of sexual abuse and had resorted to drugs to cope with her horrible secret. Doris describes tremendous progress in healing the wounds inflicted without Doris's knowledge. Doris and her husband have supported their daughter every step of the way in her recovery and are now bonded and growing ever closer.

Doris rejoices over spiritual reconnections with her other two girls, as well. They've come back to the Lord and joined church communities. One daughter fasts and prays with Doris once a week.

Doris adores the three grandchildren who eventually entered the world at the end of their mothers' tumultuous months under her roof. Siblings have made peace with each other, and cousins frolic at family gatherings. New spouses and more babies have been added to the mix. All have found satisfying career paths and manage their money well.

Of course, all is not perfect. Redheaded Doris admits she still gets triggered sometimes when one of them "badgers" her about something. Nevertheless, Doris feels confident that more healing is on the horizon, both in her own life and those of her children. Like other third-tri moms, Doris continues to keep her children and all their triumphs and difficulties constantly in her prayers.

Doris's son and the militant atheist once married to him have divorced, and Jerry subsequently married a kinder girl two years ago. Doris and her husband accepted the invitation to attend their Hawaiian wedding to give Jerry and his new wife their blessing, regardless of the ways Jerry had shut his parents out for years. Jerry recently asked his mom and dad to visit them in Idaho to meet their infant granddaughter. Doris insisted on making the trip despite recent surgery and body limitations. She senses Jerry softening now that fatherhood has helped him understand parenting better, and her husband is working on forgiving past offenses. Doris sees Jerry reevaluating and processing life differently, including acting less hostile toward his parents' Christian faith.

Doris looks for signs of God's working in her children's lives and thanks Him for each indication she sees. For example, her heart rejoiced when Jerry described his infant daughter's sleeping position with her tiny arms raised over her head, as his baby's "praise the Lord stance." It was notable in Doris's mind that Jerry saw his daughter lifting her hands to God rather than seeing his child as a referee announcing a "touchdown." Third-tri moms like Doris are always looking for hopeful signs of adult kids' movement toward God or their parents.

Jerry and his wife named Doris's new grandbaby an Irish name meaning "excessive joy or intoxicating joy." Her middle name means "answer to prayer, yielding to prayer, lovable, graceful, and beautiful lion." Doris immediately thought of the Lion of Judah.

Like all sensitive third-tri mothers, Doris doesn't want to turn off her adult son in his mini-steps toward God by overdoing "Christian vocabulary." However, the encouraging signs have led her to take a next step. Doris received in her heart a lullaby to sing over her new granddaughter. Her son told Doris he is excited to hear the lyrics and melody when Doris arrives for a visit later this month. To her amazement, Jerry says he remembers his mom singing his own special Holy Spirit-composed song when he was a young child. Doris's lullaby includes her granddaughter's name and the following chorus:

> *What a beautiful name!*
> *The cause of great, great joy!*
> *Beautiful lion!*
> *We will love you all of your days!*

Because Doris doesn't want to spook Jerry with the reality that she received her grandbaby's lullaby from the great I Am, she will wait until the right moment to reveal the next stanza to her song. It includes more words of blessing on her granddaughter and deep gratitude to her Creator.

Like Doris, many of the other women inhabiting this book have added inspiring new life chapters during the dozen years while this book has been percolating in my head. Like me, the majority have moved closer to the fulfillment of their dreams of friendship and harmony with those they birthed.

Many improvements stemmed from parents persevering in their efforts to remove the logs from their own eyes and humbly dispense unconditional love. Adult children have grown in their ability to see their mom as a person and devoted friend, and no longer as a symbol of authority or judgment. Members of all generations more readily accept one another, flaws and all. Unfailing love and enduring trust in God keep hope and progress alive.

Do you remember the Lord's questions to Abraham about his barren, ninety-year-old wife, Sarah? He asked, "Why did Sarah laugh? Why did she say, 'Can an old woman like me have a baby?' *Is there anything too hard for the* LORD? I will return about this time next year, and Sarah *will* have a son."[180]

Mark and Parker Batterson, father and son authors of the challenging book *All In,* write about Sarah's skepticism, "Isaac was God's idea. It was God who promised Abraham a son and gave the promise through Sarah. Postmenopausal octogenarians don't get pregnant. Period. But God always delivers!"[181]

Although not all third-tri mothers populating this book have experienced happily-ever-after endings, they still sense God is at work in their lives and in the lives of their grown children as they wait in faith for God to deliver. They choose to believe nothing is too hard for God as they move forward in their grand finale. And you?

Coaching Corner

1. In what ways do Doris's later life chapters speak to you?

2. What evidence of God working in your offspring's lives have you seen?

3. What adjustments has Doris made as a third trimester mom?

4. Doris found new callings from God in the later years of her third tri of life. Look back at your answers to the coaching questions in Chapter 14. What progress have you made in identifying your purpose and recognizing callings? What next step could you take in that direction?

5. Not all of our children make the U-turns we desire. Whether they've come home to you as their mother and to Jesus as their Savior, have *you* come home? Why or why not?

6. Since you have now completed reading *Life's Third Tri*, what are your biggest takeaways?

7. Would your children say, "Mom has changed recently?" To what aspects of your life would they be referring?

8. Whom do you know who needs to read *Life's Third Tri*? Will you order them a copy or give them yours? Would you like to gather a few third-tri moms to study these concepts together? If yes, how and when can you make that happen?

Notes

CHAPTER 1

1 Jane Isay, *Walking on Eggshells: Navigating the Delicate Relationship Between Adult Children and Parents* (New York: Broadway Books/Flying Dolphin Press, 2007), 209.

2 Isay, 33.

3 Isay, 34.

4 Isay, 9, emphasis mine.

5 Saint Mother Teresa of Calcutta, source unknown, emphasis mine.

6 Caleb Kaltenbach, *Messy Grace: How a Pastor with Gay Parents Learned to Love Others Without Sacrificing Conviction* (Colorado Springs: Waterbrook Press, 2015), 4.

7 Proverbs 9:10 (NLT).

8 Heidi Murkoff, *What to Expect When You're Expecting*, 5th Edition (New York: Workman Publishing, 2016).

9 Matthew 13:24 (NLT).

10 http://www.webmd.com/baby/guide/your-pregnancy-week-by-week-weeks-31-34, accessed March 6, 2013.

11 https://www.babyyourbaby.org/pregnancy/during-pregnancy/third-trimester-changes.php, accessed March 6, 2013.

12 http://www.fitpregnancy.com/pregnancy/health/all-about--third-trimester, accessed March 6, 2013.

13 http://www.parenting.com/article/third-trimester-symptoms, accessed March 5, 2013.

CHAPTER 2

14 http://www.brainyquote.com/quotes/authors/t/tomlandry.html#1Xzz113I-BUHr3.

15 http://www.goodreads.com/author/quotes/108209.Tom_Landry.

16 P. Williams & D. Menendez, *Becoming a Professional Life Coach: Lessons from the Institute for Life Coach Training* (New York: Norton & Co., 2007), 106.

17 James 1:5 (NLT).

18 Alison Gopnik, "Despite Covid-19, Older People Are Still Happier," *Wall Street Journal*, December 12-13, 2020, C4.

19 Jonathan Rauch, "The Real Roots of Midlife Crisis," *The Atlantic*, December 2014 http://www.theatlantic.,com/magazine/archive/2014/12/the_real_roots_of_midlife_crisis/382235, accessed August 18, 2015.

20 Hannes Schwandt in Jonathan Rauch article, "The Real Roots of Midlife Crisis," *The Atlantic*, December 2014 http://www.theatlantic.,com/magazine/archive/2014/12/the_real_roots_of_midlife_crisis/382235, accessed August 18, 2015.

21 Dilip Jeste in Jonathan Rauch article, "The Real Roots of Midlife Crisis," *The Atlantic*, December 2014) http://www.theatlantic.,com/magazine/archive/2014/12/the_real_roots_of_midlife_crisis/382235, accessed August 18, 2015.

22 Jonathan Rauch, "The Real Roots of Midlife Crisis," *The Atlantic*, December 2014) http://www.theatlantic.,com/magazine/archive/2014/12/the_real_roots_of_midlife_crisis/382235, accessed August 18, 2015.

23 Steven Smith, *Living Your Best: A Powerful Blueprint for Personal Transformation* (Lexington, Kentucky: Wisdom from the Heart, 2012).

24 1 Thessalonians 5:16-18 (NLT), emphasis mine.

25 Laura Whitworth, Henry Kimsey-House, & Phil Sandahl, *Co-Active Coaching* (Palo Alto: Davies-Black, 1998).

26 Psalm 111:10 (NLT).

CHAPTER 3

27 Gary Black, Facebook post, November 21, 2020.

28 2 Chronicles 7:14 (NLT).

29 2 Chronicles 7:19-22 (NLT).

30 Matthew 7:3, 5 (NLT).

31 Exodus 20:12 (NLT).

32 1 Corinthians 16:13-14 (NLT).

CHAPTER 4

33 Donald Miller, *Building a Storybrand* (New York: HarperCollins, 2017), 132.

34 Ephesians 6:4 (NLT).

35 Colossians 3:21 (NLT).

36 Ibid, pp. 35-36 (NLT).

37 Ibid, p. 36 (NLT).

38 Gary Thomas, "Good Parents, Prodigal Kids," *Focus on the Family Magazine*, August/September, 2019), 35.

39 2 Chronicles 7:13 (NLT).

40 Karl Barth, www.patheos.com/blogsrogereolson/2013/01/did-karl-barth-really-say-jesus-loves-me-this-I-k /.

41 Sabrina Tavernise and Katharine Seelye, Political Divide Splits Relationships—and Thanksgiving, Too, *NY Times*, Nov. 16, 2016, https://nytimes.com/2016/11/16/us/political-divide-splits-relationships-and-Thanksgiving-too.html.

42 Ephesians 4:31-32 (NLT).

43 Posted by Jennifer Short on Facebook November 16, 2020, and reposted by Paula Chenger on December 5, 2020.

CHAPTER 5

44 Jane Adams, *When Our Grown Kids Disappoint Us: Letting Go of Their Problems, Loving Them Anyway, and Getting On with Our Lives* (New York: Free Press, 2003), 147.

45 Ibid, 147.

46 Bonnie Tsui, "The Right Way to Learn from Your Mistakes," *Huffington Post*, February 07, 2014, https://www.huffpost.com/entry/learning-from-mistakes_n_4718445.

47 Ibid.

48 Ibid.

49 Lysa Terkeurst, *Craving God: 60 Devotions for Real Women* (Example Product Manufacturing, 2004).

50 Ibid, 118.

51 Luke 21:13-15 (NIV), emphasis mine.

52 John Gottman and Nan Silver, *The Seven Principles for Making Marriage Work: A Practical Guide from the Country's Foremost Relationship Expert* (New York: Harmony, 2015).

53 David Burns, *Feeling Good: The New Mood Therapy* (New York: William Morrow, 1999), 138.

54 Jeff Allen, Dry Bar Comedy, *YouTube*.

55 1 Corinthians 13:4-7 (NLT), emphasis mine.

56 Matthew 6:12 (NLT), emphasis mine.

57 Matthew 6:14 (NLT).

58 Luke 23:34 (NLT), emphasis mine.

CHAPTER 6

59 Alistair Begg.

60 John 15:5 (NLT).

61 Henry Blackaby, Richard Blackaby, and Claude King, *Experiencing God: Knowing and Doing the Will of God* (Nashville: LifeWay Press, 2007).

62 John 20:31 (NLT), emphasis mine.

63 John 20:27 (NLT), emphasis mine.

64 Exodus 3:4, 5, 10, 12 (NLT), emphasis mine.

65 Matthew 26:40-41 (NLT).

66 Bob Sorge, *Secrets of the Secret Place: Keys to Igniting Your Personal Time with God* (Kansas City, Missouri: Oasis House, 2001). Contact at Oasis-House.com.

67 Psalm 81:7 (NLT).

68 Sorge, 10-11.

69 Sorge, 11, emphasis mine.

70 Psalm 146:9 (NLT).

71 Psalm 32:8 (NLT).

72 John 20:30-31 (NLT).

73 Sorge, 11.

74 Matthew 13:9 (NLT).

75 Sorge, 11.

CHAPTER 7

76 2 Chron 7:14 (NLT), emphasis mine.

77 Philippians 3:8 (NLT).

78 Bob Sorge, *Secrets of the Secret Place: Keys to Igniting Your Personal Time with God* (Kansas City, Missouri: Oasis House, 2001).

79 Numbers 12:3 (NLT), emphasis mine.

80 Hebrews 11:6 (NLT).

81 Matthew 11:28 (NLT).

82 Sorge, 59.

83 Psalm 67:1 (NLT), emphasis mine.

84 Numbers 6:24-26 (NIV), emphasis mine.

CHAPTER 8

85 2 Chronicles 7:14, 19 (NLT), emphasis mine.

86 Luke 3:3 (NLT), emphasis mine.

87 Matthew 4:17 (NLT), emphasis mine.

88 Acts 2:37-38.

89 Romans 3:23 (NLT), emphasis mine.

90 Beverly Engel, *Divorcing a Parent: Free Yourself from the Past and Live the Life You've Always Wanted* (Brattleboro, Vermont: Echo Point Books, 1999).

91 Beverly Engel, "Making Amends," *Psychology Today*, July/August 2002, 40).

92 Beverly Engel, *The Power of Apology: Healing Steps to Transform All Your Relationships* (New York: John Wiley & Sons, 2001).

93 Proverbs 22:6 (NLT).

94 Ezekiel 18:2 (NLT).

95 Ezekiel 18:4 (NLT).

96 Ezekiel 18:30,32 (NLT), emphasis mine.

97 Luke 15:11-31.

98 James 4:6-9 (NLT), emphasis mine.

99 Deuteronomy 5:6-7 (NIV).

100 Ezekiel 18:2 (NLT).

101 Ezekiel 18:4 (NLT).

CHAPTER 9

102 Randy Carlson, *The Power of One Thing: How to Intentionally Change Your Life* (Carol Stream, IL: Tyndale House, 2009).

103 Matthew 7:12 (NLT).

104 Ibid.

105 Robert Emmons, *Thanks! How the New Science of Gratitude Can Make You Happier* (Boston: Houghton Mifflin Company, 2007).

CHAPTER 10

106 Joshua Coleman, *When Parents Hurt: Compassionate Strategies When You and Your Grown Child Don't Get Along* (New York: Collins Living, 2008).

107 Kathy McCoy, *We Don't Talk Anymore: Healing after Parents and Their Adult Children Become Estranged* (Naperville, IL: Sourcebooks, 2017).

108 Jane Isay, *Walking on Eggshells: Navigating the Delicate Relationship Between Adult Children and Parents* (New York: Flying Dolphin Press, 2007) 87.

109 Francine Russo, "The Science of Siblings," *Parade*, June 23, 2013, 9-17.

110 Lucy Blake, "Parents and Children Who Are Estranged in Adulthood: A Review and Discussion of the Literature," *Journal of Family Theory & Review* 9(4), 2017, 521-536.

111 Coleman, 241.

112 Coleman, 244.

113 McCoy, 284-288.

114 Dorothy Jerrome, "Family Estrangement: Parents and Children Who Lose Touch," *Journal of Family Therapy* 16, 1994, 243-258.

115 Joshua Coleman, "A Shift in American Family Values Is Fueling Estrangement," *The Atlantic*, January 10, 2021.

116 K. S. Birditt et al., "Tensions in the Parent and Adult Child Relationship: Links to Solidarity and Ambivalence," *Psychology and Aging* 24(2), 2009, 287-295.

117 McCoy, 287.

118 Laura Perry, blog "Former Transgender, Set Free in Jesus," *TransgendertoTransformed.com*, January 7, 2019.

119 Laura Perry, blog "Surrender Your Child Back to God," *Transgender-toTransformed.com*, April 16, 2020.

CHAPTER 11

120 Jim Burns, *Doing Life with Your Adult Children: Keep Your Mouth Shut & the Welcome Mat Out* (Grand Rapids: Zondervan, 2019), p. 143.

121 Jane Isay, *Walking on Eggshells: Navigating the Delicate Relationship Between Adult Children and Parents* (New York: Broadway Books/Flying Dolphin Press, 2007), 209.

122 1 Corinthians 13:4-7 (NLT).

123 Burns, 127.

124 Arthur Brooks, "How Adult Children Affect Their Mother's Happiness," *The Atlantic*, May 6, 2021.

125 Ibid., emphasis mine.

126 2 Thessalonians 3:10 (NLT).

127 Quoctrung Bui and Claire Miller, *https:///www.nytimes.com/interactive/2015/12/24/upshot/24up-family.html*.

128 Ibid.

129 Isay, 209.

130 Luke 12:52-53 (NLT).

131 Gary Thomas, Good Parents, Prodigal Kids, *Focus on the Family Magazine,* August/September 2019, 33-37.

132 2 Corinthians 2:15-16 (NLT).

133 Charles Swindoll, *Day by Day* (Nashville: Thomas Nelson, 2000), https://www.insight.org/resources/daily-devotional/individual/suffering, May 2, 2019.

CHAPTER 12

134 https://www.thoughtco.com/premack-principle-4771729.

135 Michael Greger, *How Not to Die: Discover the Foods Scientifically Proven to Prevent and Reverse Disease* (New York: Flatiron Books, 2015).

136 Ibid., 404.

137 J. Vettin and D. Todt, "Laughter in Conversation: Features of occurrence and Acoustic Structure," *Journal of Nonverbal Behavior*, 28(2), 2004, 93-115, emphasis mine.

138 R. R. Provine and K. R. Fischer, "Laughing, Smiling, and Talking: Relation to Sleeping and Social Context in Humans," *Ethology*, 83(4), 1989, 295-305), emphasis mine.

139 Ken Blanchard and Morton Shaevitz, *Refire! Don't Retire: Make the Rest of Your Life the Best of Your Life* (Oakland, California: Barrett-Koehler Publishers, 2015).

140 Nancy Hellmich, "Retiring? Book Says It's Time to 'Refire!'" *USA Today*, Feb. 3, 2015). https://www.usatoday.com/story/money/2015/02/03/refire-dont-retire-blanchard/22159407/.

CHAPTER 13

141 Robert Emmons, *Thanks: How the New Science of Gratitude Can Make You Happier* (Boston: Houghton Mifflin Company, 2007).

142 Psalm 92:14-15 (NLT).

143 Philippians 4:8 (NLT).

CHAPTER 14

144 Joan Chittister, *The Gift of Years; Growing Older Gracefully* (New York: BlueRidge, 2008), ix.

145 Ibid, xv.

146 Gail Sheehy, *New Passages: Mapping Your Life across Time* (New York: Random House, 1995), 419-420, emphasis mine.

147 Chittister, xv.

148 Sheehy, 420.

149 Westminster Assembly, *Westminster Shorter Catechism* (Westminster: United Kingdom, 1646-1647), Question #1.

150 Rick Warren, *The Purpose Driven Life: What on Earth Am I Here For?* (Grand Rapids: Zondervan, 2012), 21.

151 Mark and Parker Batterson, *All In* (Grand Rapids: Zondervan, 2014), 105.

152 Laura Whitworth, Henry Kimsey-House and Phil Sandahl, *Co-Active Coaching: New Skills for Coaching People Toward Success in Work and Life* (Palo Alto, California: Davies-Black Publishing, 1998), 222.

153 Bruce Grierson, *What Makes Olga Run: The Mystery of the 90-Something Track Star and What She Can Teach Us About Living Longer, Happier Lives* (New York: St. Martin's Griffin, 2014), 6.

154 Matthew 28:19-20 (NLT).

155 Charisse Jones, "For 6 People Over 60, Helping Change the World Is Their Purpose," *USA Today*, November 18, 2015.

156 Ibid.

157 Ibid.

158 Ibid.

159 Joe Kita, "Worth the Risk," *Parade*, November 2, 2014, 9, emphasis mine.

160 Rick Warren, *The Purpose Driven Life: What on Earth Am I Here For?* (Grand Rapids: Zondervan, 2012).

161 Laura Whitworth, Henry Kimsey-House and Phil Sandahl, *Co-Active Coaching: New Skills for Coaching People Toward Success in Work and Life* (Palo Alto, California: Davies-Black Publishing, 1998), 223.

162 Ibid.

CHAPTER 15

163 Matthew 25:21 (NLT).

164 Psalm 139:16 (NLT).

165 Luke 7:14 (NLT), emphasis mine.

166 Luke 8:54-55 (NLT), emphasis mine.

167 John 11:43-44 (NLT), emphasis mine.

168 Mark 16:6 (NLT), emphasis mine.

169 1 Thessalonians 4:16-18 (NLT), emphasis mine.

170 Hebrews 9:27 (NLT).

171 Hebrews 9:27-28 (NLT).

172 2 Tim 4:7-8 (NIV), personalized with *we* instead of *I*.

173 2 Tim 4:8 (NLT), emphasis mine.

174 Timothy Keller, *Making Sense of God: An Invitation to the Skeptical* (New York: Viking, 2016), 4.

175 J. Warner Wallace, *Cold-Case Christianity: A Homicide Detective Investigates the Claims of the Gospels* (Colorado Springs: David C. Cook, 2013).

176 1 Corinthians 13:11-13, 14:1 (NLT), emphasis mine.

177 John 3:16-18 (NLT), emphasis mine.

178 1 Corinthians 15:52, 54 (NLT), emphasis mine.

179 2 Timothy 1:14 (NLT).

CHAPTER 16

180 Genesis 18:13-14 (NLT), emphasis mine.

181 Mark and Parker Batterson, *All In* (Grand Rapids, Zondervan, 2014), 42.

About the Author

Dr. Charlotte Melcher counseled and coached hundreds of women over a span of 31 years as Clinical Director of Focus on Relationships, Inc., in Lexington, Kentucky. As a highly-lauded psychologist and marriage and family therapist, Charlotte lived in the trenches with a multitude of hurting, mystified mothers.

Prior to becoming a therapist, Charlotte ministered on the staff of Cru for 19 years with her husband, Chuck Melcher, with whom she raised three beloved children. Her 49-year marriage to her childhood sweetheart ended in 2015 when Charlotte was widowed.

God then surprised Charlotte with an amazing new Cajun husband, Tooger Smith, and they seek to glorify God together as snowbirds. During the summers, Charlotte writes while gazing out at an Indiana lake dug out by Tooger's bulldozer. They've named their 30-acre lake inhabited by swimming ducks, geese, bass, and bluegill "Mercy Lake." During Florida's sunny winters, Charlotte is inspired by looking out at an alligator and nature-rich lake they call "The Pool of His Presence."

www.CharlotteMelcherSmith.com
lifesthirdtri.com

www.ingramcontent.com/pod-product-compliance
Lightning Source LLC
Chambersburg PA
CBHW020435130626
46549CB00001B/159